Essential Native Trees and Shrubs

Essential Native Trees and Shrubs

for the Eastern United States

THE GUIDE TO CREATING
A SUSTAINABLE LANDSCAPE

TONY DOVE *and* GINGER WOOLRIDGE

Bunker Hill Studio Books

An Imagine Book
Published by Charlesbridge
85 Main Street
Watertown, MA 02472
(617) 926-0329
www.imaginebooks.net

This book was designed and produced by
Bunker Hill Studio Books LLC
285 River Road, Piermont, NH 03779.
Telephone 603 272 9221   info@bunkerhillstudiobooks.com

Library of Congress Cataloging-in-Publication Data

Names: Dove, Tony, author. | Woolridge, Ginger, author.
Title: Essential native trees and shrubs for the eastern United States :
the guide to creating a sustainable landscape / Tony Dove and Ginger Woolridge.
Description: Watertown, MA : Charlesbridge, [2018] | Includes bibliographical references and index.
Identifiers: LCCN 2017016789 (print) | LCCN 2017018661 (ebook) | ISBN 9781632892041 (ebook) |
ISBN 9781632892058 (ebook pdf) | ISBN 9781623545031 (reinforced for library use)
Subjects: LCSH: Trees—East (U.S.)—Identification. | Shrubs—East (U.S.)—
Identification. | Endemic plants—East (U.S.).
Classification: LCC QK115 (ebook) | LCC QK115 .D68 2018 (print) | DDC 582.160974—dc23
LC record available at https://lccn.loc.gov/2017016789

Printed in China

10 9 8 7 6 5 4 3 2 1

*For all the peanuts who continue to inspire me,
especially James, Mae, and Regan*
—TD

*For our readers and anyone who has the pleasure
and opportunity to improve the landscape*
—GW

Contents

Preface ix

Introduction xiii

How to Use This Book xv

PART I

Site Conditions and Plant Attributes 1

Trees *3*

Shrubs *24*

*A cross-referenced listing of select trees and shrubs
by cultural and aesthetic uses in the landscape.*

PART II

Primary Trees and Shrubs 43

*Select plant profiles. Each entry has aesthetic and cultural information,
companion plants, wildlife interest and, where appropriate, selected varieties.*

PART III

Secondary Plants 287

*A list of native plants with desirable landscape features
but limitations that may outweigh their desirable traits.*

About the Authors 295

Glossary 297

Acknowledgments 301

Sources 303

Photography and Illustration Credits 305

Index 307

Preface

Question: Who knew a peanut could have such power?

My life's work and passion, 60 years of horticulture, can be attributed to a peanut. It was a simple peanut; more importantly, it was my grandfather Owen, holding the peanut, who won me over. I was six years old, sitting on my grandfather's lap, enjoying a bag of peanuts with him. My young eye was captivated by the little plant inside the peanut. My grandfather told me that this little nugget was the embryo, and if this particular peanut hadn't been roasted, we could have grown more peanut plants by planting that embryo in soil. How exciting this thought was to me. We could grow more peanuts and have more time together for sharing stories—and peanuts!

Later that same spring, I was playing, catching the shower of "helicopter" seeds of a silver maple tree. In dissecting one of the helicopter seeds, I discovered that same-looking nugget, the embryo, that my grandfather had shown me. I planted several of these embryos in a flowerpot, and presto! Those seeds germinated and thrived to become seedlings. The seedlings flourished and grew, as did my love of horticulture. I was solidly smitten at the ripe old age of six. One of those seedlings became a stalwart in a garden bed at the back entranceway to our home and has been growing there for 60 years. Fast-forward five generations, and now my grandchildren, James, Mae, and Regan, sit on my lap enjoying that maple tree's canopy and the shower of "helicopter" seeds. It's time for me to bring out a bag of peanuts to share with them.

The leap from my interest in a peanut to my interest in native plants was a natural progression. My grandfather and I would share long walks in the woods together where he'd point out the smallest of plants emerging from the soil. His love of the native plants was the catalyst for me. I would watch for those same small plants, whether walking in woodlands or on my way to school. When I was 16 years old, I saved every penny that I earned working on a neighbor's farm and bought the woodland acres adjacent to my father's property, at a time when my other teenage friends were buying cars. And as my friends were working on their cars, I was physically clearing the debris and vines from my new property. It was an enormous task, but it was a labor of love. Various exotic and invasive plants had become the dominant vegetation and had to be controlled. But as I was manually clearing the underbrush and overgrowth of undesirables, I was unearthing native treasures. This hard work was extremely rewarding and educational.

My immersion into the enjoyment of native flora increased with every season, with every seedling and bloom. I would spend wonderful hours researching the different species of herbaceous wildflowers, native trees, and shrubs on my new property. By physically hand selecting and clearing my new property, I observed so many different traits and idiosyncrasies in a plant that would have an impact on the success or failure of the plant. For instance, I unearthed a large stand of bloodroot (*Sanguinaria canadensis*). I was fascinated by the fact that the flowering time of bloodroot could vary by as much as 10 days, depending on whether an individual plant was on the north side of a large tree or on the south side of that same tree. "Location, location, location" is a popular saying in the real estate industry, but it can also be a valuable lesson for growing native plants. Location in horticulture is realty at its most fundamental platform. It's the location and characteristics of the particular soil, the environmental factors, the nutrients, and the neighboring plant communities that determine how or even *if* a native plant thrives.

In my lifetime, I've witnessed an increased popularity and appreciation of native plants. The 21st-century trend toward sustainability has emphasized the importance of utilizing native plants in this effort. And thankfully, our industry understands and appreciates just how exacting the particular growth requirements of native plants are. Some species may be found only in certain isolated locations. Some species require a particular symbiotic (mutually beneficial) relationship with another plant—or even a fungus, or maybe a certain insect species—to be able to exist. I find our native terrestrial orchids to be this exacting, since most species can only exist in a special relationship with certain soil fungi. If the balances of pH (soil acidity or alkalinity) or moisture content or soil type (clay or sand) are not sufficient for the fungus, this native orchid will not grow. A single orchid flower may produce millions of wind-borne seeds to increase the chances that at least one seed will find a favorable location in order for the orchid to survive. In most years, few or none of the seeds will fall in a suitable location for growth.

With increased human activities and encroachment, the stress on native plant stands has become more precarious. And, like canaries in coal mines, native plants can be the harbingers of good and bad news about our current environment. Native plants are definitely affected by diseases and are certainly not impervious to insect damage. I applaud the scientists, members of the green industry, and the interested public for their increased attention to and guardianship of native plants.

When plants do evolve and thrive in a region, along with insects and pathogens organic to that particular region, natural selection will eliminate those individual plants that do not possess an inherited resistance to those native pests. The individuals that do survive and thrive produce offspring. The offspring usually have a genetic resistance to a range of pests. Native plants, when in good health, are amazingly resistant to insect pests and diseases when the plant and the pest have evolved together.

In the past, there were physical barriers such as oceans and mountain ranges that prevented exotic plants, pests, and diseases from interacting with our native species. These natural impediments are no longer keeping problems under control, because humans now freely move from continent to continent, often taking plants or plant products with them. Many of our most destructive diseases and insects hitchhiked in cargo containers from Asia and Europe and have found their way into our native ecosystems. In these cases, our native plants had little or no genetic resistance to attacks by these newly introduced pests, since they did not evolve together.

Chestnut blight, gypsy moths, and Dutch elm disease are a few of the major pests that arrived during the late 19th and early 20th centuries. Chestnut blight and Dutch elm disease have killed millions of trees and dramatically altered landscapes and ecosystems. It took almost 100 years for natural predators, intentionally introduced from Europe, to begin to effect a control in the epidemic spread of European gypsy moths. In another example, Asian long-horned beetles came into the United States in the 1990s and are still a vicious threat to many different species of trees. Sudden oak death, a fungus disease possibly of European origin, has devastated West Coast oaks and is attacking many prized ornamental trees and shrubs such as rhododendrons and camellias. Emerald ash borer is devastating the ash tree populations in America across the Midwest and the mid-Atlantic regions. Within the past few years, a new fungus that causes thousand cankers disease in black walnut trees has partnered with the native walnut twig beetle and now seriously threatens millions of native black walnut trees (*Juglans nigra*).

My intention is not to scare you—it's quite the contrary! Please don't throw down your shovel, pull your garden hat over your eyes and ears, and run to the nearest exit, abandoning any thought of using native plants in your gardens! By understanding the stresses and intricacies of native plants, we can successfully assist in the sustainability of these precious plants. As an example, we learned that the devastating effects of dogwood anthracnose can be moderated in the eastern flowering dogwood. By planting these trees in a location with good air circulation, and not in total shade (as previously thought), we can diminish instances of this disease. Through careful observation, several individuals of the eastern flowering dogwood were discovered growing free of anthracnose in shaded areas. One of those resistant plants has been introduced into the nursery trade under the name of *Cornus florida* 'Appalachian Spring.' This variety and other resistant dogwoods possess true genetic resistance and offer hope that the eastern flowering dogwood will again return to the forests in numbers seen in the past.

A major threat to native plants is the white-tailed deer. Thanks to research and sustained interest in native plants, people are becoming more aware of the detrimental overpopulation of the white-tailed deer, which is decimating species of native plants and their ecosystems. Deer consume young native tree and shrub seedlings, which directly affects the natural succession of woodlands and forests. Native wildflowers, such as trilliums and native orchids, once abundant in woodlands, are becoming scarce. One native orchid, the rattlesnake plantain, has been put on the critically endangered list in the State of New York strictly due to the decimation of the plant population by deer. Tick-borne diseases in humans are becoming more prevalent. Deaths from deer-related car accidents are on the rise. The diminishing understory due to the burgeoning deer population and their voracious foraging is causing concerns for bird and small animal habitats. Deer are taking the balance out of the ecosystem and must be considered a serious threat, especially to native plants.

I would be remiss if I failed to mention that during my lifetime, in 60 years of owning the same woodland garden, five species of woody plants and six species of herbaceous wildflowers that were once abundant in my woodlands have disappeared. My weather records indicate that the climate is generally warmer than it was 50 years ago. The warmer conditions and the current inconsistencies in the climate place considerable stress on plants native to a region. Because of these environmental stresses, many native species with proven, ironclad hardiness in the past may be weakened to the point that they fall victim to native or introduced insects and diseases. On a more encouraging note, the beauty of native plants is that many of them are resilient and even stronger for successfully adapting to these changes. I've lost five or six species, but I've enjoyed a lot more than I've lost. For the ones that I've lost, I treasure the survivors all the more.

Essential Native Trees and Shrubs for the Eastern United States identifies and highlights which natives offer the reader the best chances for gardening with success. Gleaned from the authors' combined 75 years of experience, our book is meant to provide professional landscape designers, professional horticulturists, novice gardeners, and interested native enthusiasts a palette of proven 21st-century natives that thrive in varied, diversified landscapes. These trees and shrubs are the essential plants to have in your landscapes because they've adapted well to new environmental extremes. And they offer balance, interest, and aesthetic appeal for you, your clients, and hopefully for generations to come.

—Tony Dove
Harwood, Maryland

Walking in a peanut field.

Introduction

The best time to plant a tree was 20 years ago. The next best time is now. —Anonymous

Using native plant material is important. Along with many people in our society, I am increasingly aware of the significant human footprint on our earth. So it is a real pleasure to work on a project that will contribute balance to our environment.

The Case for Planting Natives

Our unique palette. We are fortunate. The East Coast of the United States is one of the world's richest areas for native plant material. In many areas of the world, plants faced extinction as glaciers forced them up against an east–west mountain range. With the Appalachian Mountains running north to south, the advance and retreat of glaciers allowed ancient ecosystems and plants to migrate away from colder or warmer weather.

The interdependency of wildlife and natural systems. Indigenous flora and fauna have developed interdependently over the millennia. Native birds and other fauna require the nutrients provided by a healthy insect population to live and reproduce. These native insects feed primarily on native plants.

Economy. Correctly selected natives require less care. Native plants can require fewer toxins (in the form of pesticides and herbicides) and less water, fertilizer, pruning, and weeding, all translating into time and money savings.

Human health and well-being. The many benefits of plants are well-known. They clean our air and water, cool our hot environments and, as noted above, contribute to an intricate, diverse biological balance.

Natives are threatened. Native habitats and their native plants are threatened. Among the most serious threats are habitat fragmentation, overpopulation of deer, invasive plants, introduced disease, introduced pests, and climate change. Air and water pollution contribute to stress on all life forms. Our managed landscapes may be the best opportunity to preserve our native plants.

We hope *Essential Native Trees and Shrubs* helps you make informed choices for the environment you intend.

—Ginger Woolridge
Annapolis, Maryland

How to Use This Book

Essential Native Trees and Shrubs is a tool for the landscape architect, garden designer, and gardener to choose reliable native plants for particular landscape situations. Our book is purposely limited to a select list of attractive and versatile native trees and shrubs. These plants are most likely to thrive, **once established**, in varying cultural situations and have superior aesthetic attributes. They have been chosen based on Tony's 50 years managing public gardens on the East Coast. (Where the pronoun "I" is used, this is Tony's voice.)

Organization

The book is organized to make plant choice easy and logical:

Part I – Site Conditions and Plant Attributes. Each plant is listed under its appropriate application and/or attribute and cross-referenced to its other uses and attributes. Using this list, the designer is able to choose plants that suit specific needs.

Part II – Primary Trees and Shrubs. Here, once a plant is chosen from Part I, find a more complete picture of the species, including a thorough profile of its characteristics, requirements, and cultivars. Part II is described in more detail below.

Part III – Secondary Plants. These trees and shrubs have desirable features and may work in certain conditions—some are longtime favorites—but they have limitations that may outweigh their desirable traits and therefore are not included in Parts I and II (our most reliable group). Many of these limitations are

recent developments, such as attacks from exotic pests. The categories of limitations are listed for the reader's further investigation.

Part II Primary Trees and Shrubs

The following are the categories of information given for each plant in Part II:

ATTRIBUTES/USES IN THE LANDSCAPE – A brief summary of the attributes and uses for which the tree or shrub is known.

SEASONS OF INTEREST – The sketches indicate whether a plant provides significant interest in a given season. If the season entry is blank, interest is not significant during this time period.

PLANT FORM GRAPH – The form and size of trees and shrubs contribute to the architecture of gardens and other projects. These drawings describe a plant's typical form, from its youngest functional size to a mature silhouette. The images give an idea of branching habit, texture, and spacing. Plant growth over time is an important consideration for plant placement, including spacing. Our drawings assume an optimal situation for the tree or shrub, but depending on the species, there can be much variation. Growing conditions significantly affect form, size, and growth over time, and these drawings are meant as a guide. Variable conditions include sun exposure, moisture, soil texture and pH, available root space, nutrients, horticultural practices, time, and so on. For instance, plants grown in the open tend to be lower branched, denser, and more wide spreading than plants in a forest, where there is more competition. The form and size of some plants can be controlled with pruning.

FORM – Trees are defined as woody plants that grow over 15' tall; usually with a central stem, but they may have multiple stems.

Small tree	15'–35'
Medium tree	35'–50'
Large tree	50' and taller

Small shrub	1'–3'
Medium shrub	3'–8'
Large shrub	8'–15'

For an idea of maximum circumference and height for older trees, find national champions at:
americanforests.org/our-programs/bigtrees

COLOR – Foliage and flower color, and their timing, are the primary considerations for plant choices. However, buds, fruit (including nuts and seedpods), twigs, and bark provide color as well. Perceived color of flowers is often affected by a flower's form, size, abundance, persistence, and sheen, and by a plant's position in sunlight or shade.

Many natives' flowers rival those of introduced species and cultivars in color (like native azaleas, *Rhododendron* spp.) and persistence (like oakleaf hydrangea, *H. quercifolia*). Bark and twigs can provide wonderful color—for example, red twig dogwood's (*Cornus sericea*) young stems are a stunning bright red or yellow in winter. Plant bloom and leaf color, including duration, are primarily affected by sunlight, temperature, and moisture. Some natives flower in winter. Bloom and autumn color can vary year to year and by climate, so we refer to periods within a season, such as early spring or late summer.

Autumn foliage is more vibrant in regions where warm sunny days are followed by rapid temperature drops overnight. The New England climate provides these conditions perennially. Along the southeastern coastal plain, high humidity tempers the drop in overnight temperatures. Similarly, because the drop in temperature is mitigated by large bodies of water, even in the Northeast, trees near these waters may have less brilliant autumn color.

We also refer to plant fragrance in this section when significant.

TEXTURE – Texture is relative. It may also be experienced visually or through touch as rough, smooth, silky, and so on. Texture is visually identified, here, as coarse, medium, or fine.

Perception of texture is affected by distance, and texture can be used to create a false sense of perspective. For example, when coarse-leaved plants are placed in the foreground and fine-leaved plants in the background, perspective is exaggerated and a space seems larger. The reverse placement makes a space seem smaller.

Plant texture can vary depending on placement. Leaf size and shape can be affected by sun exposure. For instance, some plants, including oakleaf hydrangea (*H. quercifolia*), have leaves that are larger and thinner when grown in the shade. The leaves' surface expands in order to increase photosynthesis.

CULTURE – Here we provide a closer look into the character of our selected plants. The native range describes the natural range of the plant, provided by the USDA Forest Service. Tolerances for significant environmental and site conditions are given, including soil qualities, light levels, salt, wind, compaction, and so on. Where appropriate, we include species-specific information regarding optimal planting times. In some cases, we include naturally occurring varieties.

COMPANION PLANTS – Because the plants we have chosen are tolerant of many conditions, many of them will grow together. We specify some plants that occur together in nature and some choices for horticultural companions. The plants included in this section are generally those included among our primary plants.

WILDLIFE – An important reason for planting natives is to support a diverse ecosystem. Native insect larvae, including butterflies and moths, are particular about which plants they will feed on. The monarch butterfly is a well-known example. On the other hand, quite a wide variety of flowering trees and shrubs provide nectar and pollen for mature insects. The sterile flowers, of some varieties, that may provide pleasing aesthetics do not provide these benefits. The protein provided by native larvae and mature insects is necessary for the development of fledging birds. This is the critical link between native plants and the native bird population. We list mammals and birds that are supported with food and/or shelter by each plant. The caterpillar counts are sourced from Darke and Tallamy, 2014.

CULTIVATED VARIETIES – Not all plants have cultivated varieties. And some have many. Varieties can offer designers predictable plant material size, color, and cultural options. Where applicable, we list some of the best varieties in our experience.

Quick Reference Box

USDA Plant Hardiness Zones

Essential Native Trees and Shrubs presents plants that thrive, generally, in USDA zones 5–8. Where a plant's range is larger, we include the full range. For example, the eastern red cedar would be categorized as zones 3b–9a.

The USDA zones are based on average minimum temperature, but other important factors include sun and wind exposure, soil moisture, soil nutrients, humidity, snow cover (an insulator), maximum high temperatures, maximum nighttime high temperatures,

proximity to large bodies of water, urban heat islands, horticultural practices, and so on. On a smaller scale, the garden designer can increase a plant's tolerance to cold by placing it near a building or out of harsh winter winds.

We refer to the 2012 USDA Hardiness Zone Map. To refine your location interactively, by zip code, you may go to **planthardiness.ars.usda.gov**. The new map is meant to be sensitive to larger-scale microclimates, including urban heat islands, proximity to water, and cool mountain valley pockets. Most of the United States appears at least a half zone warmer than the previous (1990) map, and there are two new zones at the warmer end of the spectrum. This is true despite averaging back 30 years, as opposed to the prior periods of 15 and less, so that recent high temperatures are mitigated. A zone number placed in parentheses denotes the authors' dissention from the usual zone recommendations.

Sun

Full sun	A minimum of six hours of direct sun daily.
Part shade	Between two and six hours of direct sun.
Full shade	Two hours or less of direct sun, or dappled shade throughout the day.

Many plants can tolerate more sun during the growing season, when temperatures are lower or there is more soil moisture.

Some plants that are borderline cold-hardy can tolerate full sun in summer but require shade in the winter. For example, the needle palm, in zone 6, grows well with full sun and high temperatures in the summer, but the combination of full sun and cold temperatures in winter may damage its foliage. In winter shade, however, it suffers few adverse effects from the same cold temperatures.

Soil Moisture

Dry	Areas where water does not remain after a rain. These may be areas in full sun, in a windy location, on a steep slope, or with sandy soil.
Moist	Areas where the soil is damp and may be occasionally saturated.
Wet	Areas where the soil is saturated for much of the growing season, except in droughts.

pH

Soil pH affects the absorption of nutrients. Like most plants, the trees and shrubs we recommend grow optimally in a slightly acid (pH 6–6.5) soil.

As the chart below describes, acid soils are soils with pH 7 and under, and alkaline soils are pH 7 and above. Neutral soils are around pH 7. Alkaline conditions may occur around foundations due to the concentration of lime in the mortar.

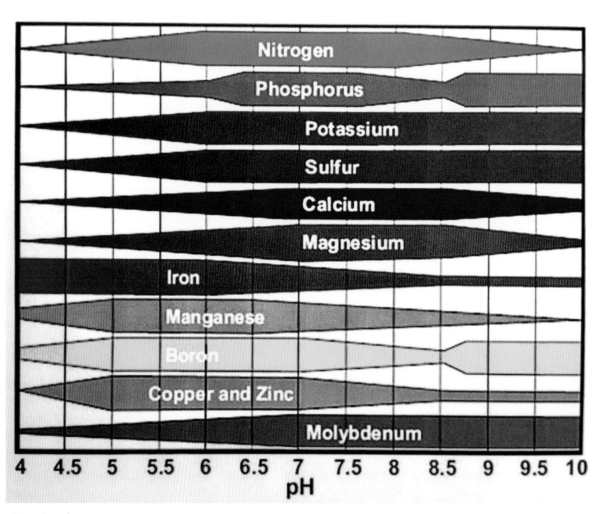

pH nutrient chart.

Essential Native Trees and Shrubs

PART I

SITE CONDITIONS *and* PLANT ATTRIBUTES

Instructions:

Certain significant landscape traits are listed for trees and shrubs. To the right of each trait is the page number where you can find a list of plants with that particular trait. Turn to that page and you will find the specific plants with this trait listed in alphabetical order, along with page numbers directing you to detailed descriptions of the plants in Part II. The trait categories of a particular tree or shrub are indexed to the right of the plant's name following the Part II page number. Note to the reader: In some genera there is enough variation in landscape traits to list them separately.

Trees

Desirable landscape traits:

A.	Trees that are salt tolerant	4
B.	Trees that are drought tolerant, once established	5
C.	Trees for poorly drained or compacted soils	7
D.	Trees suitable for rain gardens and bioretention areas	8
E.	Trees suitable for irrigated rooftop gardens	9
F.	Trees that are wind tolerant, once established	10
G.	Trees that are evergreen	11
H.	Trees that have showy flowers	11
I.	Trees that have ornamental or interesting fruit	12
J.	Trees that have good autumn foliage colors	13
K.	Trees for street tree planting	14
L.	Trees that are deer resistant	15
M.	Trees that have exceptional winter interest	16
N.	Trees tolerant of shade	17
O.	Trees that perform best in full sun	18
P.	Trees for planting beneath utility lines	19
Q.	Trees for narrow spaces	20
R.	Trees 50'+	20
S.	Trees 35'–50'	21
T.	Trees 15'–35'	22
U.	Trees that provide food and shelter for birds directly (please see native insect relationships in Part II, Primary Trees and Shrubs)	22
V.	Trees with attractive bark	23

A. Trees that are salt tolerant

Aesculus pavia	52	A, B, C, H, J, K, L, O, P, T
Amelanchier spp.	54	A, B, C, D, E, F, H, I, J, K, L, N, P, Q, T, U, V
Betula lenta	57	A, B, D, J, K, L, M, O, S, V
Betula nigra	59	A, C, D, L, M, O, R, V
Carya ovata	65	A, B, F, J, M, O, R, V
Celtis laevigata	68	A, B, C, D, F, K, L, M, N, R, U, V
Celtis occidentalis	71	A, B, C, D, F, K, L, M, N, R, U, V
Chamaecyparis thyoides	77	A, C, D, G, O, Q, S, U
Chionanthus virginicus	80	A, B, C, D, E, F, H, I, J, K, N, O, P, T, U
Cladrastis kentukea	83	A, B, H, J, L, M, O, R, V
Gymnocladus dioicus	93	A, B, C, F, J, K, M, R
Ilex decidua	96	A, B, C, D, E, F, I, M, O, P, T, U, V
Ilex opaca	98	A, B, C, E, F, G, I, K, L, M, N, R, U, V
Juniperus virginiana	102	A, B, C, E, F, G, I, K, M, O, Q, R, U
Liquidambar styraciflua 'Rotundiloba'	105	A, B, C, D, F, J, K, L, O, R
Magnolia acuminata var. *subcordata*	108	A, B, H, I, L, O, S, U
Magnolia grandiflora	111	A, B, F, G, H, I, L, M, N, R, U
Magnolia virginiana var. *australis*	117	A, B, C, D, F, G, H, I, K, M, N, P, Q, S, U
Magnolia virginiana var. *virginiana*	117	A, B, C, D, E, F, H, I, K, M, N, P, T, U
Nyssa sylvatica	120	A, B, C, D, F, J, K, L, N, R, U
Oxydendrum arboreum	126	A, B, H, J, K, L, O, P, S
Pinus palustris	129	A, B, G, L, M, O, R, U
Pinus taeda	135	A, B, C, D, G, M, O, R, U

Platanus occidentalis	141	A, B, C, D, F, L, M, O, R, V
Quercus alba	144	A, B, F, O, R
Quercus bicolor	146	A, B, C, D, F, O, R
Quercus coccinea	147	A, B, F, J, O, R
Quercus hemisphaerica	150	A, B, C, D, G, K, L, M, N, R
Quercus phellos	153	A, B, C, D, F, K, L, O, R
Quercus virginiana	156	A, B, C, D, F, G, K, L, M, O, R
Taxodium ascendens	160	A, B, C, D, E, F, K, M, O, Q, S
Taxodium distichum	159	A, B, C, D, F, K, M, O, R
Thuja occidentalis	162	A, B, C, D, E, F, G, M, N, O, Q, S, U

B. Trees that are drought tolerant, once established

ALL CATEGORIES THAT APPLY:

Acer rubrum	46	B, C, D, J, O, R, U, V
Acer saccharum	49	B, C, D, J, O, R, U
Aesculus pavia	52	A, B, C, H, J, K, L, O, P, T
Amelanchier spp.	54	A, B, C, D, E, F, H, I, J, K, L, N, P, Q, T, U, V
Betula lenta	57	A, B, D, J, K, L, M, O, S, V
Carya ovata	65	A, B, F, J, M, O, R, V
Celtis laevigata	68	A, B, C, D, F, K, L, M, N, R, U, V
Celtis occidentalis	71	A, B, C, D, F, K, L, M, N, R, U, V
Cercis canadensis	74	B, E, H, I, J, K, N, P, T
Chionanthus virginicus	80	A, B, C, D, E, F, H, I, J, K, N, O, P, T, U
Cladrastis kentukea	83	A, B, H, J, L, M, O, R, V
Cornus florida	86	B, H, I, J, M, N, O, P, T, U, V

Cotinus obovatus	90	B, H, I, J, L, O, P, S, U, V
Gymnocladus dioicus	93	A, B, C, F, J, K, M, R
Ilex decidua	96	A, B, C, D, E, F, I, M, O, P, T, U, V
Ilex opaca	98	A, B, C, E, F, G, I, K, L, M, N, R, U, V
Juniperus virginiana	102	A, B, C, E, F, G, I, K, M, O, Q, R, U
Liquidambar styraciflua 'Rotundiloba'	105	A, B, C, D, F, J, K, L, O, R
Magnolia acuminata var. *subcordata*	108	A, B, H, I, L, O, S, U
Magnolia grandiflora	111	A, B, F, G, H, I, L, M, N, R, U
Magnolia virginiana var. *australis*	117	A, B, C, D, F, G, H, I, K, M, N, P, Q, S, U
Magnolia virginiana var. *virginiana*	117	A, B, C, D, E, F, H, I, K, M, N, P, T, U
Nyssa sylvatica	120	A, B, C, D, F, J, K, L, N, R, U
Ostrya virginiana	123	B, C, F, I, J, K, L, M, N, O, P, S, U, V
Oxydendrum arboreum	126	A, B, H, J, K, L, O, P, S
Pinus palustris	129	A, B, G, L, M, O, R, U
Pinus strobus	132	B, F, G, M, O, R, U
Pinus taeda	135	A, B, C, D, G, M, O, R, U
Pinus virginiana	138	B, F, G, L, M, O, S, U
Platanus occidentalis	141	A, B, C, D, F, L, M, O, R, V
Quercus alba	144	A, B, F, O, R
Quercus bicolor	146	A, B, C, D, F, O, R
Quercus coccinea	147	A, B, F, J, O, R
Quercus hemisphaerica	150	A, B, C, D, G, K, L, M, N, R
Quercus phellos	153	A, B, C, D, F, K, L, O, R
Quercus virginiana	156	A, B, C, D, F, G, K, L, M, O, R
Taxodium ascendens	160	A, B, C, D, E, F, K, M, O, Q, S

Taxodium distichum	159	A, B, C, D, F, K, M, O, R
Thuja occidentalis	162	A, B, C, D, E, F, G, M, N, O, Q, S, U

C. Trees for poorly drained or compacted soils

		ALL CATEGORIES THAT APPLY:
Acer rubrum	46	B, C, D, J, O, R, U, V
Acer saccharum	49	B, C, D, J, O, R, U
Aesculus pavia	52	A, B, C, H, J, K, L, O, P, T
Amelanchier spp.	54	A, B, C, D, E, F, H, I, J, K, L, N, P, Q, T, U, V
Betula nigra	59	A, C, D, L, M, O, R, V
Carpinus caroliniana	62	C, D, J, L, M, N, P, S, V
Celtis laevigata	68	A, B, C, D, F, K, L, M, N, R, U, V
Celtis occidentalis	71	A, B, C, D, F, K, L, M, N, R, U, V
Chamaecyparis thyoides	77	A, C, D, G, O, Q, S, U
Chionanthus virginicus	80	A, B, C, D, E, F, H, I, J, K, N, O, P, T, U
Gymnocladus dioicus	93	A, B, C, F, J, K, M, R
Ilex decidua	96	A, B, C, D, E, F, I, M, O, P, T, U, V
Ilex opaca	98	A, B, C, E, F, G, I, K, L, M, N, R, U, V
Juniperus virginiana	102	A, B, C, E, F, G, I, K, M, O, Q, R, U
Liquidambar styraciflua 'Rotundiloba'	105	A, B, C, D, F, J, K, L, O, R
Magnolia virginiana var. *australis*	117	A, B, C, D, F, G, H, I, K, M, N, P, Q, S, U
Magnolia virginiana var. *virginiana*	117	A, B, C, D, E, F, H, I, K, M, N, P, T, U
Nyssa sylvatica	120	A, B, C, D, F, J, K, L, N, R, U
Ostrya virginiana	123	B, C, F, I, J, K, L, M, N, O, P, S, U, V
Pinus taeda	135	A, B, C, D, G, M, O, R, U

Platanus occidentalis	141	A, B, C, D, F, L, M, O, R, V
Quercus bicolor	146	A, B, C, D, F, O, R
Quercus hemisphaerica	150	A, B, C, D, G, K, L, M, N, R
Quercus phellos	153	A, B, C, D, F, K, L, O, R
Quercus virginiana	156	A, B, C, D, F, G, K, L, M, O, R
Taxodium ascendens	160	A, B, C, D, E, F, K, M, O, Q, S
Taxodium distichum	159	A, B, C, D, F, K, M, O, R
Thuja occidentalis	162	A, B, C, D, E, F, G, M, N, O, Q, S, U

D. Trees suitable for rain gardens and bioretention areas

ALL CATEGORIES THAT APPLY:

Acer rubrum	46	B, C, D, J, O, R, U, V
Acer saccharum	49	B, C, D, J, O, R, U
Amelanchier spp.	54	A, B, C, D, E, F, H, I, J, K, L, N, P, Q, T, U, V
Betula lenta	57	A, B, D, J, K, L, M, O, S, V
Betula nigra	59	A, C, D, L, M, O, R, V
Carpinus caroliniana	62	C, D, J, L, M, N, P, S, V
Celtis laevigata	68	A, B, C, D, F, K, L, M, N, R, U, V
Celtis occidentalis	71	A, B, C, D, F, K, L, M, N, R, U, V
Chamaecyparis thyoides	77	A, C, D, G, O, Q, S, U
Chionanthus virginicus	80	A, B, C, D, E, F, H, I, J, K, N, O, P, T, U
Ilex decidua	96	A, B, C, D, E, F, I, M, O, P, T, U, V
Liquidambar styraciflua 'Rotundiloba'	105	A, B, C, D, F, J, K, L, O, R
Magnolia virginiana var. *australis*	117	A, B, C, D, F, G, H, I, K, M, N, P, Q, S, U
Magnolia virginiana var. *virginiana*	117	A, B, C, D, E, F, H, I, K, M, N, P, T, U

Nyssa sylvatica	120	A, B, C, D, F, J, K, L, N, R, U
Pinus taeda	135	A, B, C, D, G, M, O, R, U
Platanus occidentalis	141	A, B, C, D, F, L, M, O, R, V
Quercus bicolor	146	A, B, C, D, F, O, R
Quercus hemisphaerica	150	A, B, C, D, G, K, L, M, N, R
Quercus phellos	153	A, B, C, D, F, K, L, O, R
Quercus virginiana	156	A, B, C, D, F, G, K, L, M, O, R
Taxodium ascendens	160	A, B, C, D, E, F, K, M, O, Q, S
Taxodium distichum	159	A, B, C, D, F, K, M, O, R
Thuja occidentalis	162	A, B, C, D, E, F, G, M, N, O, Q, S, U

E. Trees suitable for irrigated rooftop gardens

		ALL CATEGORIES THAT APPLY:
Acer pensylvanicum	44	E, J, M, N, P, T, V
Amelanchier spp.	54	A, B, C, D, E, F, H, I, J, K, L, N, P, Q, T, U, V
Cercis canadensis	74	B, E, H, I, J, K, N, P, T
Chionanthus virginicus	80	A, B, C, D, E, F, H, I, J, K, N, O, P, T, U
Ilex decidua	96	A, B, C, D, E, F, I, M, O, P, T, U, V
Ilex opaca	98	A, B, C, E, F, G, I, K, L, M, N, R, U, V
Juniperus virginiana	102	A, B, C, E, F, G, I, K, M, O, Q, R, U
Magnolia virginiana var. *virginiana*	117	A, B, C, D, E, F, H, I, K, M, N, P, T, U
Taxodium ascendens	160	A, B, C, D, E, F, K, M, O, Q, S
Thuja occidentalis	162	A, B, C, D, E, F, G, M, N, O, Q, S, U

F. Trees that are wind tolerant, once established

		ALL CATEGORIES THAT APPLY:
Amelanchier spp.	54	A, B, C, D, E, F, H, I, J, K, L, N, P, Q, T, U, V
Carya ovata	65	A, B, F, J, M, O, R, V
Celtis laevigata	68	A, B, C, D, F, K, L, M, N, R, U, V
Celtis occidentalis	71	A, B, C, D, F, K, L, M, N, R, U, V
Chionanthus virginicus	80	A, B, C, D, E, F, H, I, J, K, N, O, P, T, U
Gymnocladus dioicus	93	A, B, C, F, J, K, M, R
Ilex decidua	96	A, B, C, D, E, F, I, M, O, P, T, U, V
Ilex opaca	98	A, B, C, E, F, G, I, K, L, M, N, R, U, V
Juniperus virginiana	102	A, B, C, E, F, G, I, K, M, O, Q, R, U
Liquidambar styraciflua 'Rotundiloba'	105	A, B, C, D, F, J, K, L, O, R
Magnolia grandiflora	111	A, B, F, G, H, I, L, M, N, R, U
Magnolia virginiana var. *australis*	117	A, B, C, D, F, G, H, I, K, M, N, P, Q, S, U
Magnolia virginiana var. *virginiana*	117	A, B, C, D, E, F, H, I, K, M, N, P, T, U
Nyssa sylvatica	120	A, B, C, D, F, J, K, L, N, R, U
Ostrya virginiana	123	B, C, F, I, J, K, L, M, N, O, P, S, U, V
Pinus strobus	132	B, F, G, M, O, R, U
Pinus virginiana	138	B, F, G, L, M, O, S, U
Platanus occidentalis	141	A, B, C, D, F, L, M, O, R, V
Quercus alba	144	A, B, F, O, R
Quercus bicolor	146	A, B, C, D, F, O, R
Quercus coccinea	147	A, B, F, J, O, R
Quercus phellos	153	A, B, C, D, F, K, L, O, R
Quercus virginiana	156	A, B, C, D, F, G, K, L, M, O, R

Taxodium ascendens	160	A, B, C, D, E, F, K, M, O, Q, S
Taxodium distichum	159	A, B, C, D, F, K, M, O, R
Thuja occidentalis	162	A, B, C, D, E, F, G, M, N, O, Q, S, U

G. Trees that are evergreen

ALL CATEGORIES THAT APPLY:

Chamaecyparis thyoides	77	A, C, D, G, O, Q, S, U
Ilex opaca	98	A, B, C, E, F, G, I, K, L, M, N, R, U, V
Juniperus virginiana	102	A, B, C, E, F, G, I, K, M, O, Q, R, U
Magnolia grandiflora	111	A, B, F, G, H, I, L, M, N, R, U
Magnolia virginiana var. *australis*	117	A, B, C, D, F, G, H, I, K, M, N, P, Q, S, U
Pinus palustris	129	A, B, G, L, M, O, R, U
Pinus strobus	132	B, F, G, M, O, R, U
Pinus taeda	135	A, B, C, D, G, M, O, R, U
Pinus virginiana	138	B, F, G, L, M, O, S, U
Quercus hemisphaerica	150	A, B, C, D, G, K, L, M, N, R
Quercus virginiana	156	A, B, C, D, F, G, K, L, M, O, R
Thuja occidentalis	162	A, B, C, D, E, F, G, M, N, O, Q, S, U

H. Trees that have showy flowers

ALL CATEGORIES THAT APPLY:

Aesculus pavia	52	A, B, C, H, J, K, L, O, P, T
Amelanchier spp.	54	A, B, C, D, E, F, H, I, J, K, L, N, P, Q, T, U, V
Cercis canadensis	74	B, E, H, I, J, K, N, P, T
Chionanthus virginicus	80	A, B, C, D, E, F, H, I, J, K, N, O, P, T, U

Cladrastis kentukea	83	A, B, H, J, L, M, O, R, V
Cornus florida	86	B, H, I, J, M, N, O, P, T, U, V
Cotinus obovatus	90	B, H, I, J, L, O, P, S, U, V
Magnolia acuminata var. *subcordata*	108	A, B, H, I, L, O, S, U
Magnolia grandiflora	111	A, B, F, G, H, I, L, M, N, R, U
Magnolia macrophylla	114	H, I, N, S, U
Magnolia virginiana var. *australis*	117	A, B, C, D, F, G, H, I, K, M, N, P, Q, S, U
Magnolia virginiana var. *virginiana*	117	A, B, C, D, E, F, H, I, K, M, N, P, T, U
Oxydendrum arboreum	126	A, B, H, J, K, L, O, P, S

I. Trees that have ornamental or interesting fruit

ALL CATEGORIES THAT APPLY:

Amelanchier spp.	54	A, B, C, D, E, F, H, I, J, K, L, N, P, Q, T, U, V
Cercis canadensis	74	B, E, H, I, J, K, N, P, T
Chionanthus virginicus	80	A, B, C, D, E, F, H, I, J, K, N, O, P, T, U
Cornus florida	86	B, H, I, J, M, N, O, P, T, U, V
Cotinus obovatus	90	B, H, I, J, L, O, P, S, U, V
Ilex decidua	96	A, B, C, D, E, F, I, M, O, P, T, U, V
Ilex opaca	98	A, B, C, E, F, G, I, K, L, M, N, R, U, V
Juniperus virginiana	102	A, B, C, E, F, G, I, K, M, O, Q, R, U
Magnolia acuminata var. *subcordata*	108	A, B, H, I, L, O, S, U
Magnolia grandiflora	111	A, B, F, G, H, I, L, M, N, R, U
Magnolia macrophylla	114	H, I, N, S, U
Magnolia virginiana var. *australis*	117	A, B, C, D, F, G, H, I, K, M, N, P, Q, S, U

| *Magnolia virginiana* var. *virginiana* | 117 | A, B, C, D, E, F, H, I, K, M, N, P, T, U |
| *Ostrya virginiana* | 123 | B, C, F, I, J, K, L, M, N, O, P, S, U, V |

J. Trees that have good autumn foliage colors

ALL CATEGORIES THAT APPLY:

Acer pensylvanicum	44	E, J, M, N, P, T, V
Acer rubrum	46	B, C, D, J, O, R, U, V
Acer saccharum	49	B, C, D, J, O, R, U
Aesculus pavia	52	A, B, C, H, J, K, L, O, P, T
Amelanchier spp.	54	A, B, C, D, E, F, H, I, J, K, L, N, P, Q, T, U, V
Betula lenta	57	A, B, D, J, K, L, M, O, S, V
Carpinus caroliniana	62	C, D, J, L, M, N, P, S, V
Carya ovata	65	A, B, F, J, M, O, R, V
Cercis canadensis	74	B, E, H, I, J, K, N, P, T
Chionanthus virginicus	80	A, B, C, D, E, F, H, I, J, K, N, O, P, T, U
Cladrastis kentukea	83	A, B, H, J, L, M, O, R, V
Cornus florida	86	B, H, I, J, M, N, O, P, T, U, V
Cotinus obovatus	90	B, H, I, J, L, O, P, S, U, V
Gymnocladus dioicus	93	A, B, C, F, J, K, M, R
Liquidambar styraciflua 'Rotundiloba'	105	A, B, C, D, F, J, K, L, O, R
Nyssa sylvatica	120	A, B, C, D, F, J, K, L, N, R, U
Ostrya virginiana	123	B, C, F, I, J, K, L, M, N, O, P, S, U, V
Oxydendrum arboreum	126	A, B, H, J, K, L, O, P, S
Quercus coccinea	147	A, B, F, J, O, R

K. Trees for street tree planting

Aesculus pavia	52	A, B, C, H, J, K, L, O, P, T
Amelanchier spp.	54	A, B, C, D, E, F, H, I, J, K, L, N, P, Q, T, U, V
Betula lenta	57	A, B, D, J, K, L, M, O, S, V
Celtis laevigata	68	A, B, C, D, F, K, L, M, N, R, U, V
Celtis occidentalis	71	A, B, C, D, F, K, L, M, N, R, U, V
Cercis canadensis	74	B, E, H, I, J, K, N, P, T
Chionanthus virginicus	80	A, B, C, D, E, F, H, I, J, K, N, O, P, T, U
Gymnocladus dioicus	93	A, B, C, F, J, K, M, R
Ilex opaca	98	A, B, C, E, F, G, I, K, L, M, N, R, U, V
Juniperus virginiana	102	A, B, C, E, F, G, I, K, M, O, Q, R, U
Liquidambar styraciflua 'Rotundiloba'	105	A, B, C, D, F, J, K, L, O, R
Magnolia virginiana var. *australis*	117	A, B, C, D, F, G, H, I, K, M, N, P, Q, S, U
Magnolia virginiana var. *virginiana*	117	A, B, C, D, E, F, H, I, K, M, N, P, T, U
Nyssa sylvatica	120	A, B, C, D, F, J, K, L, N, R, U
Ostrya virginiana	123	B, C, F, I, J, K, L, M, N, O, P, S, U, V
Oxydendrum arboreum	126	A, B, H, J, K, L, O, P, S
Quercus hemisphaerica	150	A, B, C, D, G, K, L, M, N, R
Quercus phellos	153	A, B, C, D, F, K, L, O, R
Quercus virginiana	156	A, B, C, D, F, G, K, L, M, O, R
Taxodium ascendens	160	A, B, C, D, E, F, K, M, O, Q, S
Taxodium distichum	159	A, B, C, D, F, K, M, O, R

L. Trees that are deer resistant

Aesculus pavia	52	A, B, C, H, J, K, L, O, P, T
Amelanchier spp.	54	A, B, C, D, E, F, H, I, J, K, L, N, P, Q, T, U, V
Betula lenta	57	A, B, D, J, K, L, M, O, S, V
Betula nigra	59	A, C, D, L, M, O, R, V
Carpinus caroliniana	62	C, D, J, L, M, N, P, S, V
Celtis laevigata	68	A, B, C, D, F, K, L, M, N, R, U, V
Celtis occidentalis	71	A, B, C, D, F, K, L, M, N, R, U, V
Cladrastis kentukea	83	A, B, H, J, L, M, O, R, V
Cotinus obovatus	90	B, H, I, J, L, O, P, S, U, V
Ilex opaca	98	A, B, C, E, F, G, I, K, L, M, N, R, U, V
Liquidambar styraciflua 'Rotundiloba'	105	A, B, C, D, F, J, K, L, O, R
Magnolia acuminata var. *subcordata*	108	A, B, H, I, L, O, S, U
Magnolia grandiflora	111	A, B, F, G, H, I, L, M, N, R, U
Nyssa sylvatica	120	A, B, C, D, F, J, K, L, N, R, U
Ostrya virginiana	123	B, C, F, I, J, K, L, M, N, O, P, S, U, V
Oxydendrum arboreum	126	A, B, H, J, K, L, O, P, S
Pinus palustris	129	A, B, G, L, M, O, R, U
Pinus virginiana	138	B, F, G, L, M, O, S, U
Platanus occidentalis	141	A, B, C, D, F, L, M, O, R, V
Quercus hemisphaerica	150	A, B, C, D, G, K, L, M, N, R
Quercus phellos	153	A, B, C, D, F, K, L, O, R
Quercus virginiana	156	A, B, C, D, F, G, K, L, M, O, R

M. Trees that have exceptional winter interest

		ALL CATEGORIES THAT APPLY:
Acer pensylvanicum	44	E, J, M, N, P, T, V
Betula lenta	57	A, B, D, J, K, L, M, O, S, V
Betula nigra	59	A, C, D, L, M, O, R, V
Carpinus caroliniana	62	C, D, J, L, M, N, P, S, V
Carya ovata	65	A, B, F, J, M, O, R, V
Celtis laevigata	68	A, B, C, D, F, K, L, M, N, R, U, V
Celtis occidentalis	71	A, B, C, D, F, K, L, M, N, R, U, V
Cladrastis kentukea	83	A, B, H, J, L, M, O, R, V
Cornus florida	86	B, H, I, J, M, N, O, P, T, U, V
Gymnocladus dioicus	93	A, B, C, F, J, K, M, R
Ilex decidua	96	A, B, C, D, E, F, I, M, O, P, T, U, V
Ilex opaca	98	A, B, C, E, F, G, I, K, L, M, N, R, U, V
Juniperus virginiana	102	A, B, C, E, F, G, I, K, M, O, Q, R, U
Magnolia grandiflora	111	A, B, F, G, H, I, L, M, N, R, U
Magnolia virginiana var. *australis*	117	A, B, C, D, F, G, H, I, K, M, N, P, Q, S, U
Magnolia virginiana var. *virginiana*	117	A, B, C, D, E, F, H, I, K, M, N, P, T, U
Ostrya virginiana	123	B, C, F, I, J, K, L, M, N, O, P, S, U, V
Pinus palustris	129	A, B, G, L, M, O, R, U
Pinus strobus	132	B, F, G, M, O, R, U
Pinus taeda	135	A, B, C, D, G, M, O, R, U
Pinus virginiana	138	B, F, G, L, M, O, S, U
Platanus occidentalis	141	A, B, C, D, F, L, M, O, R, V
Quercus hemisphaerica	150	A, B, C, D, G, K, L, M, N, R

Quercus virginiana	156	A, B, C, D, F, G, K, L, M, O, R
Taxodium ascendens	160	A, B, C, D, E, F, K, M, O, Q, S
Taxodium distichum	159	A, B, C, D, F, K, M, O, R
Thuja occidentalis	162	A, B, C, D, E, F, G, M, N, O, Q, S, U

N. Trees tolerant of shade

ALL CATEGORIES THAT APPLY:

Acer pensylvanicum	44	E, J, M, N, P, T, V
Amelanchier spp.	54	A, B, C, D, E, F, H, I, J, K, L, N, P, Q, T, U, V
Carpinus caroliniana	62	C, D, J, L, M, N, P, S, V
Celtis laevigata	68	A, B, C, D, F, K, L, M, N, R, U, V
Celtis occidentalis	71	A, B, C, D, F, K, L, M, N, R, U, V
Cercis canadensis	74	B, E, H, I, J, K, N, P, T
Chionanthus virginicus	80	A, B, C, D, E, F, H, I, J, K, N, O, P, T, U
Cornus florida	86	B, H, I, J, M, N, O, P, T, U, V
Ilex opaca	98	A, B, C, E, F, G, I, K, L, M, N, R, U, V
Magnolia grandiflora	111	A, B, F, G, H, I, L, M, N, R, U
Magnolia macrophylla	114	H, I, N, S, U
Magnolia virginiana var. *australis*	117	A, B, C, D, F, G, H, I, K, M, N, P, Q, S, U
Magnolia virginiana var. *virginiana*	117	A, B, C, D, E, F, H, I, K, M, N, P, T, U
Nyssa sylvatica	120	A, B, C, D, F, J, K, L, N, R, U
Ostrya virginiana	123	B, C, F, I, J, K, L, M, N, O, P, S, U, V
Quercus hemisphaerica	150	A, B, C, D, G, K, L, M, N, R
Thuja occidentalis	162	A, B, C, D, E, F, G, M, N, O, Q, S, U

O. Trees that perform best in full sun

		ALL CATEGORIES THAT APPLY:
Acer rubrum	46	B, C, D, J, O, R, U, V
Acer saccharum	49	B, C, D, J, O, R, U
Aesculus pavia	52	A, B, C, H, J, K, L, O, P, T
Betula lenta	57	A, B, D, J, K, L, M, O, S, V
Betula nigra	59	A, C, D, L, M, O, R, V
Carya ovata	65	A, B, F, J, M, O, R, V
Chamaecyparis thyoides	77	A, C, D, G, O, Q, S, U
Chionanthus virginicus	80	A, B, C, D, E, F, H, I, J, K, N, O, P, T, U
Cladrastis kentukea	83	A, B, H, J, L, M, O, R, V
Cornus florida	86	B, H, I, J, M, N, O, P, T, U, V
Cotinus obovatus	90	B, H, I, J, L, O, P, S, U, V
Ilex decidua	96	A, B, C, D, E, F, I, M, O, P, T, U, V
Juniperus virginiana	102	A, B, C, E, F, G, I, K, M, O, Q, R, U
Liquidambar styraciflua 'Rotundiloba'	105	A, B, C, D, F, J, K, L, O, R
Magnolia acuminata var. *subcordata*	108	A, B, H, I, L, O, S, U
Ostrya virginiana	123	B, C, F, I, J, K, L, M, N, O, P, S, U, V
Oxydendrum arboreum	126	A, B, H, J, K, L, O, P, S
Pinus palustris	129	A, B, G, L, M, O, R, U
Pinus strobus	132	B, F, G, M, O, R, U
Pinus taeda	135	A, B, C, D, G, M, O, R, U
Pinus virginiana	138	B, F, G, L, M, O, S, U
Platanus occidentalis	141	A, B, C, D, F, L, M, O, R, V
Quercus alba	144	A, B, F, O, R

Quercus bicolor	146	A, B, C, D, F, O, R
Quercus coccinea	147	A, B, F, J, O, R
Quercus phellos	153	A, B, C, D, F, K, L, O, R
Quercus virginiana	156	A, B, C, D, F, G, K, L, M, O, R
Taxodium ascendens	160	A, B, C, D, E, F, K, M, O, Q, S
Taxodium distichum	159	A, B, C, D, F, K, M, O, R
Thuja occidentalis	162	A, B, C, D, E, F, G, M, N, O, Q, S, U

P. Trees for planting beneath utility lines

		ALL CATEGORIES THAT APPLY:
Acer pensylvanicum	44	E, J, M, N, P, T, V
Aesculus pavia	52	A, B, C, H, J, K, L, O, P, T
Amelanchier spp.	54	A, B, C, D, E, F, H, I, J, K, L, N, P, Q, T, U, V
Carpinus caroliniana	62	C, D, J, L, M, N, P, S, V
Cercis canadensis	74	B, E, H, I, J, K, N, P, T
Chionanthus virginicus	80	A, B, C, D, E, F, H, I, J, K, N, O, P, T, U
Cornus florida	86	B, H, I, J, M, N, O, P, T, U, V
Cotinus obovatus	90	B, H, I, J, L, O, P, S, U, V
Ilex decidua	96	A, B, C, D, E, F, I, M, O, P, T, U, V
Magnolia virginiana var. *australis*	117	A, B, C, D, F, G, H, I, K, M, N, P, Q, S, U
Magnolia virginiana var. *virginiana*	117	A, B, C, D, E, F, H, I, K, M, N, P, T, U
Ostrya virginiana	123	B, C, F, I, J, K, L, M, N, O, P, S, U, V
Oxydendrum arboreum	126	A, B, H, J, K, L, O, P, S

Q. Trees for narrow spaces

		ALL CATEGORIES THAT APPLY:
Amelanchier spp.	54	A, B, C, D, E, F, H, I, J, K, L, N, P, Q, T, U, V
Chamaecyparis thyoides	77	A, C, D, G, O, Q, S, U
Juniperus virginiana	102	A, B, C, E, F, G, I, K, M, O, Q, R, U
Magnolia virginiana var. *australis*	117	A, B, C, D, F, G, H, I, K, M, N, P, Q, S, U
Taxodium ascendens	160	A, B, C, D, E, F, K, M, O, Q, S
Thuja occidentalis	162	A, B, C, D, E, F, G, M, N, O, Q, S, U

R. Trees 50′+

		ALL CATEGORIES THAT APPLY:
Acer rubrum	46	B, C, D, J, O, R, U, V
Acer saccharum	49	B, C, D, J, O, R, U
Betula nigra	59	A, C, D, L, M, O, R, V
Carya ovata	65	A, B, F, J, M, O, R, V
Celtis laevigata	68	A, B, C, D, F, K, L, M, N, R, U, V
Celtis occidentalis	71	A, B, C, D, F, K, L, M, N, R, U, V
Cladrastis kentukea	83	A, B, H, J, L, M, O, R, V
Gymnocladus dioicus	93	A, B, C, F, J, K, M, R
Ilex opaca	98	A, B, C, E, F, G, I, K, L, M, N, R, U, V
Juniperus virginiana	102	A, B, C, E, F, G, I, K, M, O, Q, R, U
Liquidambar styraciflua 'Rotundiloba'	105	A, B, C, D, F, J, K, L, O, R
Magnolia grandiflora	111	A, B, F, G, H, I, L, M, N, R, U
Nyssa sylvatica	120	A, B, C, D, F, J, K, L, N, R, U
Pinus palustris	129	A, B, G, L, M, O, R, U

Pinus strobus	132	B, F, G, M, O, R, U
Pinus taeda	135	A, B, C, D, G, M, O, R, U
Platanus occidentalis	141	A, B, C, D, F, L, M, O, R, V
Quercus alba	144	A, B, F, O, R
Quercus bicolor	146	A, B, C, D, F, O, R
Quercus coccinea	147	A, B, F, J, O, R
Quercus hemisphaerica	150	A, B, C, D, G, K, L, M, N, R
Quercus phellos	153	A, B, C, D, F, K, L, O, R
Quercus virginiana	156	A, B, C, D, F, G, K, L, M, O, R
Taxodium distichum	159	A, B, C, D, F, K, M, O, R

S. Trees 35'–50'

ALL CATEGORIES THAT APPLY:

Betula lenta	57	A, B, D, J, K, L, M, O, S, V
Carpinus caroliniana	62	C, D, J, L, M, N, P, S, V
Chamaecyparis thyoides	77	A, C, D, G, O, Q, S, U
Cotinus obovatus	90	B, H, I, J, L, O, P, S, U, V
Magnolia acuminata var. *subcordata*	108	A, B, H, I, L, O, S, U
Magnolia macrophylla	114	H, I, N, S, U
Magnolia virginiana var. *australis*	117	A, B, C, D, F, G, H, I, K, M, N, P, Q, S, U
Ostrya virginiana	123	B, C, F, I, J, K, L, M, N, O, P, S, U, V
Oxydendrum arboreum	126	A, B, H, J, K, L, O, P, S
Pinus virginiana	138	B, F, G, L, M, O, S, U
Taxodium ascendens	160	A, B, C, D, E, F, K, M, O, Q, S
Thuja occidentalis	162	A, B, C, D, E, F, G, M, N, O, Q, S, U

T. Trees 15'–35'

		ALL CATEGORIES THAT APPLY:
Acer pensylvanicum	44	E, J, M, N, P, T, V
Aesculus pavia	52	A, B, C, H, J, K, L, O, P, T
Amelanchier spp.	54	A, B, C, D, E, F, H, I, J, K, L, N, P, Q, T, U, V
Cercis canadensis	74	B, E, H, I, J, K, N, P, T
Chionanthus virginicus	80	A, B, C, D, E, F, H, I, J, K, N, O, P, T, U
Cornus florida	86	B, H, I, J, M, N, O, P, T, U, V
Ilex decidua	96	A, B, C, D, E, F, I, M, O, P, T, U, V
Magnolia virginiana var. *virginiana*	117	A, B, C, D, E, F, H, I, K, M, N, P, T, U

U. Trees that provide food and shelter for birds directly
(please see native insect relationships in Part II, Primary Trees and Shrubs)

		ALL CATEGORIES THAT APPLY:
Acer rubrum	46	B, C, D, J, O, R, U, V
Acer saccharum	49	B, C, D, J, O, R, U
Amelanchier spp.	54	A, B, C, D, E, F, H, I, J, K, L, N, P, Q, T, U, V
Celtis laevigata	68	A, B, C, D, F, K, L, M, N, R, U, V
Celtis occidentalis	71	A, B, C, D, F, K, L, M, N, R, U, V
Chamaecyparis thyoides	77	A, C, D, G, O, Q, S, U
Chionanthus virginicus	80	A, B, C, D, E, F, H, I, J, K, N, O, P, T, U
Cornus florida	86	B, H, I, J, M, N, O, P, T, U, V
Cotinus obovatus	90	B, H, I, J, L, O, P, S, U, V
Ilex decidua	96	A, B, C, D, E, F, I, M, O, P, T, U, V
Ilex opaca	98	A, B, C, E, F, G, I, K, L, M, N, R, U, V

Juniperus virginiana	102	A, B, C, E, F, G, I, K, M, O, Q, R, U
Magnolia acuminata var. *subcordata*	108	A, B, H, I, L, O, S, U
Magnolia grandiflora	111	A, B, F, G, H, I, L, M, N, R, U
Magnolia macrophylla	114	H, I, N, S, U
Magnolia virginiana var. *australis*	117	A, B, C, D, F, G, H, I, K, M, N, P, Q, S, U
Magnolia virginiana var. *virginiana*	117	A, B, C, D, E, F, H, I, K, M, N, P, T, U
Nyssa sylvatica	120	A, B, C, D, F, J, K, L, N, R, U
Ostrya virginiana	123	B, C, F, I, J, K, L, M, N, O, P, S, U, V
Pinus palustris	129	A, B, G, L, M, O, R, U
Pinus strobus	132	B, F, G, M, O, R, U
Pinus taeda	135	A, B, C, D, G, M, O, R, U
Pinus virginiana	138	B, F, G, L, M, O, S, U
Thuja occidentalis	162	A, B, C, D, E, F, G, M, N, O, Q, S, U

V. Trees with attractive bark

ALL CATEGORIES THAT APPLY:

Acer pensylvanicum	44	E, J, M, N, P, T, V
Acer rubrum	46	B, C, D, J, O, R, U, V
Amelanchier spp.	54	A, B, C, D, E, F, H, I, J, K, L, N, P, Q, T, U, V
Betula lenta	57	A, B, D, J, K, L, M, O, S, V
Betula nigra	59	A, C, D, L, M, O, R, V
Carpinus caroliniana	62	C, D, J, L, M, N, P, S, V
Carya ovata	65	A, B, F, J, M, O, R, V
Celtis laevigata	68	A, B, C, D, F, K, L, M, N, R, U, V
Celtis occidentalis	71	A, B, C, D, F, K, L, M, N, R, U, V

Cladrastis kentukea	83	A, B, H, J, L, M, O, R, V
Cornus florida	86	B, H, I, J, M, N, O, P, T, U, V
Cotinus obovatus	90	B, H, I, J, L, O, P, S, U, V
Ilex decidua	96	A, B, C, D, E, F, I, M, O, P, T, U, V
Ilex opaca	98	A, B, C, E, F, G, I, K, L, M, N, R, U, V
Ostrya virginiana	123	B, C, F, I, J, K, L, M, N, O, P, S, U, V
Platanus occidentalis	141	A, B, C, D, F, L, M, O, R, V

Shrubs

Desirable landscape traits:

A.	Shrubs that are salt tolerant	25
B.	Shrubs that are drought tolerant, once established	26
C.	Shrubs for poorly drained or compacted soils	27
D.	Shrubs suitable for rain gardens and bioretention areas	28
E.	Shrubs suitable for irrigated rooftop gardens	30
F.	Shrubs that are wind tolerant, once established	31
G.	Shrubs that are evergreen	32
H.	Shrubs that have showy flowers	32
I.	Shrubs that have ornamental or interesting fruit	34
J.	Shrubs that have good autumn foliage colors	35
K.	Shrubs that are deer resistant	36
L.	Shrubs that have exceptional winter interest	37
M.	Shrubs tolerant of shade	38
N.	Shrubs that perform best in full sun	39
O.	Shrubs that are ground covers	40
P.	Shrubs that provide food and shelter for birds directly (please see native insect relationships in Part II, Primary Trees and Shrubs)	40
Q.	Shrubs with interesting bark	41
R.	Shrubs suitable for small containers	41

A. Shrubs that are salt tolerant

Aesculus parviflora	165	A, B, D, H, K, M
Aralia spinosa	170	A, B, C, D, E, H, I, J, K, L, M, P, Q
Aronia arbutifolia	173	A, B, C, D, E, H, I, J, M, P
Baccharis halimifolia	176	A, B, C, D, E, I, K, N
Callicarpa americana	179	A, B, C, D, E, H, I, M, P, R
Cephalanthus occidentalis	184	A, C, D, H, K, N
Clethra alnifolia	189	A, D, H, J, K, M, R
Comptonia peregrina	193	A, B, C, E, F, K, N, O
Cornus sericea	195	A, B, C, D, E, F, H, I, J, K, L, N, P, Q, R
Cyrilla racemiflora	201	A, B, C, D, F, G,* H, J, L, N
Fothergilla spp.	204	A, B, C, D, E, F, H, J, K, N, R
Hamamelis virginiana	211	A, B, C, D, F, H, J, K, M
Hydrangea arborescens	213	A, E, H, K, M, R
Hydrangea quercifolia	216	A, B, H, J, L, M, Q
Hypericum spp.	220	A, B, E, F, H, K, N, O, Q, R
Ilex glabra	223	A, B, C, D, E, F, G, I, K, L, M, P, R
Ilex verticillata	226	A, C, D, F, I, L, M, P
Ilex vomitoria	230	A, B, C, D, E, F, G, I, K, L, M, O,** P, R
Juniperus horizontalis	240	A, B, E, F, G, L, N, O, P, R
Lindera benzoin	242	A, B, C, D, E, H, I, J, K, M, P
Morella cerifera	245	A, B, C, D, G, I, K, L, M, P
Rhapidophyllum hystrix	250	A, B, C, D, G, K, L, M
Rhus aromatica	265	A, B, C, E, F, H, I, J, K, N, O, P, R

Rhus copallina	268	A, B, C, F, H, I, J, K, N, P
Rhus typhina	271	A, B, C, F, H, I, J, K, L, N, P
Sabal minor	274	A, B, C, D, E, F, G, K, L, M, P
Viburnum prunifolium	280	A, B, C, D, F, H, I, J, K, M, P, Q
Yucca spp.	283	A, B, E, F, G, H, K, L, N, R

B. Shrubs that are drought tolerant, once established

		ALL CATEGORIES THAT APPLY:
Aesculus parviflora	165	A, B, D, H, K, M
Aralia spinosa	170	A, B, C, D, E, H, I, J, K, L, M, P, Q
Aronia arbutifolia	173	A, B, C, D, E, H, I, J, M, P
Baccharis halimifolia	176	A, B, C, D, E, I, K, N
Callicarpa americana	179	A, B, C, D, E, H, I, M, P, R
Calycanthus floridus	181	B, C, D, E, F, H, J, K, M
Clethra acuminata	187	B, H, J, K, L, M, Q
Comptonia peregrina	193	A, B, C, E, F, K, N, O
Cornus sericea	195	A, B, C, D, E, F, H, I, J, K, L, N, P, Q, R
Cyrilla racemiflora	201	A, B, C, D, F, G,* H, J, L, N
Fothergilla spp.	204	A, B, C, D, E, F, H, J, K, N, R
Hamamelis vernalis	208	B, C, D, F, H, J, K, L, N
Hamamelis virginiana	211	A, B, C, D, F, H, J, K, M
Hydrangea quercifolia	216	A, B, H, J, L, M, Q
Hypericum spp.	220	A, B, E, F, H, K, N, O, Q, R
Ilex glabra	223	A, B, C, D, E, F, G, I, K, L, M, P, R
Ilex vomitoria	230	A, B, C, D, E, F, G, I, K, L, M, O,** P, R

Itea virginica	237	B, C, D, E, F, G,* H, J, L, M, O, R
Juniperus horizontalis	240	A, B, E, F, G, L, N, O, P, R
Lindera benzoin	242	A, B, C, D, E, H, I, J, K, M, P
Morella cerifera	245	A, B, C, D, G, I, K, L, M, P
Philadelphus inodorus	248	B, F, H, K, N
Rhapidophyllum hystrix	250	A, B, C, D, G, K, L, M
Rhododendron catawbiense	255	B, F, G, H, L, M
Rhododendron viscosum	262	B, D, F, H, J, M
Rhus aromatica	265	A, B, C, E, F, H, I, J, K, N, O, P, R
Rhus copallina	268	A, B, C, F, H, I, J, K, N, P
Rhus typhina	271	A, B, C, F, H, I, J, K, L, N, P
Sabal minor	274	A, B, C, D, E, F, G, K, L, M, P
Viburnum nudum	277	B, C, D, E, F, H, I, J, K, N, P
Viburnum prunifolium	280	A, B, C, D, F, H, I, J, K, M, P, Q
Yucca spp.	283	A, B, E, F, G, H, K, L, N, R

C. Shrubs for poorly drained or compacted soils

		ALL CATEGORIES THAT APPLY:
Aralia spinosa	170	A, B, C, D, E, H, I, J, K, L, M, P, Q
Aronia arbutifolia	173	A, B, C, D, E, H, I, J, M, P
Baccharis halimifolia	176	A, B, C, D, E, I, K, N
Callicarpa americana	179	A, B, C, D, E, H, I, M, P, R
Calycanthus floridus	181	B, C, D, E, F, H, J, K, M
Cephalanthus occidentalis	184	A, C, D, H, K, N
Comptonia peregrina	193	A, B, C, E, F, K, N, O

Cornus sericea	195	A, B, C, D, E, F, H, I, J, K, L, N, P, Q, R
Cyrilla racemiflora	201	A, B, C, D, F, G,* H, J, L, N
Fothergilla spp.	204	A, B, C, D, E, F, H, J, K, N, R
Hamamelis vernalis	208	B, C, D, F, H, J, K, L, N
Hamamelis virginiana	211	A, B, C, D, F, H, J, K, M
Ilex glabra	223	A, B, C, D, E, F, G, I, K, L, M, P, R
Ilex verticillata	226	A, C, D, F, I, L, M, P
Ilex vomitoria	230	A, B, C, D, E, F, G, I, K, L, M, O,** P, R
Illicium floridanum	234	C, D, G, H, I, K, M
Itea virginica	237	B, C, D, E, F, G,* H, J, L, M, O, R
Lindera benzoin	242	A, B, C, D, E, H, I, J, K, M, P
Morella cerifera	245	A, B, C, D, G, I, K, L, M, P
Rhapidophyllum hystrix	250	A, B, C, D, G, K, L, M
Rhus aromatica	265	A, B, C, E, F, H, I, J, K, N, O, P, R
Rhus copallina	268	A, B, C, F, H, I, J, K, N, P
Rhus typhina	271	A, B, C, F, H, I, J, K, L, N, P
Sabal minor	274	A, B, C, D, E, F, G, K, L, M, P
Viburnum nudum	277	B, C, D, E, F, H, I, J, K, N, P
Viburnum prunifolium	280	A, B, C, D, F, H, I, J, K, M, P, Q

D. Shrubs suitable for rain gardens and bioretention areas

		ALL CATEGORIES THAT APPLY:
Aesculus parviflora	165	A, B, D, H, K, M
Aralia spinosa	170	A, B, C, D, E, H, I, J, K, L, M, P, Q
Aronia arbutifolia	173	A, B, C, D, E, H, I, J, M, P

Baccharis halimifolia	176	A, B, C, D, E, I, K, N
Callicarpa americana	179	A, B, C, D, E, H, I, M, P, R
Calycanthus floridus	181	B, C, D, E, F, H, J, K, M
Cephalanthus occidentalis	184	A, C, D, H, K, N
Clethra alnifolia	189	A, D, H, J, K, M, R
Cornus sericea	195	A, B, C, D, E, F, H, I, J, K, L, N, P, Q, R
Croton alabamensis	198	D, G, J, K, L, M, R
Cyrilla racemiflora	201	A, B, C, D, F, G,* H, J, L, N
Fothergilla spp.	204	A, B, C, D, E, F, H, J, K, N, R
Hamamelis vernalis	208	B, C, D, F, H, J, K, L, N
Hamamelis virginiana	211	A, B, C, D, F, H, J, K, M
Ilex glabra	223	A, B, C, D, E, F, G, I, K, L, M, P, R
Ilex verticillata	226	A, C, D, F, I, L, M, P
Ilex vomitoria	230	A, B, C, D, E, F, G, I, K, L, M, O,** P, R
Illicium floridanum	234	C, D, G, H, I, K, M
Itea virginica	237	B, C, D, E, F, G,* H, J, L, M, O, R
Lindera benzoin	242	A, B, C, D, E, H, I, J, K, M, P
Morella cerifera	245	A, B, C, D, G, I, K, L, M, P
Rhapidophyllum hystrix	250	A, B, C, D, G, K, L, M
Rhododendron calendulaceum	253	D, F, H, J, M
Rhododendron periclymenoides	258	D, F, H, M
Rhododendron prunifolium	260	D, F, H, J, M
Rhododendron viscosum	262	B, D, F, H, J, M
Sabal minor	274	A, B, C, D, E, F, G, K, L, M, P
Viburnum nudum	277	B, C, D, E, F, H, I, J, K, N, P
Viburnum prunifolium	280	A, B, C, D, F, H, I, J, K, M, P, Q

E. Shrubs suitable for irrigated rooftop gardens

		ALL CATEGORIES THAT APPLY:
Aralia spinosa	170	A, B, C, D, E, H, I, J, K, L, M, P, Q
Aronia arbutifolia	173	A, B, C, D, E, H, I, J, M, P
Baccharis halimifolia	176	A, B, C, D, E, I, K, N
Callicarpa americana	179	A, B, C, D, E, H, I, M, P, R
Calycanthus floridus	181	B, C, D, E, F, H, J, K, M
Comptonia peregrina	193	A, B, C, E, F, K, N, O
Cornus sericea	195	A, B, C, D, E, F, H, I, J, K, L, N, P, Q, R
Fothergilla spp.	204	A, B, C, D, E, F, H, J, K, N, R
Hydrangea arborescens	213	A, E, H, K, M, R
Hypericum spp.	220	A, B, E, F, H, K, N, O, Q, R
Ilex glabra	223	A, B, C, D, E, F, G, I, K, L, M, P, R
Ilex vomitoria	230	A, B, C, D, E, F, G, I, K, L, M, O,** P, R
Itea virginica	237	B, C, D, E, F, G,* H, J, L, M, O, R
Juniperus horizontalis	240	A, B, E, F, G, L, N, O, P, R
Lindera benzoin	242	A, B, C, D, E, H, I, J, K, M, P
Rhus aromatica	265	A, B, C, E, F, H, I, J, K, N, O, P, R
Sabal minor	274	A, B, C, D, E, F, G, K, L, M, P
Viburnum nudum	277	B, C, D, E, F, H, I, J, K, N, P
Yucca spp.	283	A, B, E, F, G, H, K, L, N, R

F. Shrubs that are wind tolerant

Calycanthus floridus	181	B, C, D, E, F, H, J, K, M
Comptonia peregrina	193	A, B, C, E, F, K, N, O
Cornus sericea	195	A, B, C, D, E, F, H, I, J, K, L, N, P, Q, R
Cyrilla racemiflora	201	A, B, C, D, F, G,* H, J, L, N
Fothergilla spp.	204	A, B, C, D, E, F, H, J, K, N, R
Hamamelis vernalis	208	B, C, D, F, H, J, K, L, N
Hamamelis virginiana	211	A, B, C, D, F, H, J, K, M
Hypericum spp.	220	A, B, E, F, H, K, N, O, Q, R
Ilex glabra	223	A, B, C, D, E, F, G, I, K, L, M, P, R
Ilex verticillata	226	A, C, D, F, I, L, M, P
Ilex vomitoria	230	A, B, C, D, E, F, G, I, K, L, M, O,** P, R
Itea virginica	237	B, C, D, E, F, G,* H, J, L, M, O, R
Juniperus horizontalis	240	A, B, E, F, G, L, N, O, P, R
Philadelphus inodorus	248	B, F, H, K, N
Rhododendron calendulaceum	253	D, F, H, J, M
Rhododendron catawbiense	255	B, F, G, H, L, M
Rhododendron periclymenoides	258	D, F, H, M
Rhododendron prunifolium	260	D, F, H, J, M
Rhododendron viscosum	262	B, D, F, H, J, M
Rhus aromatica	265	A, B, C, E, F, H, I, J, K, N, O, P, R
Rhus copallina	268	A, B, C, F, H, I, J, K, N, P
Rhus typhina	271	A, B, C, F, H, I, J, K, L, N, P
Sabal minor	274	A, B, C, D, E, F, G, K, L, M, P

Viburnum nudum	277	B, C, D, E, F, H, I, J, K, N, P
Viburnum prunifolium	280	A, B, C, D, F, H, I, J, K, M, P, Q
Yucca spp.	283	A, B, E, F, G, H, K, L, N, R

G. Shrubs that are evergreen

		ALL CATEGORIES THAT APPLY:
Agarista populifolia	168	G, H, K, L, M
Croton alabamensis	198	D, G, J, K, L, M, R
*Cyrilla racemiflora	201	A, B, C, D, F, G,* H, J, L, N
Ilex glabra	223	A, B, C, D, E, F, G, I, K, L, M, P, R
Ilex vomitoria	230	A, B, C, D, E, F, G, I, K, L, M, O,** P, R
Illicium floridanum	234	C, D, G, H, I, K, M
*Itea virginica	237	B, C, D, E, F, G,* H, J, L, M, O, R
Juniperus horizontalis	240	A, B, E, F, G, L, N, O, P, R
Morella cerifera	245	A, B, C, D, G, I, K, L, M, P
Rhapidophyllum hystrix	250	A, B, C, D, G, K, L, M
Rhododendron catawbiense	255	B, F, G, H, L, M
Sabal minor	274	A, B, C, D, E, F, G, K, L, M, P
Yucca spp.	283	A, B, E, F, G, H, K, L, N, R

H. Shrubs that have showy flowers

		ALL CATEGORIES THAT APPLY:
Aesculus parviflora	165	A, B, D, H, K, M
Agarista populifolia	168	G, H, K, L, M
Aralia spinosa	170	A, B, C, D, E, H, I, J, K, L, M, P, Q

Aronia arbutifolia	173	A, B, C, D, E, H, I, J, M, P
Callicarpa americana	179	A, B, C, D, E, H, I, M, P, R
Calycanthus floridus	181	B, C, D, E, F, H, J, K, M
Cephalanthus occidentalis	184	A, C, D, H, K, N
Clethra acuminata	187	B, H, J, K, L, M, Q
Clethra alnifolia	189	A, D, H, J, K, M, R
Cornus sericea	195	A, B, C, D, E, F, H, I, J, K, L, N, P, Q, R
Cyrilla racemiflora	201	A, B, C, D, F, G,* H, J, L, N
Fothergilla spp.	204	A, B, C, D, E, F, H, J, K, N, R
Hamamelis vernalis	208	B, C, D, F, H, J, K, L, N
Hamamelis virginiana	211	A, B, C, D, F, H, J, K, M
Hydrangea arborescens	213	A, E, H, K, M, R
Hydrangea quercifolia	216	A, B, H, J, L, M, Q
Hypericum spp.	220	A, B, E, F, H, K, N, O, Q, R
Illicium floridanum	234	C, D, G, H, I, K, M
Itea virginica	237	B, C, D, E, F, G,* H, J, L, M, O, R
Lindera benzoin	242	A, B, C, D, E, H, I, J, K, M, P
Philadelphus inodorus	248	B, F, H, K, N
Rhododendron calendulaceum	253	D, F, H, J, M
Rhododendron catawbiense	255	B, F, G, H, L, M
Rhododendron periclymenoides	258	D, F, H, M
Rhododendron prunifolium	260	D, F, H, J, M
Rhododendron viscosum	262	B, D, F, H, J, M
Rhus aromatica	265	A, B, C, E, F, H, I, J, K, N, O, P, R
Rhus copallina	268	A, B, C, F, H, I, J, K, N, P
Rhus typhina	271	A, B, C, F, H, I, J, K, L, N, P

Viburnum nudum	277	B, C, D, E, F, H, I, J, K, N, P
Viburnum prunifolium	280	A, B, C, D, F, H, I, J, K, M, P, Q
Yucca spp.	283	A, B, E, F, G, H, K, L, N, R

I. Shrubs that have ornamental or interesting fruit

		ALL CATEGORIES THAT APPLY:
Aralia spinosa	170	A, B, C, D, E, H, I, J, K, L, M, P, Q
Aronia arbutifolia	173	A, B, C, D, E, H, I, J, M, P
Baccharis halimifolia	176	A, B, C, D, E, I, K, N
Callicarpa americana	179	A, B, C, D, E, H, I, M, P, R
Cornus sericea	195	A, B, C, D, E, F, H, I, J, K, L, N, P, Q, R
Ilex glabra	223	A, B, C, D, E, F, G, I, K, L, M, P, R
Ilex verticillata	226	A, C, D, F, I, L, M, P
Ilex vomitoria	230	A, B, C, D, E, F, G, I, K, L, M, O,** P, R
Illicium floridanum	234	C, D, G, H, I, K, M
Lindera benzoin	242	A, B, C, D, E, H, I, J, K, M, P
Morella cerifera	245	A, B, C, D, G, I, K, L, M, P
Rhus aromatica	265	A, B, C, E, F, H, I, J, K, N, O, P, R
Rhus copallina	268	A, B, C, F, H, I, J, K, N, P
Rhus typhina	271	A, B, C, F, H, I, J, K, L, N, P
Viburnum nudum	277	B, C, D, E, F, H, I, J, K, N, P
Viburnum prunifolium	280	A, B, C, D, F, H, I, J, K, M, P, Q

J. Shrubs that have good autumn foliage colors

		ALL CATEGORIES THAT APPLY:
Aralia spinosa	170	A, B, C, D, E, H, I, J, K, L, M, P, Q
Aronia arbutifolia	173	A, B, C, D, E, H, I, J, M, P
Calycanthus floridus	181	B, C, D, E, F, H, J, K, M
Clethra acuminata	187	B, H, J, K, L, M, Q
Clethra alnifolia	189	A, D, H, J, K, M, R
Cornus sericea	195	A, B, C, D, E, F, H, I, J, K, L, N, P, Q, R
Croton alabamensis	198	D, G, J, K, L, M, R
Cyrilla racemiflora	201	A, B, C, D, F, G,* H, J, L, N
Fothergilla spp.	204	A, B, C, D, E, F, H, J, K, N, R
Hamamelis vernalis	208	B, C, D, F, H, J, K, L, N
Hamamelis virginiana	211	A, B, C, D, F, H, J, K, M
Hydrangea quercifolia	216	A, B, H, J, L, M, Q
Itea virginica	237	B, C, D, E, F, G,* H, J, L, M, O, R
Lindera benzoin	242	A, B, C, D, E, H, I, J, K, M, P
Rhododendron calendulaceum	253	D, F, H, J, M
Rhododendron prunifolium	260	D, F, H, J, M
Rhododendron viscosum	262	B, D, F, H, J, M
Rhus aromatica	265	A, B, C, E, F, H, I, J, K, N, O, P, R
Rhus copallina	268	A, B, C, F, H, I, J, K, N, P
Rhus typhina	271	A, B, C, F, H, I, J, K, L, N, P
Viburnum nudum	277	B, C, D, E, F, H, I, J, K, N, P
Viburnum prunifolium	280	A, B, C, D, F, H, I, J, K, M, P, Q

K. Shrubs that are deer resistant

		ALL CATEGORIES THAT APPLY:
Aesculus parviflora	165	A, B, D, H, K, M
Agarista populifolia	168	G, H, K, L, M
Aralia spinosa	170	A, B, C, D, E, H, I, J, K, L, M, P, Q
Baccharis halimifolia	176	A, B, C, D, E, I, K, N
Calycanthus floridus	181	B, C, D, E, F, H, J, K, M
Cephalanthus occidentalis	184	A, C, D, H, K, N
Clethra acuminata	187	B, H, J, K, L, M, Q
Clethra alnifolia	189	A, D, H, J, K, M, R
Comptonia peregrina	193	A, B, C, E, F, K, N, O
Cornus sericea	195	A, B, C, D, E, F, H, I, J, K, L, N, P, Q, R
Croton alabamensis	198	D, G, J, K, L, M, R
Fothergilla spp.	204	A, B, C, D, E, F, H, J, K, N, R
Hamamelis vernalis	208	B, C, D, F, H, J, K, L, N
Hamamelis virginiana	211	A, B, C, D, F, H, J, K, M
Hydrangea arborescens	213	A, E, H, K, M, R
Hypericum spp.	220	A, B, E, F, H, K, N, O, Q, R
Ilex glabra	223	A, B, C, D, E, F, G, I, K, L, M, P, R
Ilex vomitoria	230	A, B, C, D, E, F, G, I, K, L, M, O,** P, R
Illicium floridanum	234	C, D, G, H, I, K, M
Lindera benzoin	242	A, B, C, D, E, H, I, J, K, M, P
Morella cerifera	245	A, B, C, D, G, I, K, L, M, P
Philadelphus inodorus	248	B, F, H, K, N
Rhapidophyllum hystrix	250	A, B, C, D, G, K, L, M

Rhus aromatica	265	A, B, C, E, F, H, I, J, K, N, O, P, R
Rhus copallina	268	A, B, C, F, H, I, J, K, N, P
Rhus typhina	271	A, B, C, F, H, I, J, K, L, N, P
Sabal minor	274	A, B, C, D, E, F, G, K, L, M, P
Viburnum nudum	277	B, C, D, E, F, H, I, J, K, N, P
Viburnum prunifolium	280	A, B, C, D, F, H, I, J, K, M, P, Q
Yucca spp.	283	A, B, E, F, G, H, K, L, N, R

L. Shrubs that have exceptional winter interest

		ALL CATEGORIES THAT APPLY:
Agarista populifolia	168	G, H, K, L, M
Aralia spinosa	170	A, B, C, D, E, H, I, J, K, L, M, P, Q
Clethra acuminata	187	B, H, J, K, L, M, Q
Cornus sericea	195	A, B, C, D, E, F, H, I, J, K, L, N, P, Q, R
Croton alabamensis	198	D, G, J, K, L, M, R
Cyrilla racemiflora	201	A, B, C, D, F, G,* H, J, L, N
Hamamelis vernalis	208	B, C, D, F, H, J, K, L, N
Hydrangea quercifolia	216	A, B, H, J, L, M, Q
Ilex glabra	223	A, B, C, D, E, F, G, I, K, L, M, P, R
Ilex verticillata	226	A, C, D, F, I, L, M, P
Ilex vomitoria	230	A, B, C, D, E, F, G, I, K, L, M, O,** P, R
Itea virginica	237	B, C, D, E, F, G,* H, J, L, M, O, R
Juniperus horizontalis	240	A, B, E, F, G, L, N, O, P, R
Morella cerifera	245	A, B, C, D, G, I, K, L, M, P
Rhapidophyllum hystrix	250	A, B, C, D, G, K, L, M

Rhododendron catawbiense	255	B, F, G, H, L, M
Rhus typhina	271	A, B, C, F, H, I, J, K, L, N, P
Sabal minor	274	A, B, C, D, E, F, G, K, L, M, P
Yucca spp.	283	A, B, E, F, G, H, K, L, N, R

M. Shrubs tolerant of shade

		ALL CATEGORIES THAT APPLY:
Aesculus parviflora	165	A, B, D, H, K, M
Agarista populifolia	168	G, H, K, L, M
Aralia spinosa	170	A, B, C, D, E, H, I, J, K, L, M, P, Q
Aronia arbutifolia	173	A, B, C, D, E, H, I, J, M, P
Callicarpa americana	179	A, B, C, D, E, H, I, M, P, R
Calycanthus floridus	181	B, C, D, E, F, H, J, K, M
Clethra acuminata	187	B, H, J, K, L, M, Q
Clethra alnifolia	189	A, D, H, J, K, M, R
Croton alabamensis	198	D, G, J, K, L, M, R
Hamamelis virginiana	211	A, B, C, D, F, H, J, K, M
Hydrangea arborescens	213	A, E, H, K, M, R
Hydrangea quercifolia	216	A, B, H, J, L, M, Q
Ilex glabra	223	A, B, C, D, E, F, G, I, K, L, M, P, R
Ilex verticillata	226	A, C, D, F, I, L, M, P
Ilex vomitoria	230	A, B, C, D, E, F, G, I, K, L, M, O,** P, R
Illicium floridanum	234	C, D, G, H, I, K, M
Itea virginica	237	B, C, D, E, F, G,* H, J, L, M, O, R
Lindera benzoin	242	A, B, C, D, E, H, I, J, K, M, P

Morella cerifera	245	A, B, C, D, G, I, K, L, M, P
Rhapidophyllum hystrix	250	A, B, C, D, G, K, L, M
Rhododendron calendulaceum	253	D, F, H, J, M
Rhododendron catawbiense	255	B, F, G, H, L, M
Rhododendron periclymenoides	258	D, F, H, M
Rhododendron prunifolium	260	D, F, H, J, M
Rhododendron viscosum	262	B, D, F, H, J, M
Sabal minor	274	A, B, C, D, E, F, G, K, L, M, P
Viburnum prunifolium	280	A, B, C, D, F, H, I, J, K, M, P, Q

N. Shrubs that perform best in full sun

		ALL CATEGORIES THAT APPLY:
Baccharis halimifolia	176	A, B, C, D, E, I, K, N
Cephalanthus occidentalis	184	A, C, D, H, K, N
Comptonia peregrina	193	A, B, C, E, F, K, N, O
Cornus sericea	195	A, B, C, D, E, F, H, I, J, K, L, N, P, Q, R
Cyrilla racemiflora	201	A, B, C, D, F, G,* H, J, L, N
Fothergilla spp.	204	A, B, C, D, E, F, H, J, K, N, R
Hamamelis vernalis	208	B, C, D, F, H, J, K, L, N
Hypericum spp.	220	A, B, E, F, H, K, N, O, Q, R
Juniperus horizontalis	240	A, B, E, F, G, L, N, O, P, R
Philadelphus inodorus	248	B, F, H, K, N
Rhus aromatica	265	A, B, C, E, F, H, I, J, K, N, O, P, R
Rhus copallina	268	A, B, C, F, H, I, J, K, N, P
Rhus typhina	271	A, B, C, F, H, I, J, K, L, N, P

Viburnum nudum	277	B, C, D, E, F, H, I, J, K, N, P
Yucca spp.	283	A, B, E, F, G, H, K, L, N, R

O. Shrubs that are ground covers

		ALL CATEGORIES THAT APPLY:
Comptonia peregrina	193	A, B, C, E, F, K, N, O
Hypericum spp.	220	A, B, E, F, H, K, N, O, Q, R
**Ilex vomitoria*	230	A, B, C, D, E, F, G, I, K, L, M, N, O,** P, R
Itea virginica	237	B, C, D, E, F, G,* H, J, L, M, O, R
Juniperus horizontalis	240	A, B, E, F, G, L, N, O, P, R
Rhus aromatica	265	A, B, C, E, F, H, I, J, K, N, O, P, R

P. Shrubs that provide food and shelter for birds directly
(please see native insect relationships in Part II, Primary Trees and Shrubs)

		ALL CATEGORIES THAT APPLY:
Aralia spinosa	170	A, B, C, D, E, H, I, J, K, L, M, P, Q
Aronia arbutifolia	173	A, B, C, D, E, H, I, J, M, P
Callicarpa americana	179	A, B, C, D, E, H, I, M, P, R
Cornus sericea	195	A, B, C, D, E, F, H, I, J, K, L, N, P, Q, R
Ilex glabra	223	A, B, C, D, E, F, G, I, K, L, M, P, R
Ilex verticillata	226	A, C, D, F, I, L, M, P
Ilex vomitoria	230	A, B, C, D, E, F, G, I, K, L, M, N, O,** P, R
Juniperus horizontalis	240	A, B, E, F, G, L, N, O, P, R
Lindera benzoin	242	A, B, C, D, E, H, I, J, K, M, P
Morella cerifera	245	A, B, C, D, G, I, K, L, M, P

Rhus aromatica	265	A, B, C, E, F, H, I, J, K, N, O, P, R
Rhus copallina	268	A, B, C, F, H, I, J, K, N, P
Rhus typhina	271	A, B, C, F, H, I, J, K, L, N, P
Sabal minor	274	A, B, C, D, E, F, G, K, L, M, P
Viburnum nudum	277	B, C, D, E, F, H, I, J, K, N, P
Viburnum prunifolium	280	A, B, C, D, F, H, I, J, K, M, P, Q

Q. Shrubs with interesting bark

		ALL CATEGORIES THAT APPLY:
Aralia spinosa	170	A, B, C, D, E, H, I, J, K, L, M, P, Q
Clethra acuminata	187	B, H, J, K, L, M, Q
Cornus sericea	195	A, B, C, D, E, F, H, I, J, K, L, N, P, Q, R
Hydrangea quercifolia	216	A, B, H, J, L, M, Q
Hypericum spp.	220	A, B, E, F, H, K, N, O, Q, R
Viburnum prunifolium	280	A, B, C, D, F, H, I, J, K, M, P, Q

R. Shrubs suitable for small containers

		ALL CATEGORIES THAT APPLY:
Callicarpa americana	179	A, B, C, D, E, H, I, M, P, R
Clethra alnifolia	189	A, D, H, J, K, M, R
Cornus sericea	195	A, B, C, D, E, F, H, I, J, K, L, N, P, Q, R
Croton alabamensis	198	D, G, J, K, L, M, R
Fothergilla spp.	204	A, B, C, D, E, F, H, J, K, N, R
Hydrangea arborescens	213	A, E, H, K, M, R
Hypericum spp.	220	A, B, E, F, H, K, N, O, Q, R

Ilex glabra	223	A, B, C, D, E, F, G, I, K, L, M, P, R
Ilex vomitoria	230	A, B, C, D, E, F, G, I, K, L, M, N, O,** P, R
Itea virginica	237	B, C, D, E, F, G,* H, J, L, M, O, R
Juniperus horizontalis	240	A, B, E, F, G, L, N, O, P, R
Rhus aromatica	265	A, B, C, E, F, H, I, J, K, N, O, P, R
Yucca spp.	283	A, B, E, F, G, H, K, L, N, R

* In the warmer parts of the South.

** Certain cultivars.

PART II

PRIMARY TREES
and SHRUBS

Acer pensylvanicum

Striped Maple, Moosewood, Snakebark

ATTRIBUTES/USE IN LANDSCAPE – The striped maple is a small, understory tree appreciated for its unique striped bark and good, although short-lived, autumn color. Use as a specimen, at the woodland edge, for naturalizing, rooftops or under utility lines.

SEASONS OF INTEREST

USDA Zones: 3–7		
SUN	**MOISTURE**	**pH**
Part shade to shade	Moist	5–7

WINTER	SPRING	SUMMER	AUTUMN
See bark photo			

FORM – The striped maple is a 15'–20' (40') deciduous large shrub or small tree. The open, vase-shaped branching pattern creates a rounded to irregular crown. It has a slower growth rate in cultivation than in a natural setting, and it is rather short-lived, to about 30 years.

COLOR – In spring, dangling pendant racemes, to 6" long, with small, ⅓" green-yellow flowers, appear below large, broad three-lobed leaves. The medium green leaves, to 7" long, have distinct red petioles. The autumn foliage is a good yellow. The thin bark is green with a pattern of white longitudinal striations.

TEXTURE – Coarse in leaf, medium in winter.

CULTURE – The striped maple's natural range is cooler areas and higher elevations from Nova Scotia to Pennsylvania and south through the Appalachians to Georgia, where it grows in well-drained acid soils.

A site with moist, well-drained soil is important for healthy growth. The striped maple performs best in climates with cool summers. It is very tolerant

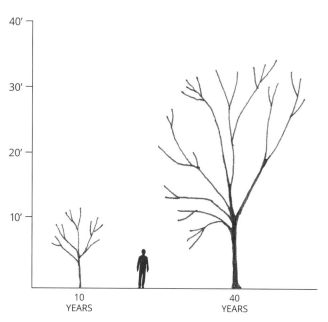

The distinctive bark of the striped maple.

Striped maple in autumn.

of shade but can tolerate more sun under cooler conditions. Protect bark from mechanical damage.

The striped maple does not tolerate flood, heat, salt, or drought. It transplants easily.

Spider mites and verticillium wilt can affect the tree but generally cause no serious damage. Moose love this maple, and deer may browse but less often. Leaves may scorch in full sun.

COMPANION PLANTS – In the wild, striped maple is associated with eastern white pine, American hornbeam, serviceberry, witch hazel, and sugar maple.

WILDLIFE – The seeds have a high value for birds, and the flowers provide nectar and pollen. The tree supports butterfly and moth larvae.

CULTIVATED VARIETIES – Choose for enhanced winter interest.

'Erythrocladum' – Young stems are a bright red with white striations that are most noticeable after leaves have fallen. The habit is more upright and can be pruned to force new red shoots. The bark ages to a yellow brown. It is usually grafted.

Acer rubrum

Red Maple

ATTRIBUTES/USE IN LANDSCAPE – The red maple is an attractive and popular shade tree, with brilliant autumn color. It makes a handsome specimen and is useful in many situations for lawns, rain gardens and bioretention areas, park plantings, golf courses, and so on. It is a good street tree where salt is not used, though its roots can lift sidewalks. It is an excellent plant for wildlife.

SEASONS OF INTEREST

| WINTER | SPRING | SUMMER | AUTUMN |

FORM – The red maple is a large, fast-growing, upright tree, 40'–60' (10'). It is pyramidal or elliptical in youth. As it ages, its strong, ascending branches form a dense oval crown.

USDA Zones: 5–8		
SUN	**MOISTURE**	**pH**
Sun to part shade	Dry to moist	4.5–8

COLOR – The small, red, profuse flowers are easily viewed from a distance in late winter to mid-spring, depending on latitude and elevation. The emerging leaves are light green, changing to medium-dark green as the summer progresses. The autumn foliage is spectacular in most individuals, with colors ranging from red, yellow, and orange to combinations of each. Young twigs are reddish in color, while the bark on most small and intermediate-sized branches is a

A young 'October Glory' in autumn.

smooth light gray. The older trunk and branches will have a furrowed, dark brown bark.

TEXTURE – Medium.

CULTURE – The familiar red maple is native to most of the eastern half of the United States. It is usually most abundant along stream and bottom-lands, where it grows rapidly to heights or spreads approaching 90'–100', but it adapts to a wide variety of conditions.

Red maple is one of the most tolerant native trees and grows very well, although more slowly, in upland locations that may be very dry. The species is tolerant of heavy clay to sandy soils, compacted soils, and a wide range of pH and air pollution. It is sensitive to salt.

Red maple grows best in full sun but is tolerant of moderate shade, especially when young. The autumn color is spectacular, particularly where there are large day to night temperature changes during autumn. The wood of red maple is relatively soft and brittle and can be damaged by heavy ice and snow loads. This problem can be exacerbated by improper pruning, including the failure to remove weak or crossing branches at an early age.

The roots are generally shallow, making the young red maple easy to transplant anytime during its dormancy. Trees should be chosen from local growers to assure cold hardiness.

There are many insects and diseases listed for red maple, including verticillium wilt, various canker diseases, leaf spots, leaf hoppers, and aphids. Usually these pests are of little concern, but when red maples are stressed, perhaps due to poor horticultural practices, the pest problem may become more severe. The introduced long-horned beetle may cause damage in areas affected by this insect. Where deer are an

'Brandywine' with dense summer foliage, as a street tree.

issue, they may browse on the foliage of seedlings and easy-to-reach branches. Young trees should be protected from deer.

COMPANION PLANTS – In nature, red maple associates with pine, sugar maple, river birch, common bald cypress, black gum, and sweet gum. The red maple produces a dense shade in maturity which, combined with shallow roots, makes it a difficult tree to grow grass or other ornamental plants beneath.

WILDLIFE – The leaves provide food for 300 species of caterpillars. Additionally, the red maple supports

The red maple's signature early-spring flowers.

pollinators and provides nectar. It also provides nesting and seeds (in female trees) for birds and small mammals.

CULTIVATED VARIETIES – There are many cultivated varieties and hybrids; some of the more well-known ones are listed below. Male clones have no seed litter. Choose for autumn color, cold hardiness, and form.

'**Brandywine**' – Consistent brilliant autumn color, scarlet turning to bright burgundy. Male.

'**Karpick**' – A narrow form 40'–50' tall, half as wide. Bright red twigs. Yellow or red autumn color. Male.

'**October Glory**' – An oval to rounded form to 40' with vibrant red fall foliage. The glossy dark green summer foliage is late to color, and brilliant autumn leaves remain late into the season. Best for locations where early autumn freezes are uncommon. Female.

'**Northwood**' – Very cold tolerant. Shiny summer foliage, but autumn color is not consistent in the South.

'**Sun Valley**' – Good symmetric oval crowned form. Brilliant red turning bright burgundy in late autumn. Male.

Acer saccharum

Sugar Maple, Rock Maple, Hard Maple

ATTRIBUTES/USE IN LANDSCAPE – The sugar maple's exceptional autumn color is the outstanding feature of this handsome, large shade tree. It is used as a specimen or grouping for large residences, parks, golf courses, and campuses; and for naturalizing and the upper edge of bio retention areas. It is excellent for wildlife.

SEASONS OF INTEREST

| WINTER | SPRING | SUMMER | AUTUMN |

See form below

FORM – Sugar maple is a large deciduous tree reaching 60'–75' (100') and about ⅔ as wide. It is dense and upright. Oval in youth, it usually forms a rounded crown with age, but there can be considerable variation between individuals. The handsome habit is appealing in winter. The tree's growth rate is medium when young and slow with maturity. It is a long-lived tree, to 200 years.

USDA Zones: 3–8		
SUN	**MOISTURE**	**pH**
Full sun	Moist	5.5–7.5

COLOR – The sugar maple leaf resembles the classic maple symbol of Canada. Palmate leaves are three to five lobed and 3"–6" long and across. They are a medium to dark green above and pale green below, both with a medium finish. The brilliant autumn colors range from bright yellow to orange to a seemingly fluorescent scarlet, sometimes on the same tree. Parts of the tree may change color ahead of other parts, but the coloring is good even in zones 7 and 8. The bark is variable. In young trees it is a smooth grayish brown. As it ages it develops

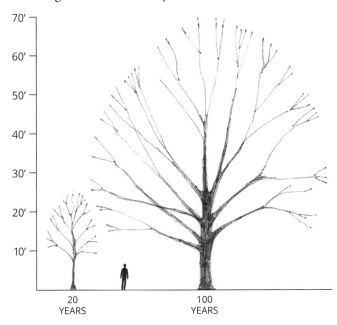

A sugar maple in early autumn.

A well-formed sugar maple in Maryland.

fissures, which ultimately deepen, so that dark gray (sometimes chalky), irregular, shaggy, longitudinal scales form. The branches can appear black against bright autumn foliage.

TEXTURE – Medium.

CULTURE – The sugar maple is an important component of rich northeastern hardwood forests. The natural range extends from Eastern Canada to Minnesota and south along the New England coast to New Jersey and west through West Virginia and the Appalachians into Tennessee.

The best autumn color, form, and growth rate are exhibited in full sun. The sugar maple is very tolerant of different soils and sites but grows best in deep, moist, well-drained, slightly acidic soils. Transplant in spring.

Among the maples, it has the strongest wood and is tolerant of snow, ice, and wind.

The sugar maple has been used as a street tree, but its shallow, sidewalk-lifting roots and its intolerance of pollution, salt, and compacted soils usually make it unsuitable. This being said, its roots are not as shallow and competitive as those of the red or silver maples. The sugar maple is moderately tolerant of drought, but intolerant of long-term flooding and chlorine. Its intolerance of chlorine may restrict its use near swimming pools.

The sugar maple produces maple syrup and high-quality wood and is the primary contributor to the autumn color in New England.

A naturally occurring subspecies or similar species is *A. barbatum* (*A. saccharum* subsp. *floridanum*). The southern sugar maple or Florida maple is a smaller tree, 25'–50' tall and half as wide with smaller foliage. It is native to rich, well-drained woods in the Piedmont and coastal plains of the southeast, zones 7–9. It is more heat tolerant than *A. saccharum*.

If it becomes established in North America, the Asian long-horned beetle will be a serious problem in maples. Young trees should be protected from deer.

COMPANION PLANTS – In nature, sugar maple associates with white oak, American hophornbeam, striped maple and others. The heavy shade and shallow root system can create a challenge for plants grown beneath a maple. Ground cover possibilities include ferns, gingers, and moss.

WILDLIFE – Sugar maple provides pollen and nectar for hummingbirds and insects. It supports 300 species of caterpillar. In addition to providing this protein source for birds, the female sugar maples provide seed for birds and small mammals through the winter. It is a good tree for nesting and shelter when in leaf.

CULTIVATED VARIETIES – There are many varieties. Consider for choice of autumn foliage color, form, size, accelerated growth, and heat tolerance. The narrow varieties are good for allées. Among the better varieties are the following:

'**Green Mountain**' – Rapid growth rate, straight central leader with a narrow oval form. Large, thick, but deeply cut dark green leaves give it a finer texture. Good bright yellow to orange and red autumn color. Hardy.

'**Legacy**' – Heat and drought tolerant, performs well in the South as well as in cold temperatures. Thick, glossy, dark green foliage turning to good yellow and orange in autumn. Dense branching for a uniform, tight oval form. Popular and vigorous.

'**Sweet Shadow**' – 50' × 50'. Large dark green leaves with somewhat drooping, deeply cut lobes for a fine, lacy texture. Autumn color is yellow to orange. Vigorous.

'**Temple's Upright**' ('**Monumentale**') – Narrow, upright, columnar habit, 40'–50' × 15' wide. It has a central leader with ascending branches, creating an elliptical form. Leathery leaves have wavy margins.

Aesculus pavia

Red Buckeye

ATTRIBUTES/USE IN LANDSCAPE – The red buckeye is a small tree or multi-stemmed shrub with showy spring flowers after early spring leaf out. It has attractive early spring and summer foliage. It may be used as a specimen, street treet, at the woodland edge, and in a rain garden for residential and park projects.

SEASONS OF INTEREST

WINTER	SPRING	SUMMER	AUTUMN

FORM – The red buckeye grows to about 10'–20' (35') tall × 10'–15' wide or more. Whether a small tree or large shrub, it usually has an irregular and open form with a rounded crown.

COLOR – Very early leaves emerge in spring followed by showy, profuse red flowers in early spring, following new leaves. The flowers are arranged on erect to

USDA Zones: 4–8		
SUN	**MOISTURE**	**pH**
Full sun to part shade	Moist	5.5–7.5

drooping terminal panicles in clusters, 3"–6" long. The palmately compound leaves have five (seven) 3"–6" long leaflets plus a 2"–5" long petiole. The leaves can be very glossy green. They emerge bronze, turning to a medium to dark green above and pubescent gray below. Leaves drop early in autumn, often by September, with no appreciable autumn coloration.

TEXTURE – Medium coarse summer and winter.

The showy, profuse, early-spring flowers of red buckeye.

20'

10'

5 YEARS	15 YEARS

The coarse mid-autumn (sometimes earlier) to winter habit of the red buckeye.

A red buckeye grown in full sun.

CULTURE – The red buckeye is native to Piedmont and coastal woodlands from Virginia to Florida and from Illinois to Texas, up to 1,500' in elevation.

The red buckeye flowers best in rich soils and full sun with moist, well-drained soil. It will flower in shade, but the habit becomes rangy with less sunlight. Red buckeye will tolerate clay and sandy soil, and is moderately tolerant of salt. It also tolerates some drought, but foliage may scorch.

Another naturally occurring variety is *A. pavia* var. *flavescens,* a usually yellow-flowering understory shrub. Naturally occurring crosses of *A. pavia* and *A. pavia* var. *flavescens* are known as *Aesculus × hybrid* and may have red and yellow blooms. *Aesculus sylvatica,* the painted buckeye, has flowers that are yellow, pink, or both colors.

The fruit has little ornamental value. Seeds, bark, and foliage are quite toxic to humans and livestock.

Red buckeye is tolerant of pollution. It is rarely bothered seriously by insect pests, disease, or deer.

COMPANION PLANTS – The red buckeye combines well with native azaleas, croton, fothergilla, smooth hydrangea, inkberry, Virginia sweetspire, and many others.

WILDLIFE – It is a good source of early-spring nectar for migrating hummingbirds, butterflies, and bees.a

Amelanchier spp.

Downy, Shadbush, Allegheny, and Apple Serviceberries

Note to the reader: The serviceberry species listed below are very similar and can be difficult to distinguish, botanically, from one another. We have grouped them together here.

USDA Zones: 4–8 (9)		
SUN	**MOISTURE**	**pH**
Full sun to part shade	Dry to wet	5.5–6.5

ATTRIBUTES/USE IN LANDSCAPE – The serviceberries are a beautiful, very early-flowering group of small trees or large shrubs with usually good autumn coloring and ornamental gray bark. They are effective as specimens, in groupings, rain gardens, rooftops, the understory, at the woodland edge, near streams and ponds, and as a street tree. They are especially effective when planted against dark backgrounds. The serviceberries are stunning in flower in very early spring. They are excellent for wildlife.

Amelanchier arborea **var.** *arborea* – The downy serviceberry or common serviceberry is the largest of the *Amelanchiers*. It is a small, graceful, short-trunked or multi-stemmed tree or large shrub. The multi-stemmed plant is vase shaped with an open branch structure. At 12'–20' (30'), it can be wider than tall. Its 1"–3" long, lanceolate to obovoid leaves are lightly serrated and emerge silvery, becoming a medium green in summer. The ¼"–⅓" green to red to purple fruit mature in hanging clusters in late summer to early autumn.

SEASONS OF INTEREST

WINTER
See bark photo

SPRING

SUMMER

AUTUMN

30'

20'

10'

15 YEARS

40 YEARS

The very early spring flowers of a multi-stemmed shadbush.

Amelanchier canadensis – The shadbush or shadblow serviceberry grows to about 25'–30' by half as wide and spreads by suckering. It grows in the Piedmont and coastal wetlands along the East Coast. The shadblow has an upright, dense habit with a narrow crown, 1"–3" leaves, upright flower clusters, and red to purple berries that ripen to black.

Amelanchier laevis – The Allegheny serviceberry grows to about 15'–25' (40') by the same width and is usually multi-stemmed. Its leaves, 1½"–3", begin bronze in color. The red fruit ripens to purple or black and is sweeter and juicier than shadbush. This plant is less likely to sucker and has superior autumn color to the shadbush.

Amelanchier × grandiflora – The apple serviceberry, 15'–25' × 12'–15', is a cross between *A. arborea* and *A. laevis*.

The serviceberries have a medium growth rate and relatively short life span, 30–40 years.

COLOR – Showy, profuse, pendulous 2"–4" racemes of small white flowers emerge in very early spring before the leaves. They are lightly fragrant. The duration of bloom is dependent on weather but is usually five to seven days. The autumn leaf color can be a yellow to orange to red, but it is quite variable and can sometimes be nondescript, especially if the foliage has been damaged by spider mites. The cultivated varieties (hybrids) listed below offer a more consistent fall coloration than seed-grown plants. The handsome gray bark is smooth with vertical striations in youth, and develops shallow furrows with maturity.

TEXTURE – Fine in winter, medium to fine in leaf.

CULTURE – The native range is most of the East

A serviceberry in autumn.

Coast with the exception of the coastal areas of the Carolinas south through Florida.

Serviceberry tolerates a wide range of soils, including clay, but performs best in slightly acidic, moist soils in full sun. Drier soils are tolerated with more shade and cooler temperatures. It is one of the earliest trees to bloom in the spring.

All of the serviceberries have some issues when in a challenging environment, but we felt their attributes warranted them a place on our primary list. They are tolerant of salt, soil compaction, drought, and heat but somewhat intolerant of pollution.

The attractive, smooth, light gray bark of serviceberries.

As members of the rose family, they can be susceptible to occasional rust diseases. Most of the rust diseases affecting rose family members have an alternate host in junipers. If there are no species of juniper within a radius of several miles, there will be no rust problems. However, this is rarely the case, so some method of control may need to be used. Spider mites can affect the appearance when grown in a hot, dry location. Deer occasionally browse the foliage.

COMPANION PLANTS – Serviceberries exist in nature and combine well with sugar maple, hornbeam, flowering dogwood, sourwood, black gum, Virginia sweetspire, spicebush, winterberry, and inkberry.

WILDLIFE – The flowers provide pollen and food for hummingbirds, butterflies, and bees. The serviceberries host hundreds of species of caterpillar. Birds love the berries.

CULTIVATED VARIETIES – Choose cultivated varieties for size, autumn color, heat and drought tolerance, and disease and insect resistance.

Amelanchier × *grandiflora* 'Autumn Brilliance' – 20'–25'. Grows quickly. Leaves tend to remain healthy through the summer on well-sited plants. Excellent red autumn color.
Amelanchier × *grandiflora* 'Princess Diana' – 25' × 15'–20'. Leaves tend to remain healthy through the summer on well-sited plants. Excellent red autumn color. Very hardy.

Betula lenta

Sweet Birch, Black Birch, Cherry Birch

ATTRIBUTES/USE IN LANDSCAPE – Sweet birch is an attractive, medium-sized canopy tree notable for its excellent yellow autumn color and appealing bark. It is effective as a specimen and in groupings for parks, bioretention areas, golf courses, highways, and large residences. It is an excellent plant for wildlife.

USDA Zones: 3–7		
SUN	**MOISTURE**	**pH**
Full sun to very light shade	Moist to wet	4.8–6.8

SEASONS OF INTEREST

WINTER	SPRING	SUMMER	AUTUMN
See form below			

FORM – Sweet birch is a single-trunked tree, 40'–50' (90') and spreading 35'–45'. It grows fast in youth, when it is conical in shape. In maturity, growth becomes more moderate, and it develops an oval to rounded shape, with ascending limbs and slightly pendulous branchlets. Sweet birch has a medium lifespan, to 100 years and more.

COLOR – The leaf is a simple, ovate, serrated (or doubly serrated) shape, shiny, dark green on the upper surface in summer, 2½"–6" long and 1½"–3½" wide. Foliage is lighter green at leaf out in late spring and a reliably golden yellow in autumn. Sweet birch flowers are small, tan catkins in spring. In youth the bark is thin and red brown with horizontal lenticels like a young cherry. Older bark remains gray, with vertical, scaly plates, unusual in birches.

A mature sweet birch grown in full sun.

ABOVE: *Sweet birch mature bark texture.*
RIGHT: *The smooth cherrylike bark of a young sweet birch.*

with cool summer nights, unlike river birch, which tolerates the heat and humidity of the southeastern coastal plain. Sweet birch is deer resistant.

COMPANION PLANTS – Sweet birch combines well with our native azaleas and hydrangeas, fothergilla, summersweet, Virginia sweetspire, and ferns.

WILDLIFE – According to Darke and Tallamy, birches support more than 400 species of caterpillars as well as providing food for migrating birds in spring and autumn. The seeds appeal to songbirds and upland ground birds. The catkins provide pollen for bees and other insects.

TEXTURE – Medium in leaf. In winter, sweet birch has an attractive, fine, uniform texture with shiny, tan twigs.

CULTURE – Sweet birch is native from Maine to Pennsylvania and south through the Appalachians to northern Georgia and Alabama, often along small streams and rivers.

It prefers moist, well-drained soils, but will tolerate drier soils. It will grow in a wide range of soils from sandy to moderately heavy clay. While found commonly on limestone soils, it also tolerates moderately acidic soils and salt. It performs best in cooler climates.

Sweet birch is moderately resistant to ice storm damage, more so than the river birch or red maple. If pruning is required, it should be done in the summer, when their sap is not flowing. In fact, birch sap is used as syrup, like maple sap, particularly for birch beer. The bark smells and tastes of wintergreen. *B. allegheniensis*, yellow birch, is a similar species with less interesting young bark.

Like river birch, sweet birch is resistant to bronze birch borer. But sweet birch grows best in climates

A mature sweet birch grown among younger trees.

Betula nigra

River Birch

ATTRIBUTES/USE IN LANDSCAPE – River birch is a popular, large shade tree with exceptionally attractive bark, interesting form, and rapid growth. It is effective as a specimen, shade tree, and in small groupings along streams and ponds. It is used in parks, estates, campuses, golf courses, and other large sites. See the cultivated varieties below for plants suitable to smaller-scale projects including rain gardens. River birch has good wildlife value.

SEASONS OF INTEREST

| WINTER | SPRING | SUMMER | AUTUMN |

See bark photo

FORM – River birch is a single-trunked or, often preferred, multi-trunked tree. It grows 40'–50' (70') and taller in cultivation with a spread of 40'–60'. The multi-trunked forms tend to be shorter than the single-trunked tree. In youth it is pyramidal

USDA Zones: 3–9		
SUN	**MOISTURE**	**pH**
Full sun to part shade	Moist to wet	4–6

with arching branches. As it ages, it develops a more rounded shape. River birch is a vigorous, fast-growing tree. Birches are generally relatively short-lived, but a properly placed tree may be enjoyed for more than 100 years.

COLOR – The bark of the river birch is its exceptional and distinguishing feature. The thin, curling as they peel, dark gray-brown to tan patches reveal

The showy bark of 'Cully' ('Heritage').

50'
40'
30'
20'
10'

15
YEARS

60
YEARS

A clump form of river birch in full sun.

a smooth peach- to buff-colored trunk. The leaves, 1½"–3½" in length, emerge a light green and mature to a shiny dark green and sometimes a variable yellow, before dropping in mid-autumn. If the summer is quite dry, the leaves may drop earlier.

TEXTURE – Medium in leaf, fine without leaves. The foliage texture is lively in a breeze.

CULTURE – Primarily a coastal plain tree, river birch spreads into the Piedmont from northern New Jersey south to Florida and west into Ohio and Texas and up the Mississippi River. It is very tolerant of the high heat and humidity of the southeast coastal plain.

The river birch prefers acid, consistently moist, fertile, well-drained soils. Once established, though, it is tolerant of drought and periodic standing water. It has adapted to drought by dropping some of its leaves in dry years. It will grow in a wide range of soils, including heavy clay. The river birch is the most southern and the most culturally adaptable of the birches, including excellent cold tolerance. It is resistant to air pollution, soil compaction, and salt. The best growth is achieved when planted in full sun.

The many fine, wiry branches can catch snow and ice and lead to some significant loss of small and mid-sized branches. But the tree recovers within a season or two. If pruning is required, it should be done in the summer, when the tree's sap is not flowing.

River birch is resistant to the bronze birch borer, a serious pest for some other birches. Deer do not favor river birch. In higher pH soils, the tree can suffer from chlorosis.

COMPANION PLANTS – In nature it associates with sweet gum, sycamore, and swamp white oak. Many native shrubs combine well with river birch.

WILDLIFE – River birches support more than 400 species of caterpillars. Additionally, they provide food for migrating birds in spring and autumn with their seeds. The seeds appeal to songbirds and upland ground birds including wild turkey and grouse. River birch provides cover and nesting sites as well. The catkins appeal to pollinators.

River birch planted in a parking lot bioswale.

A river birch in autumn, in a rain garden.

CULTIVATED VARIETIES – Select for size and hardiness.

B. nigra 'BNMTF' ('Dura-Heat') – 30'–40' tall × 25'–35'. This variety is known for tolerating heat and humidity particularly well. Good leaf retention.

B. nigra 'Cully' ('Heritage') – A popular and superior variety to the species. Especially resistant to bronze birch borer and leaf spot diseases. It can have nice yellow autumn color.

B. nigra 'Little King' ('Fox Valley') – 10' × 12'. A multi-stemmed shrub for use in smaller sites. Dense, oval, and compact. Orange-brown bark peels to tan inner bark.

Carpinus caroliniana

American Hornbeam, Ironwood, Musclewood, Blue Beech

ATTRIBUTES/USE IN LANDSCAPE – The American hornbeam is a small understory tree noted for its smooth, sinewy trunk, attractive form, and autumn foliage. It is useful as a specimen, in a grouping, at the woodland edge, and for naturalizing. The hornbeam makes a nice small shade tree, hedge, or understory woodland tree for many uses including rain gardens. It works well under transmission wires, but it is not tolerant of salt. It is a good plant for wildlife support.

SEASONS OF INTEREST

WINTER	SPRING	SUMMER	AUTUMN
See form below			

FORM – American hornbeam is a deciduous, slow-growing, single- or multi-stemmed tree, 20'–30' (50') tall and wide. In either case, the form can be very attractive. Its habit is most dense, shorter, wider, and more uniform in full sun. In the woodland understory, it is quite open and branching is elevated. The trunk and branches can be twisted,

USDA Zones: 3–8 (9)		
SUN	**MOISTURE**	**pH**
Full sun to full shade	Dry to moist	5.5–7

but the overall outline is a clean, rounded shape, particularly in the sun. As with most understory trees, it is generally short-lived, usually to around 50 years, but it can live up to 125 years. Smaller branches take pruning well. It is neither as large nor as formal as the European hornbeam.

COLOR – Thin, light green leaves become a shiny medium green in summer. The American hornbeam leaves are similar in shape and texture to their close relatives the beech and hophornbeam. The fruit consists of clusters of involucres hanging at the tip of the branches. Each involucre encloses a small oval nut. The fruits are evident through late spring to early autumn. The smooth, light blue or brown-gray bark is similar to that of a beech, and the trunk is often described as muscular and sinewy. The autumn foliage colors of

Summer foliage with fruit.

30'

20'

10'

15 YEARS

50 YEARS

A grove of American hornbeam at Longwood Gardens, Pennsylvania.

yellow or orange are most common, but some trees are reliably red. In some cases, a tree will not color well; this can be cultural but may also be genetic. Choose plants for good autumn color if possible.

TEXTURE – Fine in leaf. Medium in winter.

CULTURE – The American hornbeam is native to the eastern half of the United States excepting northern Maine and Vermont and Florida. It is common and found in bottomlands, swamps, and river and stream margins, as well as moist upland forests.

Moist (mesic) soils are preferred, but it can tolerate periodic flooding as well as short-term drought. The form is more dense and the autumn coloring best in full sun. The hornbeam is sensitive to soil compaction, road salt, and damage by turf equipment.

The trunk can spiral, and the branches are finely

Autumn foliage.

The smooth, sinewy trunk of our native hornbeam.

textured. While smaller branches take pruning very well, the recovery from pruning large branches is slow, and despite the heavy weight of the wood, wounds are prone to rot. Transplant from root-pruned stock.

American hornbeam is usually not bothered by any serious pests or diseases, but it has been attacked by ambrosia beetle in nurseries in very wet conditions. It is not a preferred plant of deer.

COMPANION PLANTS – In nature, our hornbeam associates with red oak, willow oak, sugar maple, shagbark hickory, river birch, downy serviceberry, flowering dogwood, American holly, and spicebush. It combines well with ephemeral wildflowers, ferns, and ground covers.

WILDLIFE – The native hornbeam supports dozens of caterpillar larvae, including the tiger swallowtail. For birds, it provides understory cover and nesting and supports spring migrants. Ducks and warblers enjoy the seeds. It is a pollen source. Small mammals eat the seed as well.

CULTIVATED VARIETIES – Choose plants for form and autumn color.

'**Native Flame**' – Select for red autumn coloring and an upright oval form, 30' tall × 20' wide.
'**Firespire**' – An attractive upright form, 20' tall × 10' wide, with very good, red-orange autumn color.

Carya ovata

Shagbark Hickory

ATTRIBUTES/USE IN LANDSCAPE – The shagbark hickory is one of our most handsome large shade trees. It is notable for its unique shaggy bark and attractive autumn foliage. Use as a specimen and shade tree for large lawns, parks, and highway plantings. The shagbark hickory performs well in urban settings but does produce litter. It is an excellent plant for wildlife.

SEASONS OF INTEREST

WINTER	SPRING	SUMMER	AUTUMN
See bark photo and form			

FORM – The shagbark hickory is a large tree, 70'–90' (120') tall × 50'–70' wide, with a regular oval outline. The trunk is straight, and branching is open, ascending and descending. Growing at less than 6" per year, it is generally even slower than oaks. The

USDA Zones: 4–8		
SUN	**MOISTURE**	**pH**
Full sun to part shade	Dry to moist	4–7

shagbark hickory is long-lived, to 250 or 300 years. Its wood is exceptionally strong.

COLOR – The medium green, pinnately compound leaves emerge pale and velvety in spring. The flowers are fairly inconspicuous. The autumn color can be an excellent early and persistent golden yellow. The distinctive gray bark peels away from the main trunk in thick, long, wide, longitudinal strips.

TEXTURE – Medium coarse. The signature shaggy bark texture provides interest in all seasons.

Distinctive "shagbark."

20 YEARS	80 YEARS

A fine, mature specimen on a busy town street.

CULTURE – The shagbark hickory is an upper-story woodland tree. It is native to most of the eastern half of the country with the exception of northern Maine, Vermont, New Hampshire, and New York, and the coastal plain from New Jersey south. Older trees are common in woodlands of the east, but younger trees are more and more scarce as deer populations increase.

The shagbark hickory is adaptable to a variety of soils. Easily grown, it is tolerant of clay soils and drought, but it does not tolerate flooding. It performs well in urban settings, but litter from leaves and nuts must be considered. The shagbark hickory's coarse branching and strong wood withstand snow and ice well. It is moderately salt tolerant.

The compound leaves have five leaflets including a larger terminal leaf. The green to brown, 1"–1½", globular fruit is a hard-husked, edible nut. It is sweet and enjoyed by humans and wildlife. Additionally, a delicious syrup is made by incorporating powdered bark.

The interesting shaggy bark on older specimens and bright autumn color make this a good tree to plant, if you have the space, despite its slow growth rate. It can be difficult to locate in nurseries due to its slow growth and deep taproot, but it is worth seeking out. The taproot grows 2'–3' in the first three years, so it is important to access trees that have been root pruned in the nursery. Transplant balled and burlapped in early spring or fall.

There are a number of related useful *Carya* species. *C. cordiformis* (bitternut or swamp hickory) is suitable for moist to wet sites. *C. glabra* (pignut hickory) is useful in a variety of habitats and has bright yellow autumn color. *C. illinoinensis* (pecan) grows and fruits best in the South (zones 6–9). There are many cultivated varieties for nut production. *C. laciniosa* (shellbark hickory) is similar to

Shagbark hickory autumn foliage.

C. ovata, but with less dramatic bark. It has a very sweet nut and is suitable for wet sites.

I have never seen any serious pests or diseases on this tree. Deer usually will not bother trees taller than 8', but smaller plants should be protected from browsing and antler rubbing.

COMPANION PLANTS – Many native shrubs, ground covers, and turf grow well under this high-branching, taprooted tree. Shagbark and other hickories produce a chemical called juglone. This chemical is known to be toxic to other plants. However, juglone is not as concentrated in hickories as it is in black walnut (*Juglans nigra*), and hickories rarely cause harmful effects in other plant species.

WILDLIFE – The tree is very valuable for larvae of moths and butterflies, feeding about 200 species and providing protein for young birds. Many mammals enjoy hickory nuts.

Celtis laevigata

Sugarberry, Southern Hackberry

ATTRIBUTES/USE IN LANDSCAPE – Sugarberry is a hardy, large shade tree with mostly smooth, thin gray bark and a tolerance for many environmental conditions. It is effective as a shade tree for large properties and highway plantings, as a street tree, and in windbreaks, rain gardens, and bioswales. Sugarberry is a good tree for wildlife support.

SEASONS OF INTEREST

WINTER   SPRING   SUMMER   AUTUMN

FORM – While the species form may be variable, sugarberry is usually a large, straight-trunked tree, 60'–80' (100') × 40'–60' wide, with upright limbs and arching branches that become slightly drooping while forming an open, spreading, rounded crown. It has a medium to fast growth rate. The trunk may

USDA Zones: 6–9		
SUN	**MOISTURE**	**pH**
Full sun to part shade	Dry to wet	5.5–7.8

be up to 3' in diameter, and the tree can live several hundred years.

COLOR – The simple, glossy green, 2'–4', mostly lanceolate leaves leaf out early. The autumn color is usually an undistinguished yellow. The tree is

The thin, light gray bark of sugarberry.

60'

50'

40'

30'

20'

10'

15 YEARS   50 YEARS

named for its sweet, ¼", inconspicuous berries. The unique light gray-brown bark is thin, with perhaps some corky warts and ridges, though fewer than *C. occidentalis*.

TEXTURE – Medium to fine in winter, medium in leaf. The main branches are stout with numerous small twigs.

CULTURE – Sugarberry is native throughout the east from southern Virginia south through Florida and west beyond the Mississippi River. Most commonly it inhabits stream banks and floodplains.

The sugarberry, or southern hackberry, differs in several traits from the northern hackberry. The sugarberry (1) is larger, (2) is less cold-hardy, (3) is more moisture tolerant, (4) has glossier and narrower leaves, (5) has less corky bark, and (6) is resistant to witches'-broom. Where their native ranges overlap, the two *Celtis* species can cross and become confusing to tell apart.

Sugarberry will grow in a wide range of soils from sandy to moderately heavy clay. It tolerates both moderately acidic and moderately alkaline soils. Soils are usually well-drained, but it is also tolerant of recurring seasonal short-term flooding that is common adjacent to small streams and rivers. I have seen sugarberry grown beautifully as a street tree in New Bern, North Carolina, in spite of periodic saltwater flooding in hurricanes, prolonged droughts, and road salts. It also tolerates poor, compacted soils and general urban neglect.

The spring flowers are inconspicuous. The fruits are sweet and edible with a very hard seed. The berries can create a light litter load beyond the deciduous leaves. The thin, beech-like bark should be protected from mechanical injury associated with turf equipment.

Sugarberry in early autumn.

Nipple gall on leaves may be an issue in some situations, affecting the appearance but not the health of the tree. Sugarberry is moderately resistant to deer browsing.

COMPANION PLANTS – Sugarberry combines well with summersweet, spicebush, and Virginia sweetspire.

WILDLIFE – The flowers provide spring pollen and nectar for hummingbirds, butterflies, and bees. Sugarberry provides food for wintering birds, spring and fall migrations, and breeding birds including songbirds and game birds. Several butterfly larvae use *Celtis* exclusively. Young stands provide shelter for game birds and small mammals.

CULTIVATED VARIETIES – Choose for foliage type.

'**All Seasons**' – Shiny leaves turning a bright yellow in autumn. This variety has a well-balanced growth habit.

Celtis occidentalis

Common Hackberry, Northern Hackberry

ATTRIBUTES/USE IN LANDSCAPE – The common hackberry is a tough, sturdy, medium to large shade tree with distinctive bark, especially interesting in winter. It is effective as a shade tree for large properties, as a street tree, and in rain gardens and bioswales. The hackberries are excellent trees for wildlife.

USDA Zones: 3–9		
SUN	**MOISTURE**	**pH**
Full sun to part shade	Dry to wet	5.6–7.8

SEASONS OF INTEREST

WINTER	SPRING	SUMMER	AUTUMN
See bark photo			

FORM – The common hackberry is a medium to large tree, 40'–60' (100'). Its stout branches ascend and arch forming an open, spreading, rounded crown. This hackberry is usually nearly as wide as tall until old age, where it can become spreading and picturesque, with the pendulous branch tips nearly reaching the ground. It grows at a slow to medium rate and can live several hundred years.

COLOR – The simple, glossy to dull green, 2"–5", ovate, pointed-tip leaves become an undistinguished yellow in autumn. The ¼" berries are inconspicuous, ripen in autumn, and are enjoyed by birds. The unique light gray bark is thin with protruding, corky warts and ridges, adding to winter interest. As the tree ages, the ridges become a thick and scaly, highly textured bark.

The unique texture of hackberry bark.

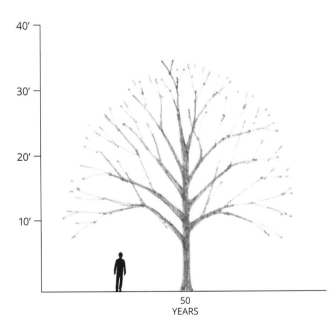

50
YEARS

A 75-year-old common hackberry in autumn.

TEXTURE – Medium. The main branches are stout with numerous small twigs.

CULTURE – The common hackberry is native from southern New England into Virginia and Tennessee and west beyond the Mississippi River. (See *C. laevigata*, the sugarberry or southern hackberry, for a southern native and a summary of differences between these two hackberries. Both species can grow well through most of the range of our book.)

Hackberry will grow in a wide range of soils from sandy to moderately heavy clay. While found commonly on limestone soils, it also tolerates moderately acidic soils. Soils are usually well drained, but the tree is also tolerant of the sporadic seasonal flooding that is common adjacent to small streams and rivers. It is tolerant of salt, occasional drought, heat, air pollution, wind, and compacted soils.

The spring flowers are inconspicuous. The fruits are sweet and edible with a very hard seed. The berries can create a light litter load beyond the deciduous leaves.

Hackberry is a member of the elm family, but it is highly resistant or immune to Dutch elm disease. It can host psyllids, insects that cause nipple gall—small round pockets—on the leaves. When a tree is

This Hackberry is one of the oldest trees in Washington, DC.

near a residence, the psyllids may be a brief nuisance in autumn. In areas affected by witches'-broom, it is not unusual for the hackberry to become a host. This disease can affect appearance and vigor, but resistant varieties of hackberry are available.

COMPANION PLANTS – The common hackberry is shallow rooted. It combines well with hickory spp., American holly, maple spp., redbud, summersweet, Virginia sweetspire, and spicebush.

WILDLIFE – The flowers provide spring pollen and nectar for hummingbirds, butterflies, and bees. The sweet berries are enjoyed by many birds. Several butterfly larvae use hackberry exclusively. Young stands provide shelter for game birds, small mammals, and deer.

CULTIVATED VARIETIES – Choose for foliage color, form, and immunity to witches'-broom.

'Prairie Pride' – Immune to witches'-broom and lower fruit yield. Shiny, dark green, dense foliage.
'Prairie Sentinel' – A columnar form.

Cercis canadensis

Eastern Redbud

ATTRIBUTES/USE IN LANDSCAPE – The eastern redbud is a small, picturesque tree with excellent spring flowering and good autumn color. It is effective as a specimen, in groupings, rooftops, under utility lines, as a woodland edge, in the understory, and many other types of projects.

SEASONS OF INTEREST

USDA Zones: 5–9		
SUN	**MOISTURE**	**pH**
Full sun to full shade in all seasons	Dry to moist	5–7.5

SEASONS OF INTEREST

WINTER   SPRING   SUMMER   AUTUMN

FORM – The redbud is a small, short-trunked or multi-stemmed tree. It grows to about 25' tall in cultivation and is generally wider than tall. Redbud grows fastest in youth, when it is vase shaped with arching branches. As it ages, at a medium growth rate, its crown becomes more rounded. It is usually a relatively short-lived tree, to 30 years.

COLOR – The profuse, purplish pink (not red) to occasionally white, early-spring flowers appear before leaves. Distinctive heart-shaped leaves (up to 6" in length) are a light green in spring and then a shiny medium green before turning yellow in autumn. The autumn color is not dependable and can vary from year to year and location to location. Dark, dry, 2"–3" seedpods can be profuse in some years and persist into winter. The dark, rough bark, usually not a striking ornamental characteristic, can be featured well against a light background.

TEXTURE – Medium coarse in leaf, finely textured in winter and early spring.

CULTURE – The eastern redbud is native throughout the mid-Atlantic to southern New England, the Ohio Valley, and southeastern states. It will grow in a wide range of soils from sandy to moderately

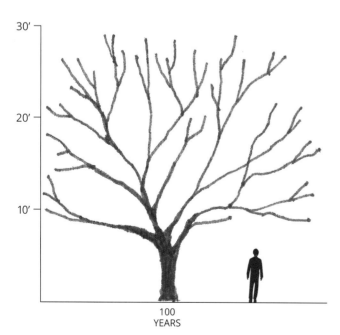

30'

20'

10'

100
YEARS

Redbud flowers close-up.

An old multi-stemmed redbud in shade.

heavy clay. While found commonly on limestone soils, it also tolerates moderately acidic soils. Soils are usually well drained, but it tolerates the occasional short-term flooding that is common adjacent to small streams and rivers.

Redbud is a fairly easy species to establish in the garden; the best time to plant is while the tree is dormant in late winter or early spring in the northern regions (zones 5–6). Further south (zones 7–8), it can be moved successfully in autumn as well. Choosing trees from local growers will help assure that buds are not damaged in late frosts.

Redbud with flowering dogwoods.

Seedling trees produce a taproot for the first few years, after which a fibrous lateral root system develops. It is common for many volunteer seedlings to appear, but they are not a serious maintenance issue. The wood is hard and strong, but the sharp crotches formed in this species can lead to breakage under snow and ice loads. It is not tolerant of salt spray at the seashore, but I have seen many trees along the highway tolerate salt during their dormancy. The redbud may be significantly affected by the Asian long-horned beetle if it becomes an established pest. Deer love the young foliage and can cause significant damage when within their reach.

COMPANION PLANTS – In nature, eastern redbud is usually found as an understory plant beneath oaks, pines, and other deep-rooted native trees, and it thrives in the same limestone regions as eastern red cedar. Redbud combines well and enjoys the same growing conditions as Virginia sweetspire, summersweet, oakleaf hydrangea, and winterberry holly. It is especially striking in the spring with our native serviceberries and flowering dogwoods.

WILDLIFE – The flowers provide early spring pollen and nectar for hummingbirds, butterflies, and bees. It is a host for butterfly larvae, including Henry's elfin butterfly. The seeds are eaten by birds.

CULTIVATED VARIETIES – Select for size, hardiness, and color of leaves and flowers.

'**Alba**' (**forma** *alba*) – White flower form.
'**Dwarf White**' – To 10' tall and slower growing than 'Alba.' White flowers.
'**Forest Pansy**' – New leaves are a bright, deep red-purple, fading toward a shiny, dark reddish green during the season. Rose-purple flowers bloom later than in the wild species.
'**Hearts of Gold**' – Vigorous grower to 20' tall. Leaves emerge yellow with a red tint and mature to yellow and sometimes a chartreuse green.
'**Royal White**' – More cold resistant and larger white flowers than 'Alba.'
'**Tennessee Pink**'–Clear pink flowers.

Redbud autumn foliage color.

Chamaecyparis thyoides

Atlantic or Southern White Cedar, False Cypress

ATTRIBUTES/USE IN LANDSCAPE – The Atlantic white cedar is a colorful, narrow, upright, evergreen conifer. It is valued as a specimen as well as for grouping, screening, bioretention, and naturalized plantings. The varieties provide versatility of color and form and support additional smaller-scale projects including rain gardens and formal plantings. White cedar is tolerant of salt and even brief saltwater flooding.

SEASONS OF INTEREST

WINTER	SPRING	SUMMER	AUTUMN

FORM – The Atlantic white cedar species is a medium or large, narrow, columnar, even spire-like evergreen, 20'–40' (55') tall, 6'–15' wide, but there is variety of form in the species. It is similar in form to

USDA Zones: 4–9		
SUN	**MOISTURE**	**pH**
Full sun	Moist to wet	3.5–6.5

the eastern red cedar. Atlantic white cedar is larger in the South and along the northern coast, where the climate is milder and there is less 'pruning' by winter storms. It has a medium growth rate. The cultivated varieties have more uniformity and include some dwarf and shrub forms.

COLOR – The color, in wild trees, varies with site conditions. Southern white cedar may be blue-green to a glaucous green intermixed with older leaves of brown. Cultivated varieties provide more reliable coloring, which may or may not be affected to varying degrees by site conditions. The light reddish brown bark peels in long, fibrous strips. With age the bark becomes ridged, often with a longitudinal twist.

TEXTURE – Medium.

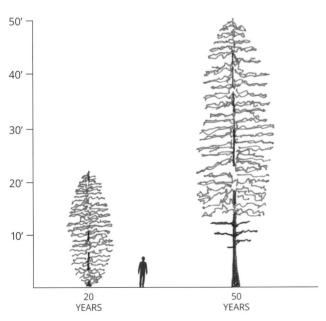

Southern white cedar foliage and fruit.

A young southern white cedar.

CULTURE – The Atlantic white cedar is primarily native to freshwater swamps along a narrow coastal band from southern Maine to northern Florida and west to southern Mississippi. Typically the soils are peaty soils of varying depth over sand, but not over clay or silt.

Full sun is preferred, but Atlantic white cedar will grow very slowly in partial to moderate shade. It is more shade tolerant in youth. Like the eastern red cedar, juvenile plants have needlelike foliage, while adult foliage is scalelike and feathery. Once the plants have attained the adult foliage, they will not tolerate shade.

The Atlantic white cedar is not a true cedar but a false cypress. Its valuable timber is lightweight and rot resistant.

As noted above, for the wild species, snow and ice can cause severe limb breakage or even cause a tree to uproot. White cedar handles the urban conditions of heat and pollution well and is moderately tolerant of road salt.

Few diseases and insects bother this plant, but deer will browse its foliage.

COMPANION PLANTS – In its native range it often grows in pure stands but can be accompanied by red maple, black gum, sweetbay magnolia, and shrubs including summersweet, sweet pepperbush, swamp azalea, highbush blueberry, and winterberry holly. It can be difficult to establish turf and understory plants beneath existing trees due to root competition and dense shade.

WILDLIFE – Atlantic white cedar provides cover for birds and is the sole host of the rare Hessel's hairstreak butterfly.

CULTIVATED VARIETIES – Select for size, form, texture, and color.

'Shiva' – A shrub form with a central leader and fine blue-green foliage that is brown in the winter. 4'–5' tall and wide.

'Andelyensis' – A dense and very upright miniature tree, to 10'. It forms a neat pyramid of dark blue-green.

'Aurea' – A bright yellow form, with a dense cone shape, to 15'. The feathery foliage creates a bronze-yellow accent in winter. It tolerates some shade.

'Glauca Pendula' – A weeping form with silvery blue foliage. This plant has a dense, upright, pyramidal form with pendulous branches.

'Red Star' – Choose for red coloring in winter.

'Top Point' – Blue foliage, slow growing at 3" per year, up to 5' in height, juvenile foliage, plum-bronze in winter. Full sun only.

'Heatherbun' – Dwarf 3' × 3', juvenile foliage, plum-bronze in winter.

Chionanthus virginicus

White Fringe Tree

ATTRIBUTES/USE IN LANDSCAPE – The white fringe tree is an excellent, reliable small tree or large shrub. Despite its stunning and usually fragrant flower display, it is underused. White fringe tree is effective as a specimen. It is also useful as a street tree, in parking islands, under utility wires, in rain gardens, and in residential, park, campus and highway plantings. The white fringe tree withstands compacted soils, poor drainage, and windy locations.

SEASONS OF INTEREST

WINTER	SPRING	SUMMER	AUTUMN

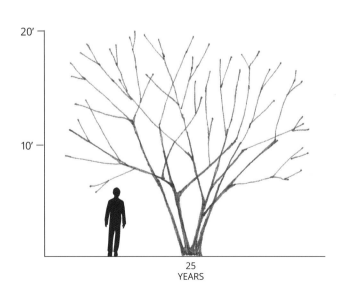

FORM – White fringe tree is a small, short-trunked or multi-stemmed tree or large shrub. It reaches 12'–20' (30') tall and can be wider than tall. The regular, upright, oval shape of youth becomes more spreading, open, and arching with age. It is relatively slow growing.

USDA Zones: (4) 5–9		
SUN	**MOISTURE**	**pH**
Full sun to part shade	Dry to moist	4.6–6.5

COLOR –The fringe-like flowers are profuse, showy, creamy white, 6"–8" loose panicles, emerging in late spring with the new yellow-green leaves. White fringe tree is one of the last trees to leaf out, with medium green, 6" long × 2"–3" wide, oblong to oval leaves. The flowers, on female plants, are followed by blue drupes in late summer. The autumn color can be a yellow-green to a clear or golden yellow, depending on location. The gray-brown bark is thin when young, aging to low, broad ridging. Some individuals have a strong lilac-like fragrance.

TEXTURE – Medium.

CULTURE – The native range of white fringe tree is from southern Pennsylvania through the southeast

Yellow autumn foliage and dark blue fruit on a female white fringe tree.

20'

10'

25
YEARS

White fringe tree in a shrub border.

to Texas. While its native range covers a broad area, the tree is not common. Still, it is hardy in colder climates. White fringe tree is found in rich, moist woodlands, floodplains, and stream edges as well as dry upland woods and rocky bluffs.

White fringe tree performs best on acidic, moist soils in full sun. It will tolerate relatively dry soils but not prolonged drought. Its drought tolerance increases with shade, but the white fringe tree habit is more dense in full sun.

Male fringe tree pruned for a single trunk.

Both sexes must be present for fruit production on the female trees, but differentiating between the sexes of young trees, prior to flowering, is difficult. If fruiting is an important feature, it is best to plant several trees.

The white fringe tree rarely requires pruning unless training for a single stem. Because the tree has deep lateral rooting, it is best to transplant young, balled and burlapped plants in the spring.

White fringe tree is tolerant of air pollution and moderately tolerant of soil salts but is intolerant of root compaction and aerosol salts.

Today, the tree has no serious insect or disease problems, but it can be susceptible to scale and borers, particularly when grown in dry locations. It is only occasionally browsed by deer.

COMPANION PLANTS – In nature it is found in the understory of deciduous forests, including oaks and cucumber tree. It combines well with dogwoods, serviceberries, smooth witherod, winterberry, native azaleas, and many others.

The plant is dioecious, with sexes on separate plants. The male flowering is somewhat showier, with longer petals, but only the female flowers are followed by the ½"–⅔" dark blue, fleshy, olive-shaped fruits. The fleshy drupes are produced in late summer.

WILDLIFE – The flowers provide pollen and ample nectar for hummingbirds, butterflies, and bees. The tree is a host to some sphinx moth larvae, including rustic sphinx moth, as well as Henry's elfin butterfly. The fruit is eaten by dozens of bird species.

Cladrastis kentukea

American Yellowwood

ATTRIBUTES/USE IN LANDSCAPE – The yellowwood is a very attractive, multi-season, flowering shade tree for residential and park plantings, where it is appreciated as a specimen, in a group, and in a raised bed or median strip. It has beautiful, fragrant flowers; smooth, light gray, attractive bark; and good autumn foliage coloring.

SEASONS OF INTEREST

WINTER	SPRING	SUMMER	AUTUMN

FORM – The yellowwood's very upright branching pattern creates a broad, rounded to irregular crown. It is a medium to large tree and typically grows to about 30'–50' (75') × 40'–55'. Branching will tend to be low in full sun, but it can be trained higher with pruning. The trunk can be 4' in diameter. Pruning can improve longevity by removing sharp crotches

USDA Zones: 4–8		
SUN	**MOISTURE**	**pH**
Full sun	Dry to moist	5.5–8

formed by very acutely angled branches, which break easily in ice loads. It has a medium growth rate.

COLOR – In spring the pinnately compound, yellow-green leaves emerge, turning a bright green as summer progresses. Gorgeous white 1" flowers on 8"–16" drooping terminal panicles bloom in late spring, resembling wisteria. The yellowwood is typically 10 years old or older before blooming occurs, and the extravagance of the bloom varies from year to year. The splendid yellow autumn color is reliable. The bark is smooth, thin, and light gray, like a beech. See Cultivated Varieties for a pink-blooming cultivar.

Yellowwood flowers.

40 YEARS

Yellowwood tree in bloom.

TEXTURE – Medium. It casts a dense shade.

CULTURE – The yellowwood is native to the southern Appalachian Mountains, where it grows on sunny, moist limestone outcroppings. It is rare in the wild but readily available in nurseries. The common name is derived from the color of the wood, which is a dull to bright yellow.

In seasons when it blooms prolifically, the yellowwood is stunning, and few trees can rival its beauty. However, a season of heavy bloom is usually followed by a season with few or no flowers. In fact, it may be up to three years before the exquisite show of flowers is produced again. Additionally, new growth can be susceptible to, and sometimes damaged by, late spring frosts. Freeze damage will reduce or eliminate flowering. The autumn foliage is a golden yellow and provides a beautiful display annually. Full sun is required for the best flowering and color. It may bloom faster in planters, where roots are somewhat restricted. When yellowwood is planted in a raised planter, good drainage can be provided and the effect of low branching can be mitigated.

The medium growth rate is enhanced with full sun, moisture, and rich organic soils. Rapid growth, however, can lead to weaker branch structures. Branching at acute angles can increase breakage. Do not prune in winter or spring as the plant is likely to bleed excessively. Prune after growth has commenced in spring and into early summer. The thin bark is susceptible to mechanical damage.

Very tolerant of drought, this tree also grows well in moist, well-drained soils. It grows well in both acid and alkaline soils and is easily transplanted in the spring. It is reported to be moderately tolerant of salt. I have grown trees that perform very well in both sandy and clay loam soils.

Although small saplings have a taproot, they ultimately develop a shallower root system and sometimes surface roots. Transplant when young, balled and burlapped or from container-grown plants.

Clay soils may pose an indirect problem in years of heavy spring rains. The recently introduced invasive Asian ambrosia beetle attacks many thin-barked trees, especially when the surrounding soil is saturated. Ethanol is produced in saturated soils, and in the warm spring weather, ambrosia beetles are attracted to the ethanol and may readily attack the thin-barked yellowwood. Planting in sharply drained soils or in raised beds, such as elevated parking lot islands, will reduce the chances of ambrosia beetle damage. The native locust leaf miner may sometimes feed on yellowwood, but it rarely requires control measures. Yellowwood is not a preferred plant of deer.

COMPANION PLANTS – In nature, yellowwood associates with sugar maple, white oak, cucumber tree, viburnums, dogwood, redbud, and smoke tree. In cultivation, many plants will survive and grow well in its company, including bottlebrush buckeye, red buckeye, serviceberry, eastern redbud, and eastern red cedar.

The tree's tendency to low branching and dense

Autumn foliage and form.

shade may preclude the choice of some companion plants.

WILDLIFE – Pollinators, including bees and hummingbirds, enjoy the flowers. The yellowwood provides nesting sites for birds.

CULTIVATED VARIETIES

'Perkins Pink' – Pendulous terminal panicles of light pink flowers.

Cornus Florida

Flowering Dogwood

ATTRIBUTES/USE IN LANDSCAPE – The familiar flowering dogwood is a beautiful, multi-season, flowering tree with excellent autumn color and attractive winter form. It is appreciated as a specimen, in groupings, and as a woodland edge. The flowering dogwood is useful in many landscape applications including residential plantings, beneath utility lines, near patios, in park landscapes, and as highway plantings. It is an excellent plant for wildlife.

SEASONS OF INTEREST

WINTER	SPRING	SUMMER	AUTUMN

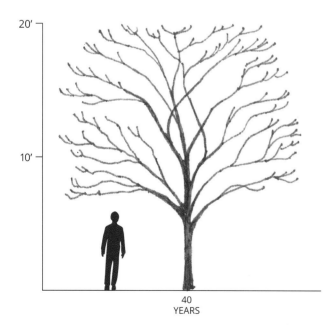

FORM – The flowering dogwood is a small, short-trunked tree or large, multi-stemmed shrub, 15'–30' (40') tall × 15'–25'. It grows fastest in youth, when it is vase shaped with arching branches. As it ages,

USDA Zones: 5–9		
SUN	**MOISTURE**	**pH**
Sun to part shade	Moist	5.5–6.5

at a medium growth rate, its branches become more horizontal and the crown becomes more rounded. Flowering dogwood is usually not long-lived, but may live to 100 years. The horizontal branching of the mature tree is very attractive.

COLOR – Showy, profuse, creamy white, early-spring "flowers" bloom before and during the emergence of foliage. The 3"–6" leaves are a light green becoming a medium to dark green before turning an attractive red to burgundy early in autumn with ripening of fruits. Clusters of bright red ½" drupes, persisting for at least one month, are loved by birds. In winter, the horizontal branching habit, dark

A close-up of flower with bracts on 'Appalachian Spring'.

Autumn foliage and drupes.

state tree twice. It can succeed if its needs are met as described below.

The plant prefers a moist, slightly acid soil. Established trees are moderately tolerant of drought. It will grow in a wide range of soils from sandy to moderately heavy clay. It may be a bit slow to establish in clay soil and will not withstand flooding. Flowering dogwood grows well in urban pollution as long as other cultural needs are met.

While it grows easily in many situations, when it is stressed it can suffer from pests and disease. The species prefers part sun and a well-drained loam soil with an above-average organic matter content. High

A young specimen of 'Appalachian Spring'.

checkered bark, purple-brown young branches, and nearly round buds can be striking against a dark wall or evergreen background.

TEXTURE – Medium in leaf, medium fine in winter. Mature bark has a checkered texture.

CULTURE – Native from southern New England to the Ohio Valley, south to northern Florida, and west into Texas.

Note to the reader: The flowering dogwood is not as resilient or culturally flexible as the majority of plants on our primary list. We have included it because it is very attractive, abundant, in high demand, and is a

An entrance drive lined with flowering dogwood in spring.

shade with good air circulation is an optimal situation. The tree is, however, less prone to the dogwood borer, ambrosia beetle, and cankers in light shade. There are fewer problems with ambrosia beetle in well-drained soil. When grown in full sun or part shade, again with good air circulation and moist soil, dogwoods are not as affected by anthracnose (*Discula* spp.). But in full sun they may be more sensitive to drought stress, which may lead to increased insect attack. Increase in sun exposure will increase plant density and decrease the size of the leaves. Powdery mildew may be an issue in some locations and in some individuals and varieties. This disease may be prevented or reduced by spraying with an antitranspirant, which will also reduce the water use by the tree. Additionally, deer do not browse the foliage as frequently when antitranspirants are applied.

In the colder parts of zones 5 and 6, it is advisable to choose plants grown from local sources and cultivated varieties proven to be cold-hardy in those zones.

The dogwood develops a large lateral root system but is easy to transplant in spring; choose nursery-grown, balled and burlapped or container-grown stock. Dogwood borers are attracted to mechanical injuries and can damage or kill trees by entering the tree through these wounds. During the first few years, maintain an evenly distributed 3"–4" mulch under the branch spread to protect from mechanical injury and turf competition. The mulch should

The distinctive autumn foliage of flowering dogwood.

be kept several inches from the trunk. Transition the area under the tree into a planting bed for soil-cooling plants including ferns and perennials.

The showy, 3"–4" white "flowers" are actually clusters of small green-yellow flowers surrounded by four large white bracts. In some varieties, including naturally occurring forms, the bracts are pink to red.

Deer browse seedlings and leaves.

COMPANION PLANTS – Flowering dogwood combines well with other understory woodland plants such as native azaleas, pawpaw, and shadbush. It is especially striking in the spring with redbud. Ground covers and ferns help cool the soil beneath the plant and do not compete with the roots for moisture. It does not compete well with turf.

WILDLIFE – The flowers provide early-spring pollen and nectar for hummingbirds, butterflies, and bees. The native *Cornus* spp. support 118 different species of moths and butterflies while the non-native *C. kousa* dogwood only supports six. Birds use the tree for cover, nesting, and food. The tight clusters of shiny red fruit are a favorite of many songbirds and small mammals like chipmunk, eastern gray squirrel, fox, and skunk. The new leaves are a larval host plant for spring azure butterflies.

CULTIVATED VARIETIES – Cultivated varieties of flowering dogwood may be selected for disease resistance, flower size, flower color, and form. At this time, we are only recommending *C. florida* 'Appalachian Spring,' the variety with the best resistance to the most destructive disease, dogwood anthracnose.

'Appalachian Spring' – Considered highly resistant to anthracnose, it is susceptible to powdery mildew. This variety performs well in shady as well as sunny landscapes. Dark green, larger leaves and an upright habit.

Cotinus obovatus

American Smoke Tree

ATTRIBUTES/USE IN LANDSCAPE – The American smoke tree is an underused small flowering tree or large shrub. It has superior, vibrant, and persistent autumn color as well as high tolerance for heat, drought, and poor, dry soils. Use as a specimen, a small shade tree, for massing, in a shrub border, in raised parking islands, under utility lines, and as a woodland edge. American smoke tree is useful in residential, park and campus settings. It is not very tolerant of salt.

SEASONS OF INTEREST

WINTER	SPRING	SUMMER	AUTUMN
See form below			

FORM – The American smoke tree is a small, short-trunked or multi-stemmed tree or large shrub, 15'–30' (40') × 20'–30'. It grows fastest in youth when it is vase shaped with irregular, arching branches. As

USDA Zones: 4–8		
SUN	**MOISTURE**	**pH**
Full sun to part shade	Dry to moist	5.2–8

it ages it usually has a slow to medium growth rate. With maturity its branches become more horizontal and its crown becomes more rounded. American smoke tree is most dense in full sun. It can live for 100 years.

COLOR – The flower display appears in mid- to late spring. Although the flowers themselves are insignificant, the billowy, "smoky" namesake bloom follows in shades of pink to purple to silver and persists through summer. The frothy, cloud-like display results from many tiny hairs on the multibranched 5"–10" terminal floral and fruit panicles.

The distinctive, attractive 2"–6" × 3½" leaves are oval and blunt tipped or notched. The 1½" petiole is attached at the narrow base of the leaf. They are a blue-green to dark green in summer. In early autumn, the leaves turn an exceptional yellow, orange, scarlet, and purple, often on the same

The spoon-shaped foliage of our native smoke tree.

15 YEARS · 40 YEARS

A young specimen smoke tree grown in full sun.

tree, lasting three to four weeks. Both the twigs and leaves are aromatic.

The attractive bark is a thin gray-brown when young, and darker gray with an interesting scaly texture in maturity.

TEXTURE – Medium in leaf, medium fine in winter.

CULTURE – The American smoke tree occurs in a few isolated, small locations in poor, alkaline, rocky soils in Kentucky, Missouri, Alabama, Arkansas, and Texas. But this tough plant grows easily outside of its natural range. Use of the inner bark for an orange-yellow dye during the 1800s may have contributed to its reduced range.

Like its relative the sumac, the American smoke tree will grow in a wide range of well-drained soils, from sandy to moderately heavy clay and in acid to alkaline conditions. It is tolerant of drought, heat, and humidity once established. It is intolerant of

The excellent autumn foliage of the American smoke tree at Mt. Cuba Center, Delaware.

A closer view of the smoky effect at Scott Arboretum, Swarthmore College, Pennsylvania.

overwatering, overfertilizing, salt, and root compaction. Flowering and autumn color are best in full sun.

Flowering occurs on new growth, so pruning should take place in late winter or early spring. The smoke tree sprouts easily from its trunk and can take heavy pruning, even to the ground, but flowering may be prevented during that year. The resinous sap has a strong odor and has been known to cause contact dermatitis.

The American smoke tree is fairly pest and disease resistant and is less prone to verticillium wilt than the Asian *C. coggygria*. Our native plant is also larger and has more outstanding autumn foliage. It is usually not browsed by deer.

COMPANION PLANTS – In nature it associates with eastern red cedar, eastern redbud, fragrant sumac, and blackhaw viburnum.

WILDLIFE – The flowers provide pollen and nectar for hummingbirds, butterflies, and bees. American smoke tree provides cover and nesting sites for birds. The seeds are eaten by birds and small mammals in winter.

Gymnocladus dioicus

Kentucky Coffee Tree

ATTRIBUTES/USE IN LANDSCAPE – The Kentucky coffee tree is a handsome, underused, large tree with picturesque, coarse, open branching. It is notable for its winter profile, beautiful summer foliage, and nice but brief autumn coloring. The Kentucky coffee tree is a superb specimen for large lawns, parks, streets, highway plantings, and golf courses. It performs well in urban settings.

SEASONS OF INTEREST

WINTER	SPRING	SUMMER	AUTUMN
See form below	*See form below*		

FORM – The Kentucky coffee tree is a large tree with upright, open, coarse branching, to 60'–80' × 40'–50'. The excellent, bold architecture of this tree is present much of the year. It has a medium growth rate and a long life span of several hundred years.

USDA Zones: 3–8		
SUN	**MOISTURE**	**pH**
Full sun all seasons	Dry to wet	5–8

COLOR – The large leaves are doubly compound and up to 40" × 24". Dark green to blue-green leaves emerge late in spring and drop early in fall. The autumn color can be an excellent though short-lived yellow. The thick, leathery, purplish brown seedpods are held into winter on female plants. The bark is an attractive gray-brown, rough, vertically fissured and ridged.

TEXTURE – The texture is coarse in winter and medium fine in summer. In contrast to the stout, coarse branching, the large doubly pinnate leaves provide the medium-fine, tropical texture.

CULTURE – The Kentucky coffee tree is a beautiful and easy-to-grow large shade tree. Rare in nature and uncommon in the modern landscape, it is considered endangered in New York State. It is native east of the Mississippi River from southern Ontario

The large doubly compound leaf of the Kentucky coffee tree.

15 YEARS — 50 YEARS

60'
50'
40'
30'
20'
10'

A 15-year-old specimen leafing out following other trees, Bartholdi Park at the US Botanic Garden, Washington, DC.

southward to Georgia. Where it occurs naturally, it is usually found near streams and rivers.

This tree is tolerant of both acidic and slightly alkaline soils and many soil types, but the fastest growth will occur in moist alluvial soils. Kentucky coffee tree tolerates some flooding as well as drought. It performs well in urban settings. It is storm tolerant, as the coarse branching does not allow wet snow to accumulate and the wood is fairly strong. It is also salt tolerant.

Because it is late to leaf out in the spring, this species may be devoid of foliage for five to six months of the year. Male and female flowers are fragrant and usually borne on separate plants. The female flowers are 10"–12" long, greenish white panicles, but are inconspicuous as they are lost among the foliage. The equally inconspicuous male flower is a 4" cluster. The seeds are found in 6"–12" pods and were used as a coffee substitute in colonial times and sometimes eaten. Unless roasted, the seed is poisonous for humans, pets, and livestock.

I have never seen any serious pests or diseases on this tree. And it is rarely bothered by deer.

COMPANION PLANTS – The light shade and brief leafing of the tree are excellent for growing with turf. In a naturalized environment, it might be seen grouped with maples, hickories, and redbud. Many different species of flowering shrubs, both native and introduced, will succeed and flower well when planted beneath the Kentucky coffee tree.

WILDLIFE – The Kentucky coffee tree is used by nesting birds, but the toxicity of the fruit prevents it from being a common food source. It is a larval host for both bicolored and bisected honey locust moths.

CULTIVATED VARIETIES – Select for gender and form. Male cultivars are generally preferred because they do not produce the large seedpods. It is not commonly available but is worth seeking out.

'**Espresso**' – 50' × 35'. Beautiful male clone; oval to vase shaped with upright to arching branches.
'**Prairie Titan**' – 60' × 70'. Male clone, very symmetrical upright spreading branches.
'**Stately Manor**' – Narrow growth, 50' × 10' (20'). Male clone, very good for street tree planting.

A 25-year-old specimen at White Hall, Annapolis, Maryland.

Ilex decidua

Possum Haw

ATTRIBUTES/USE IN LANDSCAPE – The possum haw is an underused, deciduous small tree or large shrub holly, valued for a stunning profusion of red berries on female plants and for its silvery bark. Possum haw is used as a specimen, for massing, and in hedging. It can be used for residential and commercial projects, woodland gardens, rooftop gardens, park and highway plantings, and rain gardens. The possum haw is tolerant of many soil conditions. It is very good in the early winter garden with a background of evergreens or snow. Branches are frequently used in holiday decorations.

SEASONS OF INTEREST

| WINTER | SPRING | SUMMER | AUTUMN |

FORM – Possum haw is a deciduous, upright, multistemmed plant in youth, becoming more open with age. In cultivation, it is usually 7'–15' tall and nearly as wide with a more dense habit. In the wild, it may grow 20'–30' tall. The growth rate is slow to medium but can be enhanced with nutrition and water. In moist locations, this tree spreads by root suckers to form

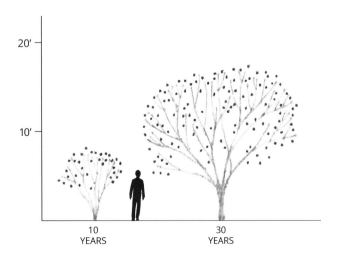

20'

10'

| 10 | 30 |
| YEARS | YEARS |

USDA Zones: 5–9		
SUN	**MOISTURE**	**pH**
Full sun to part shade	Moist to wet	4.5–6.5

thickets. It may be pruned to shape in early spring. Please see cultivars for a variety of consistent forms.

COLOR – Profuse, showy ¼"–⅜" red berrylike drupes on bare branches are revealed with leaf drop (at first freeze), in autumn through late winter. The foliage is a glossy light green in spring, dark green in summer. The slender obovate leaves, with gentle undulating margins, are 2"–3" long. The handsome, thin bark is silvery gray and smooth with some warty texture. Cultivars provide foliage and berry color options.

TEXTURE – Fine all seasons.

CULTURE – The possum haw is native to river floodplains of the Piedmont region south from Washington, DC, to northern Florida and west to most of Mississippi and Alabama and the Mississippi River. It is also found along stream and pond borders.

A soil rich in organic matter suits it best. It will tolerate clay soil, air pollution, and salt, and is tolerant of moderate drought as well as periodic flooding.

The berries are produced most abundantly when plants are grown in full sun, but adequate crops of berries may be expected on plants grown in partial shade. The sexes are separate, so at least one male plant must be present for female plants to produce berries.

There are few insect and disease pests. Deer may browse the leaves in certain locales.

COMPANION PLANTS – In nature, possum haw may be found in association with American holly, serviceberry, American hornbeam, silky dogwood,

ABOVE: *Possum haw in leaf.*

RIGHT: *The abundant, showy winter berries of the possum haw.*

spicebush, inkberry, arrowwood viburnum, and other understory plants that thrive in moist soil and shade. It combines well and thrives in the same growing conditions as summersweet, oakleaf hydrangea, needle palm, bald cypress, Virginia sweetspire, and southern magnolia.

WILDLIFE – The drupes provide winter fodder for many different species of birds. The plant provides cover for nesting. It is a pollen source and a nectar source.

CULTIVATED VARIETIES – The many named cultivated varieties provide variation in form, size, fruit color, leaf color, finish, and retention. For fruit, a male is generally required. American hollies will also pollinate.

Female (fruited) varieties:

'Council Fire' – An upright, rounded shrub, 6'–15' tall. Fruit is orange-red. Retains its narrow, dark green foliage longer.

'Finches Golden' – To 30' tall, an upright form. Bright yellow fruit. Dark green foliage.

'Warren's Red' – 12'–18'. Very glossy, dark green, with persistent foliage and abundant bright red fruit. Upright while young.

Male cultivars for pollination:

'Red Escort' – 18'. Dense and upright. Very glossy, dark green foliage.

Ilex opaca

American Holly

ATTRIBUTES/USE IN LANDSCAPE – The American holly is a handsome, medium to large, dense, broad-leaved evergreen tree known for its attractive fruit and foliage. It is popular as a specimen, hedge, grouping, or screening in residential, park, street, and highway plantings. It is also useful for sound attenuation and in woodland gardens. The many varieties offer size and color choices. American holly is an excellent plant for wildlife.

SEASONS OF INTEREST

| WINTER | SPRING | SUMMER | AUTUMN |

FORM – The American holly is a medium to large tree with a pyramidal form, particularly in youth, and dense low branching. In cultivation, it typically grows slowly to about 50' and by up to ⅔ in width. A long-lived tree, it may exceed 200 years. American

USDA Zones: (5) 6–9		
SUN	**MOISTURE**	**pH**
Full sun to part shade	Dry to moist	5.5–6.8

holly tolerates pruning well. There is great variation in the species, but hundreds of reliable varieties allow for a wide selection of form.

COLOR – The evergreen, 1½"–3½" leaves are usually yellowish green to olive green to dark green with a smooth, dull finish. They are thick and usually have spiny tips and margins. New leaves emerge soft and lighter green in spring and become leathery and dark through the summer. Clusters of small, mildly fragrant, white flowers appear in spring. Globular berries (drupes) that are ¼"–½" and red (rarely yellow or orange) are borne on female trees from autumn through winter. The attractive, thin bark is smooth and light gray. Cultivated varieties below offer options in foliage color and finish, berry color, size, and sex.

50'
40'
30'
20'
10'

20
YEARS

80
YEARS

Fruit on a female American holly.

Fruit on a yellow-fruited form of American holly.

leaves. Also, plants may grow faster, under these conditions, in a protected location.

Hollies are usually dioecious, so a male plant is required in the vicinity, less than ¼ mile, for the females to provide their showy fruit display. While the males do not fruit, they have more flowers and are more fragrant. Flowering is on new wood. The berries, while enjoyed by birds, are toxic to humans, cats, dogs, and horses.

Depending on one's intended use, select high- or low-branching plants from the nursery. Holly trunks should be pruned when young. When mature plants are limbed up, the scars can be unattractive and the tree may be harmed. American

TEXTURE – Medium in all seasons. Some varieties are finely textured.

CULTURE – The native range is south from the coast of Massachusetts through New Jersey and west into Kentucky and Tennessee, then south to northern Florida and west to Texas. American holly is a common understory tree of southeastern mesic forests, and it grows well in nearly the entire East Coast.

Full sun is best for maximum berry production and most compact growth. Moist, well-drained, slightly acid soils are also preferred. Growth is slower in wet or very dry soils. American holly is tolerant of periodic flooding and drought. It is also very shade tolerant, but is rangy with sparse foliage in the understory of a forest.

The waxy leaves of American holly are resistant to salt spray and air pollution. In the northern range, in an exposed location and frozen soil, providing a protected location may be helpful. In a windy location, in the spring, leaf damage may be the result of older, tougher leaf spines piercing tender young

An American holly with an upright habit and pendulous branches.

An American holly with a rounded form and dense branching.

holly can be difficult to transplant from the wild and in large sizes. Use of antitranspirants when digging plants will greatly enhance reestablishment. Transplant in spring, balled and burlapped or container grown. Depending on site location, the leaf drop and spiny tips may be considered a nuisance. Leaf drop occurs mainly in spring, with the emergence of new growth.

Numerous insects and diseases may affect the American holly, including leaf miner, berry midge, and tar spot, but they do not affect the health of the tree. The superior cultivated varieties are chosen for resistance to insects and disease and their ability to put on a consistent, good show. American holly is not a favored plant of deer.

COMPANION PLANTS – Growing plants beneath a holly may be difficult unless it is pruned up from the ground. *Asarum* spp., ephemeral wildflowers, ferns, and dwarf shrubs may be planted but must be tolerant of competition and dense shade.

WILDLIFE – Many pollinators, including butterflies and bees, are attracted to the flowers. The species is larval host to Henry's elfin butterfly. In winter the berries are eaten by songbirds and game birds as well as small mammals. Trunk cavities provide nesting for the endangered red-cockaded woodpecker.

CULTIVATED VARIETIES – There are numerous varieties. Select for plant form and size as well as leaf shape, finish, color, and size; fruit color; cold hardiness; and sex.

Female Cultivars

'Croonenburg' – This is a heavy fruiter with shiny, dark green, less spiny leaves. It is unique in that it is monoecious and does not require a male plant to flower and set seed.

'Dan Fenton' – Oval leaves are a shiny dark green. Vigorous. Profuse dark red fruit.

'Jersey Delight' – 15'–20' tall × 15' wide, with a narrow, conical habit. Shiny foliage and abundant, bright red-orange fruit.

'Jersey Princess' – Shiny, dark foliage and abundant, persistent red fruit.

'Menantico' – 15'–20' tall × 10'–12' wide. Upright and spreading. Shiny, smaller dark green leaves. Dark red berries persisting into winter.

'Maryland Dwarf' – A low shrub form, 2'–3' tall × 3'–10' wide. Useful for rooftop gardens.

'Miss Helen' – To 40'. Large olive-green leaves with excellent, large berry production.

'Old Heavy Berry' – To 30'. Dark leaves, profuse red fruit, and very winter hardy.

Yellow Berried

'Canary' – Light yellow berries. This plant has shiny, medium green leaves.

'Goldie' – Especially heavy fruited with clear yellow berries. Leaf finish is dull.

'Princeton Gold' – 30' × 15'. Good, abundant bright yellow fruit. Leaves are smaller and darker than the species and have a dull finish.

Males

'Jersey Knight' – 30' tall × 20' wide. Handsome, shiny, dark green foliage.

Juniperus virginiana

Eastern Red Cedar

ATTRIBUTES/USE IN LANDSCAPE – The eastern red cedar is a handsome, colorful, evergreen conifer for specimen, grouping, or with screening, streets, and windbreak use. It may also be used for topiary work. Eastern red cedar is an excellent plant for wildlife.

SEASONS OF INTEREST

WINTER	SPRING	SUMMER	AUTUMN

FORM – Eastern red cedar is a large evergreen, 50'–60' (90') tall. The dense growth habit varies in wild plants from very narrow and upright to slightly weeping, broader than tall individuals. Cultivated varieties offer specific, reliable habits including columnar, pyramidal, and spreading. The tree develops a picturesque form and trunk as it ages. It can reach 800 years old and is medium to slow growing.

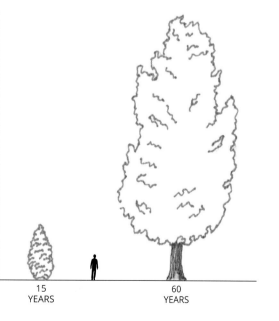

USDA Zones: 3b–9a		
SUN	**MOISTURE**	**pH**
Full sun to part shade	Dry to wet	4.5–8

COLOR – The summer foliage in wild trees may be dark green to gray or bluish green, varying with site conditions. In winter, it may develop a rich bronze or purple cast and may be subject to winter burn. Cultivated varieties can be acquired with more reliable, specific coloring, but they may also be affected by site conditions. The sexes are usually separate. Flowers are inconspicuous on females in spring and are not an ornamental feature. In fall and winter, the female plants may be covered with bluish gray, waxy, berry-like cones. Quantities may vary from year to year. The male plants have numerous small, tan cones that give the tree a yellowish tint when pollen is released in late winter or early spring. The attractive trunk has light tan to gray fibrous bark, exfoliating in thin strips and sometimes revealing a reddish bark beneath.

TEXTURE – Fine in all seasons.

CULTURE – Eastern red cedar is a very common pioneer species and is native throughout most of the eastern United States. It is among the first trees to appear after a forest is cleared. It dominates, almost to the exclusion of other tree species, in neglected pastures where limestone lies close to, or at, the soil surface. The US Forest Service notes that it is the most widely distributed conifer tree in the east. Along the coasts of the southern range, where it grows in sand dunes and marsh edges, the tree can be more open and broad in habit and greener in color. Some authorities consider this naturally occurring variety to be a separate species, *J. silicicola* or southern red cedar.

Full sun is preferred, but the species will grow very

Eastern red cedar as a lawn specimen.

slowly in partial to moderate shade. It is more shade tolerant in youth. Juveniles, with their needlelike foliage, can exist for decades in shade, barely growing at all. The foliage may be primarily scalelike (adult), needlelike (juvenile), or a mix of the two. Once the plants have attained the adult foliage, they will not tolerate shade.

The red cedar tolerates heavy clay, almost pure sand, gravelly soils, or very dry and wet soils. I have seen specimens survive frequent inundations of water, with high soil salt levels, in brackish marshes along the Chesapeake Bay. Yet, it can also tolerate extreme drought. Alkaline to acid soils are tolerated. Snow and ice can cause severe limb breakage or even cause a tree to uproot. Red cedar handles the urban conditions of heat, drought, and pollution well and is tolerant of road salt.

Like the cedar it is named for, the aromatic wood is moderately lightweight and soft, and the heartwood is a deep red color and very resistant to decay.

The young red cedar is fairly easy to transplant, but success rates can decline with age. 70-year-old specimens, however, were transplanted at The Westchester apartments campus in Washington, DC, in the 1930s and exist today.

Eastern red cedar is an alternate host of cedar-apple rust, a serious disease of apples. In many areas where apples are produced, red cedars are destroyed to help prevent this disease from appearing in apples. Junipers may also be alternate hosts of other rust diseases, many of which affect other members of the rose family. Bag worms can be an issue, but trees usually recover from their damage. Deer frequently browse the foliage, and male deer can cause serious damage by rubbing their antlers on the thin bark of small trees.

COMPANION PLANTS – There are many potential companions because the red cedar grows in

Female and male eastern red cedars.

A group of old eastern red cedars showing variation in form.

many environments, in some cases in pure stands. In nature it is found with other sun-loving pioneer species, such as hickories, various sumacs, and devil's walking stick. Eastern red cedar is frequently found with redbud, especially in limestone-soil regions. It can be difficult to establish turf and understory plants beneath existing trees due to root competition.

WILDLIFE – The eastern red cedar is an important plant for native insects, birds, and mammals. It provides good nesting and roosting cover for many species of birds including juncos, myrtle warblers, and mourning doves, as well as cover for mammals. The fruit is eaten by many wildlife species including cedar waxwings, finches, warblers, songbirds, game birds, small mammals, and coyote. Eastern red cedar supports many butterfly larvae and is the primary host for the juniper hairstreak.

CULTIVATED VARIETIES – There are many,

increasing smaller project options such as rooftops. Select for size, form, color, and fruit set.

'**Blue Arrow**' – Upright, narrow to 15' × 2' wide, silvery blue foliage, dense. A fruiting, cultivated variety.

'**Burkii**' – Pyramidal clone to 20', fine-textured, blue-green foliage with a purple cast in winter. Male.

'**Canaertii**' – An irregularly pyramidal clone, 25'. Deep green foliage year-round. Profuse fruiting. A slow grower. Female.

'**Emerald Sentinel**' – Narrow, columnar growth 20' × 8' with dark green color and little to no winter discoloration. Female.

'**Grey Owl**' – Low, spreading to 3' × 10'–12', silver-blue feathery foliage, abundant fruit. Female.

'**Hillspire**' – Pyramidal growth to 25', remains deep green in winter. Male.

'**Manhattan Blue**' – Pyramidal to 12', about half as wide as tall. Brilliant bluish foliage, fading through summer. Female.

Liquidambar styraciflua
Sweet Gum

ATTRIBUTES/USE IN LANDSCAPE – The sweet gum is a beautiful, medium to large lawn or shade tree known for its stunning autumn color and signature star-shaped leaf. It is appreciated as a specimen or grouping for large residences, parks, and campuses; also as a street tree with ample room. Sweet gum is an important wetland restoration tree. Because of the profuse, prickly, spherical fruit, the basic species is only recommended for informal landscapes and wetland projects, away from pedestrian traffic. For general landscapes, we recommend using the most commonly available fruitless variety, *Liquidambar styraciflua* 'Rotundiloba'.

USDA Zones: 5b–9a		
SUN	**MOISTURE**	**pH**
Full sun	Dry to moist	3.5–6.5

FORM – The sweet gum is a medium to large, straight-trunked, symmetrical tree reaching 60'–75' (100'). Pyramidal in youth, it develops an oval-rounded to spreading crown in maturity. The tree's growth rate is fast when young, especially in full sun, and moderate as it matures. Growth is enhanced in moist soils. It is long-lived, up to 300 years. 'Rotundiloba' is smaller than the species at 45'–50'.

SEASONS OF INTEREST

WINTER   SPRING   SUMMER   AUTUMN

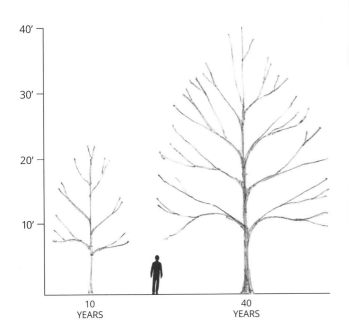

Summer foliage on 'Rotundiloba'.

A young specimen 'Rotundiloba'.

red, scarlet, burgundy, or purplish, or a combination of colors, often on the same tree. Autumn color is less reliable in 'Rotundiloba'. The early-spring flowers are inconspicuous. Round, prickly seed capsules, 1"–1½", become apparent in the species in autumn and often persist and drop throughout winter and into early spring. They can create a considerable litter issue. The mature bark is gray and deeply furrowed with narrow, scaly plates or ridges.

TEXTURE – Medium in all seasons. Prominent, up to 1" high, corky "wings" may develop along branches.

CULTURE – The sweet gum is native to the eastern United States from southern Connecticut to central Florida and west, then north to southern Illinois, Indiana, and Ohio, with the exception of the Appalachian Mountains. It is one of the most common hardwoods of the southeast.

While the sweet gum performs best in full sun, it will tolerate partial shade when young. It is very tolerant of different soils and sites but grows best on the rich, moist, alluvial clay and loamy soils of river bottoms. Once established, it tolerates drought. The sweet gum also tolerates compacted soils and is moderately tolerant of salt and saltwater inundation.

This tree has a shallow root system. In the northern reaches of its range (6a–5b) it should be transplanted in the spring when young, balled and burlapped. Prune after leaf drop.

The wood is very difficult to split and so resistant to breaking during ice and snow loads. Sweet gum is an important timber tree and is even harvested for Popsicle sticks and exported to China for chopsticks.

The durable, spiky seed capsules of the species drop in winter and can be a hazard for walkers. Few insects or diseases pose a serious problem. Deer will browse occasionally foliage within reach.

COLOR – The leathery, medium to dark green, 4"–8" leaves have a glossy upper surface. The species' leaves are distinctly star shaped with five to seven deep, pointed lobes. The leaves of the seedless *L. styraciflua* 'Rotundiloba' have unique rounded lobes. Their fragrance is camphor-like when crushed. The brilliant autumn color of the species can be yellow, orange,

COMPANION PLANTS – In nature, sweet gum occurs with bald cypress, sycamore, tulip poplar, black gum, river birch, red maple, shagbark hickory, and sugarberry. Common understory associates include buttonbush, dogwood spp., possum haw, eastern redbud, and shade-tolerant turf.

WILDLIFE – The seeds are eaten by birds and small mammals.

CULTIVATED VARIETIES – Options include reduced seed production, foliage (leaf color and shape), and plant habit. The narrow variety is good for allées. A variegated form might be interesting for collectors.

'**Grazam**' ('**Grandmaster**') – A new pyramidal selection growing 50' tall and wide with glossy green leaves that turn shades of red, purple, and orange in fall. A fruiting variety.

'**Gumball**' **and** '**Oconee**' – These cultivars are notable for their dwarf, multi-stemmed shrubby habit to 15' tall with a smaller spread. They exhibit good fall color, with 'Oconee' expressing better cold hardiness. These are fruiting varieties.

'**Hapdell**' – Rarely sets the "gum ball" fruit. Autumn color is an attractive maroon.

'**Moraine**' – The most common cultivar and relatively faster growing. Very hardy and has a dependable red autumn color. It has a uniform, oval habit. It is fruit producing.

'**Rotundiloba**' – This form rarely sets fruit and is named for the rounded lobes of the leaves. The

Autumn foliage on 'Rotundiloba'.

autumn color varies with the year. Its branches can develop at a sharp angle to the tree, risking storm damage. Discovered in North Carolina in the 1930s, in zone 5 it should be planted in a protected location.

'**Slender Silhouette**' – Very narrow columnar form. The few fruits that form are not considered a litter problem, as they fall over a confined area.

Magnolia acuminata var. *subcordata*

Yellow Cucumber Tree

ATTRIBUTES/USE IN LANDSCAPE – The yellow cucumber tree is an excellent, underused, small to medium-sized, flowering tree. It is deciduous and may be single- or multi-stemmed. The yellow cucumber tree works well as a specimen, shade tree, or in a grouping for residences, parks, streets, campuses, and golf courses. It is mildly tolerant of salt.

SEASONS OF INTEREST

WINTER	SPRING	SUMMER	AUTUMN

FORM – A small to medium, single- or multi-stemmed deciduous tree, yellow cucumber tree reaches 25'–30' (50') with a spread of 10'–20'. The rounded to symmetrically oval form is attractive, and the tree has a medium to fast growth rate. Faster growth can be expected in consistently moist, fertile soils.

COLOR – The lightly fragrant flowers are relatively

USDA Zones: 5–9		
SUN	**MOISTURE**	**pH**
Full sun to part shade	Moist, well drained	4.5–6.5

small, 2"–2½", clear golden yellow, blooming in mid-spring, with sporadic flowering in autumn. The flower buds are ovate and densely covered with white hairs, opening with emerging leaves. The medium green, ovate leaves are large, 6"–7" long and 3"–4" wide. Fall foliage color is a dull yellow. The 2"–3" green, then red, cone-like fruits resemble small cucumbers and open to reveal small red seeds in late summer. The young bark is smooth and pale gray. In maturity it is brown, deeply furrowed and ridged.

TEXTURE – Coarse in summer, medium all other seasons.

CULTURE – The yellow cucumber tree is native to small areas of the Piedmont and coastal plain in Georgia and North and South Carolina, but it is hardy much farther north.

The species *M. acuminata* is the hardiest and most widely distributed of our native magnolias. *M. acuminata* var. *subcordata* is a smaller, more rare tree whose brighter yellow flowers are more visible. It is slightly less cold tolerant than *M. acuminata*. In nature, both plants are found on wooded hillsides near small streams in fertile, well-drained soils.

Yellow cucumber tree flowers best in full sun. In cultivation, it tolerates clay loam soils as well as sandy soils. It is moderately tolerant of drought and salt.

While the wood is moderately brittle and may be subject to damage from ice and heavy, wet snow, it is less susceptible than other magnolia species, especially the evergreen forms.

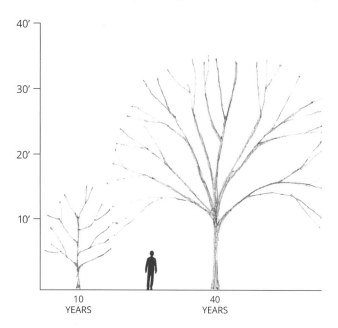

10 YEARS	40 YEARS

A yellow cucumber tree in spring.

The yellow cucumber tree flower in spring.

Developing fruit in autumn.

Yellow cucumber magnolia, as with all magnolias, has fleshy roots that are subject to rot when transplanted in late autumn or winter in colder regions. It is advisable to plant magnolias in spring or summer in USDA zone 7b and north, for root establishment during summer. The thin bark should be protected from mowing mechanical damage.

Few insects or diseases pose a serious problem. Woodpeckers and sapsuckers seem to enjoy the sweet inner bark of magnolias and drill many holes along the trunk. This damage usually heals rapidly in spring and rarely causes major damage to the tree. Deer rarely browse the aromatic foliage.

COMPANION PLANTS – In nature, yellow cucumber tree is found with red maple, white oak, sugar maple, sweet gum, sweet birch, ash, beech, sourwood, sweetbay, flowering dogwood, redbud, *Viburnum* spp., witch hazel, *Rhododendron* spp.,

and spicebush. The yellow cucumber magnolia casts dense shade, where ferns and ephemeral wildflowers may be well suited.

WILDLIFE – Many bird species and small mammals eat the red fleshy-coated seeds of magnolias. Woodpeckers in particular are fond of magnolia seeds. Magnolias also support the larvae of butterflies and moths.

CULTIVATED VARIETIES

'**Miss Honeybee**' – A more compact habit, 20'–30'. The fragrant flowers are large, 2½"–3", and the tree blooms at a young age. This variety has been used extensively in breeding programs for yellow-flowered cultivars.

'**Mister Yellow Jacket**' – Bright canary yellow flowers. Rounded habit.

Magnolia grandiflora

Southern Magnolia, Bull Bay

ATTRIBUTES/USE IN LANDSCAPE – The southern magnolia is a grand, imposing symbol of the South. This dense, flowering evergreen tree is appreciated as a specimen and for grouping, screening, and espalier. It is useful for residential, commercial, park, golf course, street, and highway projects.

SEASONS OF INTEREST

WINTER   SPRING   SUMMER   AUTUMN

FORM – The southern magnolia is a large evergreen with a pyramidal to oval form typically growing to about 60'–70' (90'), with an equal branch spread. It is dense and low branching in cultivation. The southern magnolia is a long-lived tree with a medium growth rate.

USDA Zones: 6–8 (9)		
SUN	**MOISTURE**	**pH**
Summer: full sun to partial sun Winter: full sun to full shade	Moist to wet	4.5–6.5

COLOR – The large, glossy evergreen leaves are varying shades of green on the upper surface and a dull tan to copper brown beneath. The smooth, leathery, 5"–10" leaves are held for two years. The gorgeous white flowers are large, 6"–12", very fragrant and bloom from late spring, diminishing through the summer. Conspicuous greenish, cone-like, tan pods, to 4" long, reveal bright red seeds in mid-autumn for about a month. Mature trunks are a mottled, slightly flaking brownish gray, and usually covered with lichens and moss. Many trees reveal the scarring of woodpeckers' activity.

TEXTURE – Coarse in all seasons.

A large, late-spring through summer flower.

A mature specimen grown in full sun.

CULTURE – The southern magnolia is one of the most well-known and extensively grown American trees throughout the world. The natural range is from eastern North Carolina south along the coast to central Florida, and west to eastern Texas. Generally, it grows best in regions with hot, humid summers and where winter temperatures do not fall much below 0°F. Hot summers increase winter hardiness. See Cultivated Varieties for increased cold hardiness.

Full sun is preferred, but the species is quite shade tolerant. It grows best in a well-drained, moist, sandy loam, but when established, it is tolerant of sandy to heavy clay soils. In northern areas, where hardy, it benefits from additional winter shade and wind protection. Once established, it is relatively drought tolerant. The degree of drought tolerance varies in seedling populations. The species also inhabits bottomlands along streams and is tolerant of short-term flooding. The waxy leaves of the southern magnolia protect it from salt spray and air pollution.

Older leaves drop during late spring and summer. In fact, it is frequently considered a litter tree, dropping leaves, dead twigs, or old fruit throughout the year. This can be a problem in well-manicured landscapes. The leaves may be light green, dark green, wavy, or flat and may also be broad or narrow. In individual trees of seed origin, the underside of the leaf may have a range of indumentum, from sparse to a thick coppery brown covering.

Magnolia wood is relatively brittle. I have seen trees hold up well in high winds, only to be heavily damaged from the weight of snow or ice. This primitive genus can live 400–500 years. A tree planted during the early 1800s is still growing happily on the south façade of the White House in Washington, DC. The tree survived the crash of a small airplane in 1994 with only minimal damage.

Because roots of all magnolias are fleshy and easily broken, it is best to transplant them in the spring in colder regions (zones 6 and 7), when roots have an entire growing season to recuperate. Transplanting in late autumn and winter, in colder areas within its range, may lead to rotting of the damaged roots. Additionally, in colder regions, it is best not to apply nitrogen fertilizers after mid-June to avoid seasonal growth that may not harden before winter. This is particularly true when grown in moist, loamy soils.

Few insects or diseases pose a serious problem. Magnolia scale may occasionally be an issue. Deer rarely bother southern magnolia.

COMPANION PLANTS – In the wild, the southern magnolia is usually found growing in association with

A robin feasting on southern magnolia seeds.

oaks, sweet gum, tupelo, cabbage palmetto, dwarf palmetto, and pines. In cultivation, shade-loving plants, such as ferns, woodland wildflowers, and ground covers, can grow very nicely under the dense shade of the tree, particularly if the lower branches are pruned off of the ground and the soil is not too sandy and dry. The shallow roots, dense year-round shade, and tendency for branching to the ground may make it difficult to grow turf beneath this tree. I have had success growing dwarf palmetto and needle palm beneath the branches in my zone 7 garden.

WILDLIFE – The southern magnolia provides shelter and food for many animals, including native birds. The seeds are relished by mourning dove, pileated woodpecker, red-cockaded woodpecker, yellow-bellied sapsucker, red-eyed vireo, quail, and wild turkey. They are also eaten by small mammals. The tree provides cover and nesting sites for birds as well. The southern magnolia also produces pollen.

CULTIVATED VARIETIES – In recent years, many new cultivated varieties have arrived in the nursery trade. As a result, southern magnolia can be seen in landscapes previously thought to be too far north

for survival. Trees grown in colder regions (zones 6–7a) should be planted in locations that are sheltered from cold winter winds. Trees grown from northern inland parents of the native range are usually the most cold tolerant. Some of the new varieties have proven to be especially cold-hardy, surviving temperatures to –20°F. Select for size of plant, leaf, and flower as well as cold hardiness.

'Bracken's Brown Beauty' – Up to 30' (50') × 25' (30'). A dense, compact, pyramidal form. Narrow leaves have a rusty brown indumentum beneath. It is noted for cold hardiness—through zone 5b in a wind-protected area. Tolerant of snow burden.

'D. D. Blanchard' – Up to 50' × 25'–35'. Noted for its strong central leader. Glossy, dark green leaves have a notable coppery-brown indumentum.

'Edith Bogue' – Up to 60' × 30'. Leaves are more narrow than species. Noted for winter hardiness—through zone 6. Light indumentum.

'Little Gem' – To 25' × 15' with a compact, narrow, upright form. Can be multi-stemmed. Smaller leaves, to 4" long with bronze indumentum. Smaller, prolific flowers, up to 4"–6". Cold-hardy through zone 7.

'Majestic Beauty' – To 50' × 30'. A coarser texture due to large leaves. Flowers are up to 12" in diameter. Not as wind and cold tolerant as others. Dense red-brown indumentum.

'Russet' – Up to 20' tall and wide. Very compact and a good variety for espalier use. Leaves have a bronze indumentum. Cold-hardy through zone 7 (6).

'Samuel Sommer' – To 30' tall and wide. Broad pyramidal form with large leaves. Rusty indumentum. Large flowers to 14". Very bright red fruit. Cold-hardy through zone 7.

Magnolia macrophylla

Bigleaf Magnolia

ATTRIBUTES/USE IN LANDSCAPE – The big-leaf magnolia is a medium-height, single-trunked, deciduous tree. Its unique large leaves and flowers provide a dramatic tropical effect. Use as a specimen or a shade tree where it can be protected from wind, in residences, parks, campuses, and large enclosed courtyards.

SEASONS OF INTEREST

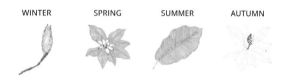

WINTER   SPRING   SUMMER   AUTUMN

FORM – A 30'–40' (60') tall × 30'–40', single-stemmed, upright, globe-shaped, deciduous magnolia. The tree has a medium to fast growth rate. Faster growth can be expected in consistently moist, fertile soils.

COLOR – The large, showy, creamy white flowers,

USDA Zones: 6–8		
SUN	**MOISTURE**	**pH**
Full sun to part shade	Moist, well drained	5–6.5

8"–10" (12"), are produced in mid-spring after the leaves have fully expanded. The flowers are fragrant but not as much as many other species of magnolia. Many flowers are located high above the ground in a mature tree and may be obscured by the foliage. The large, 12"–36" × 12", shiny green leaves are broader at the apex than at the base. They are thin with a silver-gray underside; the color contrast is notable when the leaves blow in a breeze. The flowers are followed by dark olive, 3", ovoid, cone-like fruits that open to reveal dark red seeds in late summer. The bark is thin and gray.

TEXTURE – Coarse in all seasons. Bigleaf magnolia has the largest flower and simple leaf of any native plant in the United States.

CULTURE – The bigleaf magnolia is native to central Alabama and Mississippi with scattered populations into the southern Appalachians. It is rare in nature

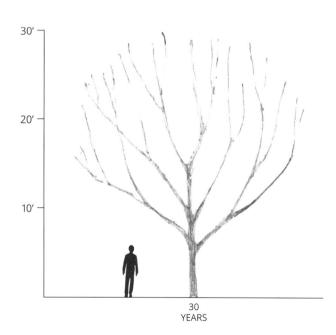

30'

20'

10'

30
YEARS

The large, showy bigleaf magnolia flower in spring.

Bigleaf magnolia form.

and usually found in partially shaded ravines and other protected areas.

The bigleaf magnolia prefers acidic, moist, rich, organic, well-drained soils. In cultivation, it tolerates clay loam soils as well as sandy soils and is moderately tolerant of drought. It has a tendency to drop leaves during dry weather. A location in full sun or partial shade suits it best. In partially

Bigleaf magnolia in bloom.

that are protected by large buildings or other trees. I have seen bark split from cold on young trees when winter temperatures drop suddenly from relatively warm to very cold, and the tree is exposed to sun or high wind. Therefore, it is best to locate the bigleaf magnolia in a site that is shielded from wind and in partial shade, even in winter when leaves are not present. The leaves can create a maintenance issue at leaf drop in autumn. The branches are brittle and may be susceptible to wind storm damage. In winter, the coarse branches rarely catch enough snow or ice to cause severe damage.

M. macrophylla subsp. *ashei* is a naturally occurring variety, native to northern Florida. It is a large shrub to small tree with an open habit, up to 20' × 20'. Its leaves and flowers are also smaller than the species.

Few insects or diseases pose a serious problem. Deer may browse the foliage and the large winter buds on lower branches.

COMPANION PLANTS – Bigleaf magnolia casts a moderate to dense shade. Shade-tolerant herbaceous perennials, ferns, azaleas, and evergreen ground covers may be planted beneath the tree.

WILDLIFE – Bigleaf magnolia provides pollen and nectar, and supports caterpillars. Many bird species and small mammals eat the red fleshy-coated seeds.

CULTIVATED VARIETIES

'Palmberg' – Flowers are exceptionally large.
'Purple Spotted' – Flowers have unusually prominent purple markings.

shaded areas, the leaves will be slightly larger. More flowering can be expected in full sun. It is not salt tolerant.

The large leaves are easily damaged by high winds. The best locations are large courtyards or park areas

Magnolia virginiana varieties

Northern and Southern Sweetbay Magnolias

ATTRIBUTES/USE IN LANDSCAPE – The sweetbay is an excellent medium-sized, multi-stemmed shrub or single-trunked tree with attractive, fragrant flowers. It can be deciduous, semievergreen, or evergreen. Sweetbay is useful as a specimen or grouping for patios, larger residences, parks, campuses, and rain gardens. See Part I for other uses.

SEASONS OF INTEREST

NORTHERN VARIETY (*M. Virginiana* var. *virginiana*)

| WINTER | SPRING | SUMMER | AUTUMN |

SOUTHERN VARIETY (*M. virginiana* var. *australis*)

| WINTER | SPRING | SUMMER | AUTUMN |

FORM – There are two distinct varieties: *M. virginiana*

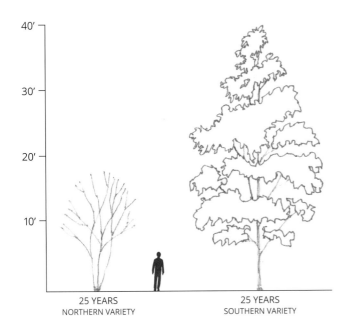

25 YEARS
NORTHERN VARIETY

25 YEARS
SOUTHERN VARIETY

USDA Zones: 5–11		
SUN	**MOISTURE**	**pH**
Full sun to shade	Dry to wet	4.5–6.5

var. *virginiana* in the northern part of its range, and *M. virginiana* var. *australis* in the southern part. In the North, sweetbay is generally a graceful, deciduous to partially evergreen large shrub or small tree: multi-stemmed, 10'–20' by same, loose, open, and upright with a rounded crown. In the South, the usually single-trunked tree can reach 60' by half as wide with an upright pyramidal crown. The growth rate is medium to fast, with var. *australis* being a faster grower. Faster growth can be expected in consistently moist soil in the southern portions of the respective ranges. Sweetbay casts a light to medium shade.

COLOR – The extremely fragrant, white flowers, 2"–3" in diameter, are produced in mid-spring and throughout the summer. The lemony scent is especially noticeable at night in the southern variety, *australis*. Each bloom lasts for a few days and is like a smaller version of the southern magnolia

Close-up of the leaves and fruit of the northern form of sweetbay magnolia.

A 10-year-old specimen of the southern form of the sweetbay magnolia.

younger trees. In some locations, the wood of older trees is scarred by woodpeckers and sapsuckers.

TEXTURE – Medium all seasons. Mature bark texture can be variable.

CULTURE – Sweetbay is native to the Atlantic and Gulf coastal plains from Long Island south through most of Florida and west into Louisiana. It grows in wet (seasonal inundation) to moist soils in ravines and along streams, generally below 200' elevation. But it is hardy further north and at higher elevations.

In cultivation, it tolerates clay loam soils as well as sandy soils. Salt spray and moderately saline soils are tolerated.

Close-up of the leaves and flower of the southern form of the sweetbay magnolia.

flower, but more fragrant. The 4"–8" ovate to elliptical leaves are a glossy, medium to dark green with a grayish white underside that flashes attractively when the wind blows. The leaves are more evergreen in the variety *australis*, even in the northern locations where it is hardy.

The 2" green, then brown cone-like fruits open to reveal many dark red seeds in late summer. The bark is handsome, thin, smooth, and silvery gray on

The wood is brittle and may be subject to damage from snow and ice, especially in the more evergreen varieties. Some individuals seem to be more tolerant of snow and ice loads than others, including *M. virginiana* var. *australis* 'Henry Hicks.' This cultivated variety also appears to be more cold tolerant than other southern varieties.

Like all magnolias, sweetbays have fleshy roots subject to rot when transplanted in late autumn or winter. Therefore, it is advisable to plant the species in spring in the cooler regions (zones 5, 6, and 7) to allow for root establishment before winter.

Few insects or diseases pose a serious problem. Deer rarely browse the aromatic foliage. Woodpeckers and sapsuckers seem to enjoy the sweet inner bark of magnolias and drill many holes along the trunk. This damage usually heals rapidly in spring and rarely causes major harm to the tree.

COMPANION PLANTS – In nature, sweetbay associates with red maple, bald cypress, sweet gum, willow oak, loblolly pine, *Viburnum* spp., spicebush, summersweet, swamp azalea, titi, and so on. Grasses, herbaceous perennials, and low shrubs are easily grown under and around sweetbay.

WILDLIFE – Sweetbay provides pollen and nectar for pollinators. Many bird species and small mammals eat the red fleshy-coated seeds. It is a host plant for the tiger swallowtail butterfly and the sweetbay silkmoth.

CULTIVATED VARIETIES – The species varies greatly in the degree of evergreen foliage, number of stems, and height. As one goes farther south in the tree's range, the taller, more evergreen trees with a single stem increase in dominance. Given that the

The multi-stemmed habit of the northern form of sweetbay magnolia.

species has such a wide range, one would expect the tolerance of winter cold to decrease in the more southern variety.

'Henry Hicks' – An evergreen single-stemmed tree to 40', a southern variety, cold-hardy into zone 5.
'Jim Wilson' ('Moonglow') – A multi-stemmed shrub, semi-evergreen, with slightly larger, very fragrant flowers; more cold-hardy.

Nyssa sylvatica (*N. sylvatica* var. *sylvatica*)

Black Gum, Tupelo, Sour Gum

ATTRIBUTES/USE IN LANDSCAPE – The black gum is a popular shade tree with exceptional autumn color. It is appreciated as a specimen or grouping, for bioretention areas, large residences, parks, and campuses, as well as a street tree.

USDA Zones: 3–11		
SUN	**MOISTURE**	**pH**
Full sun to part shade	Dry to wet	4.5–6.5

SEASONS OF INTEREST

WINTER	SPRING	SUMMER	AUTUMN
See form below			

COLOR – The 3"–6" leaves are ovate to elliptical and emerge light green in spring, maturing to a lustrous dark green in summer. The brilliant orange-yellow to red autumn color arrives early and may defoliate early. Dark blue fruits follow inconspicuous flowers on the female trees only. There can be considerable variation in bark color and texture—it can be gray to dark gray; with narrow, scaly plates or deeply furrowed, blocky, ridged, or even peeling.

FORM – The black gum is a small to medium single-trunked deciduous tree reaching 30'–60' (100' rarely) with a spread of 20'–30'. Its branching habit is horizontal, picturesque, dense, and variable. Pyramidal when young, it develops an oval to irregularly rounded crown in maturity. The medium growth rate is enhanced in moist soils. The growth rate can be slow after transplanting, until established, and also in maturity.

TEXTURE – Medium in all seasons. Bark texture variable.

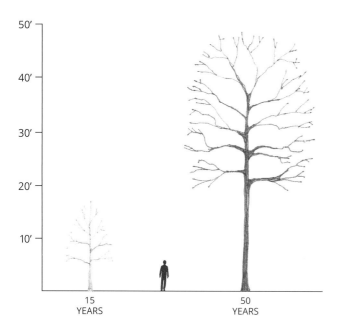

Autumn foliage.

A majestic, mature black gum specimen.

CULTURE – The black gum is native from south-western Maine and New York, west to southern Illinois and central Missouri, and south to Florida.

It grows in a wide range of locations ranging from wet (seasonal inundation) to dry soils. The black gum tolerates compacted soils as well. It is moderately tolerant of both aerosol and soil salt. The leaves of the black gum are firm and glossy; they have brighter autumn color when grown in full sun. With more shade, the leaves are thinner and with a less shiny finish. Although the wood is very resistant to split-ting, I have seen individual trees, with sharp-angled crotches, break at the crotch from ice and snow.

This tree has a taproot and must be root pruned by

Two mature black gums showing furrowed and checkered bark characteristics.

grower for transplanting. The best results are when planted in the spring, under 10' tall, and transplanted from containers or balled and burlapped.

Few insects or diseases pose a serious problem, but leaf spot, while not generally a perennial problem, can cause early defoliation in autumn. Deer will occasionally browse the leaves of young trees.

COMPANION PLANTS – In nature, black gum is found with red maple, bald cypress, sweet gum, willow oak, loblolly pine, hickory species, flowering dogwood, hophornbeam, yaupon, native azaleas, titi, arrowwood viburnum, and spicebush.

WILDLIFE – The flowers are an excellent source of nectar for honeybees, wild bees, and other pollinators. The nutritious fruit is eaten by a variety of birds and mammals.

CULTIVATED VARIETIES – The black gum has several close relatives, which are generally known as tupelos in their regions. Choose cultivars for variety of form, leaf color, and disease resistance.

'**Autumn Cascade**' – A weeping form with an irregular/informal habit. Leaves are larger, and the autumn colors are yellow, orange, and red.
'**Green Gable**' ('**NSUHH**') – An upright, pyramidal form with regular branching. It has shiny green summer foliage and excellent bright red autumn color.
'**Red Rage**' – Autumn color is an excellent red. Strong pyramidal habit. Very resistant to leaf spot.
'**Wildfire**' – New growth emerges reddish and persists through summer.
'**Zydeco Twist**' – Somewhat contorted branches add winter interest.
'**JFS-Red**' ('**Firestarter**') – Taller than wide, fruitless.
'**Gum Drop**' – Taller than wide, fruitless.

Ostrya virginiana

American Hophornbeam, Ironwood

ATTRIBUTES/USE IN LANDSCAPE – The American hophornbeam is a worthy, underused small to medium deciduous tree that is very resilient in urban and suburban landscapes. It has a nice form and autumn color, and its interesting bark and charming catkin clusters are attractive in winter. Hophornbeam is effective as a specimen in raised parking lot tree islands and parking lot buffer strips, around decks and patios as a shade tree, in reclamation areas, and along residential streets, including under utility lines, where salt treatment is not an issue.

USDA Zones: 3–9		
SUN	**MOISTURE**	**pH**
Full sun to full shade	Dry to moist	4.2–7.6

SEASONS OF INTEREST

WINTER   SPRING   SUMMER   AUTUMN

FORM – Hophornbeam grows slowly to 30'–40' with a 25'–30' spread. Hophornbeam is typically pyramidal in youth. As it ages, it develops an oval to rounded outline, with a moderately dense crown with many fine-textured twigs. The elliptical or ovate single leaves are 4"–8" long × 2"–4" wide. The average life span is up to 150 years.

COLOR – The thin bark of the hophornbeam is usually orange to reddish brown with a distinctive shedding character. The 4"–8" long × 2"–4" wide leaves are medium green in summer and turn a quiet yellow-brown in autumn. They are finely serrated, like some other members of the birch family. The drooping, pale green "hop-like" papery fruits are very attractive in summer. At leaf drop the abundant fruits, now light brown, become apparent and remain into winter. They provide nice interest and food for wildlife.

TEXTURE – Medium in leaf, fine in winter.

30'

20'

10'

15 YEARS   40 YEARS

American hophornbeam catkins.

A hophornbeam specimen at Mt. Cuba Center, Delaware.

CULTURE – The hophornbeam is native to a wide area of eastern North America from Nova Scotia south to northern Florida, west to Texas, and north to Manitoba.

Hophornbeam grows most rapidly in a well-drained, moist soil, but it is tolerant of dry sands or compacted clays. It is very drought tolerant and will not stand prolonged flooding. It tolerates moderately acid and moderately alkaline soils and pollution. Hophornbeam is generally not very tolerant of high concentrations of salt. The wood and branches are very resistant to breakage from wind, ice, and snow.

In average soils, hophornbeam can be expected to reach 15' in 15 years. This tree can sometimes be slow to recover from transplanting. It is best to select balled and burlapped or container-grown specimens for early-spring planting. Young trees respond well to additional watering for the first two years after transplanting.

Hophornbeam has very few insect or disease problems, but it can be defoliated by gypsy moths if the pest is present. On rare occasions, the two-lined chestnut borer may attack hophornbeam. Deer rarely browse hophornbeam, but they do enjoy the nutlike seeds.

COMPANION PLANTS – In nature, American hophornbeam is found in association with shagbark hickory, oaks, sugar maple, American holly, dogwoods, redbud, and many other native species.

WILDLIFE – The buds and catkins are eaten by many birds, small mammals, and deer. The American hophornbeam is a larval host to nearly one hundred butterfly and moth larvae, including the

The distinctive shedding bark as an attractive winter feature.

eastern swallowtail. The trees support spring migrations as well.

CULTIVATED VARIETIES – Cultivated varieties are not available commercially at this writing.

Oxydendrum arboreum

Sourwood, Sorrel Tree

ATTRIBUTES/USE IN LANDSCAPE – The sourwood is a superior, colorful, medium-sized tree with multi-season interest. It is stunning in midsummer flowering and in autumn with its fruits against excellent prolonged, scarlet foliage. Fruit retention adds winter interest. Sourwood is effective as a specimen, in groupings, as a street tree, under utility lines, and at the woodland edge.

SEASONS OF INTEREST

| WINTER | SPRING | SUMMER | AUTUMN |

FORM – The sourwood is a slow-growing, medium-sized, single-trunked tree, 25'–30' (50'–75') and nearly as wide. In youth, it is typically pyramidal with drooping branches. With age, it develops more regular branching and a narrowly oval form. In the forest, it is straight, relatively limbless, and tall.

USDA Zones: 5–9		
SUN	**MOISTURE**	**pH**
Full sun to partial sun	Dry to moist	3.5–6.5

COLOR – The attractive, firm, glossy leaves, up to 6" long, are lightly serrated, lanceolate to obovate. They emerge light green in spring, becoming a medium to dark green in summer. The underside is pale green. In mid- to late summer, profuse, small, showy, creamy white flowers on slightly pendulous spikelets, 4"–10" long and wide, splay over the mature leaves. The flowers resemble lily of the valley. Pale yellow peppercorns develop in late summer and prolong the flowering appearance even after the early leaf change to brilliant red. The seeds persist into winter following leaf drop, enhancing the winter form of the tree. The sourwood's distinctive dark gray and brown bark becomes deeply furrowed and checkered with age. The slender, flexible twigs

The lily-of-the-valley-shaped blossoms.

50'

40'

30'

20'

10'

15
YEARS

40
YEARS

A mature sourwood, in flower, grown in full sun.

A young sourwood in a shady garden.

and young branches are olive green to red in color. Flowers are fragrant.

TEXTURE – Fine in winter, medium other seasons.

CULTURE – The sourwood's native range is from southern Pennsylvania through the southeast to Texas.

The sourwood flowering and autumn color are best in full sun. It also performs best in acidic, moist soils with protection from afternoon sun, but it tolerates dry soil and short-term drought when mature. Sourwood will not grow in heavy clay soils with poor drainage.

Sourwood is best transplanted as a small, 6'–8'

A 25-year-old sourwood, Grove Street Cemetery, New Haven, Connecticut.

container-grown tree in spring or autumn. It is intolerant of pollution, soil compaction, root disturbance, and flooding. Sourwood is listed as moderately salt tolerant.

There are no serious insect or disease problems, though fall webworm may be an issue from time to time. Deer are usually not a serious issue.

COMPANION PLANTS – The sourwood is found in nature with black gum, scarlet oak, flowering dogwood, and oakleaf hydrangea.

WILDLIFE – The sourwood is an important source of midsummer nectar and pollen and provides nesting for birds. The seeds are eaten by birds and small mammals. Humans consider sourwood honey a delicacy.

CULTIVATED VARIETIES – Today, the few existing varieties do not improve upon the species.

Pinus palustris

Longneedle or Longleaf Pine

ATTRIBUTES/USE IN LANDSCAPE – The long-needle pine is a uniquely attractive, large evergreen conifer that grows under a variety of conditions. The combination of long needles and unusual growth habit make longneedle pine a first choice for a large specimen or accent plant. It may also be used in groupings and windbreaks for parks, golf courses, and other large properties. It is an excellent tree for wildlife.

SEASONS OF INTEREST

WINTER	SPRING	SUMMER	AUTUMN

FORM – A tall, slow to start but eventually fast-growing tree, 70'–90' (historically 100'–120') with width about half the height. Trunks may reach 2' and more in diameter. In my Maryland garden, one tree raised from seed grew to 35' tall, with a trunk diameter of 18", in 25 years.

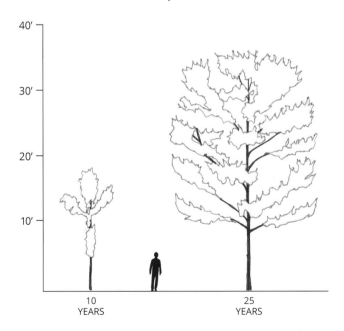

USDA Zones: 6b–9		
SUN	**MOISTURE**	**pH**
Full sun	Dry to moist	4–6.5

Longneedle pine has a unique growth habit when young that is not duplicated elsewhere in native plants. Young plants first develop a "grass stage," resembling a clump of grass rather than a tree. It remains in this stage for several years, not producing any visible increase in size, while developing a deep (up to 8') taproot. Once a source of water is encountered, the top begins to expand rapidly. Lateral branches are slow to expand, so a plant recently growing out of the grass stage may resemble a pencil with 10"–12" needles.

At 5–10 years from seed, longneedle pine begins

The 10"–12" long, evergreen needles.

A mature specimen longneedle pine in winter.

to develop lateral branches, while retaining a dominant central leader.

The tree eventually develops into a tall, pyramidal
and open-branched evergreen tree. It self-prunes for
a long, bare trunk. Longneedle pine generally lives
75–100 years but can live 150 years and more. It is
more short-lived in zones 6b–7.

COLOR – The longneedle pine's bright green needles
are the longest of any native pine species, typically
10"–18" on mature trees. The needles are in bundles
of three (rarely two). The cones are very large, ranging from 8"–10". The branches are quite rough and
textured, with regular woody protuberances. The
mature trunk bark is gray brown. It is thick, rough,
and plated with a reddish under-bark.

TEXTURE – Medium coarse in all seasons.

CULTURE – The longneedle pine is native to the
southeastern states on the coastal plain from southeast Virginia to Florida, west to eastern Texas. I grew
this plant very successfully on Long Island, NY.

Longneedle pine grows most rapidly in rich, well-
drained, moist, sandy soil, high in organic matter, but
it will grow almost as well in sandy clay, dry sand, and
gravelly soils. It will withstand very dry or seasonally
wet, sandy soils and poorly drained soils. However, it
will not thrive in heavy clay or extremely compacted
soils. Longneedle pine survives heat, wind, cold, and
urban conditions very well. It is intolerant of shade
in all phases of life.

Longneedle pine is not as susceptible to damage

by heavy loads of ice and snow as most other pines. A tree in my garden was repeatedly bent nearly in half by wet snow or ice, only to spring back to its original shape after growth commenced the following spring.

Longneedle pine is a member of the group of two- or three-needled pines collectively known as hard pines or yellow pines. The needles fall after two years, generally in autumn, and provide a good mulch for acid-loving plants below. Every two to three years, trees of cone-bearing age may produce exceptionally heavy crops of large cones.

The surface roots are deep and far-reaching. It can be difficult to transplant. For the best results, plant nursery-grown trees that were frequently root pruned to develop a more compact root system. Plant only in the spring in the northern areas where it may be cultivated.

Longneedle pines usually do not have serious disease and pest concerns. However, when under stress, they may be attacked by southern pine bark beetle. It is usually tolerant of deer and rabbits.

COMPANION PLANTS – The hardwoods most closely associated with longneedle pine include southern red oak, flowering dogwood, black gum, sweet gum, yaupon, and sweetbay. The more common shrubs include inkberry, southern bayberry, shining sumac, and titi.

The dappled shade cast by longneedle pine provides an excellent environment for growing acid-loving understory ornamental shrubs such as native azaleas, rhododendrons, Florida leucothoe, and holly.

WILDLIFE – The seeds of pines offer shelter and food for many mammals and bird species. Birds

The interesting bark and unique branching detail of the longneedle pine.

are also drawn to the more than 200 butterfly and moth larvae that use the tree, including pine-specific species.

CULTIVATED VARIETIES – There are no cultivated varieties in the trade as of this writing.

Pinus strobus

Eastern White Pine

ATTRIBUTES/USE IN LANDSCAPE – The eastern white pine is a beautiful, large, evergreen conifer. It is a member of the five-needled pine group collectively known as the soft or white pines. It is useful as a handsome specimen, in groupings and windbreaks, for parks and large properties. The size of this fast-growing tree may be controlled for a hedge by shearing the new growth while it is actively expanding. Eastern white pine is an excellent tree for wildlife.

SEASONS OF INTEREST—GREEN FOLIAGE:

WINTER	SPRING	SUMMER	AUTUMN

USDA Zones: 3–8a		
SUN	**MOISTURE**	**pH**
Full sun (to part shade in youth)	Dry to moist	4.5–6.5

30" in 45 years. Eastern white pine is the tallest pine in the eastern United States. The dense, pyramidal form of young trees gives way to an open, wide-spreading, irregular-crowned form in maturity. The horizontal and ascending branches are distinctly whorled around the trunk. The eastern white pine generally lives 75–100 years but can live 150 years and more. It is more short-lived in zones 7–8.

FORM – The eastern white pine is a tall, fast-growing tree, 50'–80' (historically 150'–200') with width about half the height. Trunks may reach 3' in diameter. In my Maryland garden, one tree raised from seed grew to 75' tall with a trunk diameter of

COLOR – The soft light to blue-green needles, 3"–5" long, come in bundles of five. The brown 4"–8" cones open in their second autumn to release seeds. They frequently hang on for several months to a year after seed release and can be a maintenance issue in manicured landscape situations. Additionally, the cones exude plenty of dripping pitch, which can be an issue on maintained surfaces. The bark is a smooth green-gray on young trunks and upper branches and twigs.

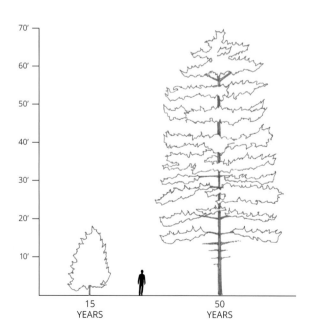

The handsome foliage of eastern white pine.

A 20-year-old grouping of white pine at the US National Arboretum, Washington, DC.

The mature dark gray-brown bark has thick blocks with deep longitudinal fissures.

TEXTURE – Medium fine in all seasons.

CULTURE – The eastern white pine is native to the northeastern states through Pennsylvania and throughout the Appalachians into Georgia.

Eastern white pine grows most rapidly in rich, well-drained, moist soil, high in organic matter. However, it will grow almost as well in clay, sand, gravelly soils, or compacted urban soils. It will withstand very dry soils but does not thrive in poorly drained soils. It survives heat, wind, cold, and urban conditions very well. Eastern white pine always succeeds best in full sun, but partial shade is tolerated in youth, until about 10 years old. I have read numerous articles stating white pine is intolerant of salt and air pollution. I have, however, seen plants encrusted with salt at the edges of highways after particularly snowy winters that survive happily year after year. The same is true for many older trees located in the urban confines of Washington, DC. On the other hand, white pine will not survive the constant aerosol salt spray near the ocean, nor will it survive consistently polluted air in low-lying urban areas with poor air circulation. Eastern white pine is susceptible to damage by heavy loads of snow and ice. Other native pines, mentioned in this book, will be more vigorous in the South.

The needles fall after two years, generally in autumn, and provide a good mulch for acid-loving understory plants. The surface roots are shallow and far-reaching. It is easily transplanted in spring or early autumn.

A young eastern white pine in a native shrub border.

White pine, like other five-needle pines, is subject to white pine blister rust. The alternate hosts are currants and gooseberries, so these should not be planted near white pine. Blister rust affects the bark and may kill the tree. White pine weevil, which deforms the tree, can sometimes be a serious pest in landscape situations where uniformity is important. Young white pines are occasionally browsed by deer.

COMPANION PLANTS – Mature white pine, with branches removed to at least 15 feet above the soil surface, provides an excellent environment for growing acid-loving understory shrubs such as azaleas, rhododendrons, and holly.

WILDLIFE – The seeds of pines feed many mammals and bird species. Birds are also drawn to the more than 200 butterfly and moth larvae that use the tree, including pine-specific species.

CULTIVATED VARIETIES – There are many cultivars. Select for size, form, and needle color.

'Blue Shag' – 2'–4' × 2'–4', very compact, rounded form. Blue-green, short, soft needles.
'Fastigiata' – 30'–40' (70') × 7'–10' (20'). Narrow, upright growth habit.
'Glauca' – Light blue-green needles.
'Horsford' – A dwarf shrub, rounded to 1'. Yellow-green foliage.
'Macopin' – 3' × 3', upright, irregular shrub. Silver-blue foliage.
'Nana' Group – A dwarf group of varieties, generally compact and rounded or spreading. Most to about 2' in height.
'Pendula' – 6'–15' × 10'–20'. A semi-dwarf cultivar. The branching is horizontal, then drooping, sometimes trailing to the ground. Pruning and training define form.

A mature white pine at Wave Hill Garden, NY.

Pinus taeda

Loblolly Pine

ATTRIBUTES/USE IN LANDSCAPE – The loblolly pine is a large evergreen conifer, very common in the southeast, with an attractive form and tolerance for many soil conditions. It is effective as a specimen and fast-growing screen for windbreaks. It is useful for bioretention areas, parks, golf courses, and other large properties and projects. Loblolly pine is an excellent tree for wildlife.

SEASONS OF INTEREST

WINTER   SPRING   SUMMER   AUTUMN

FORM – Loblolly pine begins to form branches at a young age. The lower branches are rapidly lost as the tree grows, due to the lack of shade tolerance. A tall, straight trunk with a high crown usually develops. It reaches heights of 90'–115' (160') with trunk diameters of 1'–4'. The tree casts a medium shade, as the branches are never very dense.

USDA Zones: 6–10		
SUN	**MOISTURE**	**pH**
Full sun	Dry to wet	4–6.5

COLOR – The green needles are in bundles of three (rarely two), 4"–9" long, and sometimes twisted. There is a slight bluish green tinge, with the overall effect being a light green.

The reddish brown 3"–6" cones are produced in large numbers every year. They frequently hang on for several years. The bark is grayish brown and furrowed with elongated and broad irregular plates. The young twigs are scaly and reddish brown in color.

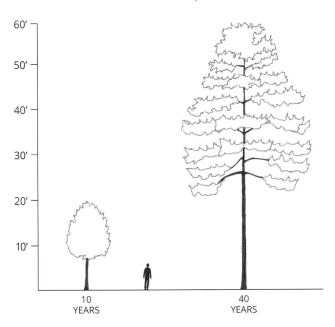

A young volunteer loblolly growing in a sediment pond.

A perfectly formed, 45-year-old loblolly along a well-travelled road in North Carolina.

TEXTURE – Medium in all seasons.

CULTURE – The loblolly pine is native to the coastal plain from southern New Jersey to Florida, west to eastern Texas. It is the largest and one of the most common pines in the southeastern states. Loblolly is a member of the group of two- or three-needled pines collectively known as hard pines or yellow pines.

The loblolly pine will withstand very dry or seasonally wet soils. It grows most rapidly in rich, well-drained, moist sandy soil high in organic matter. But it will grow almost as well in sandy clay, dry sand, and gravelly soils. It is very tolerant of poor drainage and compacted soil.

Loblolly is intolerant of shade in all phases of its life. It is best to plant this tree away from more formal planting areas, as the fallen cones can be a maintenance issue in manicured landscapes when they fall. The needles fall after two years, generally in autumn, and provide a good mulch for acid-loving understory plants. It is easy to transplant.

Loblolly is moderately soil-salt tolerant and slightly tolerant of airborne salt. It provides very fast screens and windbreaks but is susceptible to breakage in strong winds, ice, and snow. Unlike longneedle pine, loblolly pine is intolerant of fire.

Pinus resinosa, red pine, has a similar appearance and is suitable for more northern areas (zones 2–5). A two-needled pine, red pine is intolerant of heat and humidity, requiring relatively cool summers. It superficially resembles loblolly pine and provides many of the same attributes to more northern locales. Red pine is more tolerant of breakage from wind, ice, and snow than loblolly, but it is not as tolerant of poor drainage. There is very little diversity among red pines. Even when grown from seed the offspring resemble one another very closely.

Loblolly pine, when not stressed, does not have significant disease and pest concerns. Deer are rarely a serious issue, although they will occasionally feed on the needles.

COMPANION PLANTS – Hardwood trees most closely associated with loblolly pine include southern red oak, flowering dogwood, black gum, sweet gum and sweetbay. The more common shrubs include inkberry, yaupon, spicebush, southern bayberry, shining sumac, and titi. The dappled shade cast by loblolly pine provides an excellent environment for growing acid-loving understory ornamental shrubs such as azaleas, rhododendrons, and Florida leucothoe. Many species of native ferns and herbaceous wildflowers thrive with loblolly pine.

WILDLIFE – The loblolly offers shelter and food for many mammals and bird species. Birds are also drawn to the more than 200 butterfly and moth larvae that use the tree, including pine-specific species.

CULTIVATED VARIETIES

'**JC Raulston**' – Lower growing, 15'–30', much more dense, slower growing, and more picturesque than the species. 'JC Raulston' was selected and named by JC Raulston Arboretum at NC State University. Difficult to locate in the trade, but it is well worth the search.

'JC Raulston' at JC Raulston Arboretum, North Carolina.

Pinus virginiana

Virginia or Scrub Pine

ATTRIBUTES/USE IN LANDSCAPE —The Virginia pine is a medium-sized, relatively short-lived evergreen conifer. It is not considered to be as ornamental as other native pines, but it is very tolerant of adverse growing conditions, including dry, sterile soil. Virginia pine is used, usually in groupings, for reclamation plantings, soil erosion cover, wildlife habitat, windbreaks, parking lot islands, and for large properties. Virginia pine is an excellent tree for wildlife.

USDA Zones: 5–8		
SUN	**MOISTURE**	**pH**
Full sun	Dry	4–6.5

develops a 40'–50' single trunk, with the remains of dead branches lining the trunk almost to the ground. The open crown of the tree is usually irregular, with the branches containing numerous old cones that are not concealed by the short, 1½"–3" needles.

SEASONS OF INTEREST

WINTER	SPRING	SUMMER	AUTUMN

COLOR – Needle color ranges from dark green to a yellowish green. They are twisted and in two-needle bundles. The oval brown 1"–3" cones are produced in large numbers each year. They frequently hang on for years and sometimes never fall. The bark is

FORM – Virginia pine remains relatively low branched and compact when growing as a specimen in full sun. With competition from other plants, Virginia pine rapidly loses its lower branches and

The small cones and short, two-needled bundles of Virginia pine.

40'

30'

20'

10'

10
YEARS

40
YEARS

A young Virginia pine in full sun.

cinnamon brown with irregular plates. The young twigs are scaly and orange-brown in color.

TEXTURE – Fine in all seasons.

CULTURE – The Virginia pine is native from southern Pennsylvania and New Jersey southward to northern Georgia and Alabama. It is quite common in dry, sandy, gravelly, acid soils in the mid-Atlantic states.

Virginia pine will withstand very dry clay and compacted soils as well. Like most other pines, it is intolerant of shade. It is also intolerant of wet, poorly drained soils. It is slightly tolerant of soil salt but has a low tolerance for aerosol salt. The cones and growth habit make it best suited for less formal landscapes. It is relatively easy to transplant.

Virginia pine does not have significant disease and pest concerns. Deer are rarely a serious issue, although they will occasionally feed on the needles.

COMPANION PLANTS – Virginia pine's associates include southern red oak, scrub oak, red maple, sweet gum, bayberry, shining sumac, and staghorn sumac.

WILDLIFE – Virginia pine offers shelter and food for many mammals and bird species. Birds are also drawn to the more than 200 butterfly and moth larvae that use the tree, including pine-specific species.

CULTIVATED VARIETIES – Currently there are no cultivated varieties.

Old Virginia pine with good form.

Platanus occidentalis

Sycamore, American Planetree

ATTRIBUTES/USE IN LANDSCAPE – The sycamore is a handsome, large, deciduous lawn or shade tree with unique, showy bark and a distinctive leaf shape. It is appreciated as a specimen, in an allée, or in a grouping for parking strips, highway plantings, large residences, parks, campuses, and bioretention projects. The sycamore is a good plant for wildlife.

USDA Zones: 4–9		
SUN	**MOISTURE**	**pH**
Full sun to part shade	Dry to wet	4.9–6.5

SEASONS OF INTEREST

WINTER SPRING SUMMER AUTUMN

FORM – The sycamore is a large tree reaching 75'–100' (150') tall, with spreads typically ½ to ⅔ of its height, and several large, horizontal branches. In rare cases spread may be equal to the height. The sycamore is a massive tree and may have trunk diameters of up to 8', with records higher. Pyramidal in youth, it develops an irregular crown in maturity. It is fast growing and long-lived.

COLOR – The large, leathery, medium to dark green leaves are 4"–9" wide and have three to five shallow, pointed lobes. The tree leafs out late in spring and may hold its undistinguished, yellow-brown autumn foliage into winter. The early-spring flowers are inconspicuous and followed by 1" spherical fruits that become long-stemmed fuzzy balls. These are apparent in fall and often persist and shatter

The distinctive sycamore bark on a mature tree.

70'
60'
50'
40'
30'
20'
10'

10 YEARS   40 YEARS

A mature specimen grown in full sun.

throughout winter. The bark on the lower trunk is brown and rough. This bark peels away with height from the ground, on both the trunk and upper branches, to a smooth, mottled pale green and whitish bark.

TEXTURE – Coarse in all seasons.

CULTURE – The sycamore is native to the eastern United States from southwest Maine to northern Florida, west to the Mississippi River, excepting

A sycamore allée, Baltimore, Maryland.

A sycamore thriving in an urban setting.

Minnesota. It is abundant and distinctive in alluvial soils, river bottoms, floodplains, and near waterways, where it withstands flooding.

The sycamore performs best in full sun but will tolerate partial shade. It is very tolerant of different soils and sites but grows best on the rich, moist, alluvial clay and loamy soils of river bottoms. When mature it tolerates drought. It also tolerates compacted soils and is moderately tolerant of salt.

The sycamore can be used as a street tree, with its tolerance of pollution, drought, heat, and soil compaction. However, it presents a maintenance issue when it sheds large leaves, twigs, peeling bark, and fruits.

Anthracnose can be a serious problem in wet, cool springs, when it may kill the early foliage. The foliage recovers with the warmer temperatures of summer. Deer are not a serious problem.

COMPANION PLANTS – It associates in nature with sweet gum, river birch, and swamp white oak, spicebush, itea, winterberry, titi, and summersweet.

WILDLIFE – The sycamore provides shelter for birds and food for wintering birds (finches love the seed), and supports 45 common caterpillars.

CULTIVATED VARIETIES – Cultivated varieties can be hard to find in the trade at the time of this writing.

Quercus alba

White Oak

ATTRIBUTES/USE IN LANDSCAPE – The white oak is a handsome, large tree with a massive trunk and spreading branches. It is notable for its scale, picturesque winter profile, beautiful summer foliage, and its strong, storm-resistant trunk and branching. It is a superb specimen or shade tree for large lawns, parks, highway plantings, median strips, and golf courses. The oaks are exceptional trees for wildlife.

SEASONS OF INTEREST

WINTER	SPRING	SUMMER	AUTUMN
See form below			

FORM – The white oak is a large tree, to 60'–100' × 50'–90', with a massive trunk. The branching habit is coarse, open, and wide spreading. When grown in full sun, the strong lower branches, on an older specimen, are nearly horizontal. A slow-growing tree, it can live up to 600 years.

USDA Zones: 3–8		
SUN	**MOISTURE**	**pH**
Full sun to part shade	Dry to moist, but well drained	4–7

COLOR – The leaves are thick and 4"–8" long by half as wide. They are a dark green to a blue-green on the upper surface with a light green underside. They are oblong to obovate with five to seven rounded, often deep lobes, with smooth margins. The autumn foliage is reddish brown, and leaves may hang on the branches throughout winter after dying, especially on young trees or on the lower branches of older trees. The thick bark is pale gray and vertically fissured to flaking. Light brown ¾"–1" acorns have a rough cap covering about a quarter of the acorn.

TEXTURE – Medium to coarse in summer, it is coarse in winter, with a massive trunk and branches on older specimens.

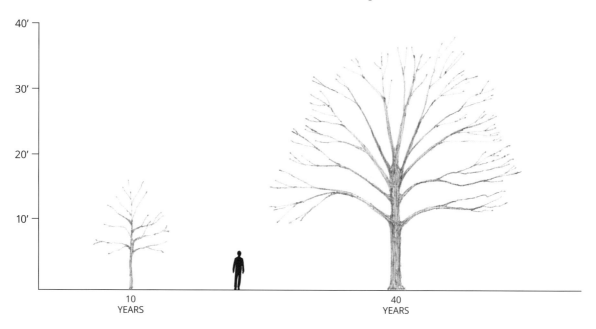

40'

30'

20'

10'

10 YEARS

40 YEARS

A 35-year-old white oak.

CULTURE – The white oak is native east of the Mississippi River, from southern Ontario southward into Georgia. It is one of the most durable trees in the forest, resisting wind and ice storms with ease.

The white oak is a beautiful and, once established, an easily grown large shade tree. This tree grows best in full sun and acidic soil. The fastest growth will occur in moist alluvial soils, but it tolerates many soil types ranging from sand to clay. White oak is not very tolerant of consistently poorly drained soils and intolerant of flooding. It is tolerant of drought and of both soil and aerosol salt. It may not perform well in urban settings, where it is intolerant of compaction around its roots. It should be well protected if there is construction disturbance near the tree.

The oaks are a wind-pollinated species, producing both male and female flowers on the same plant. Copious amounts of pollen are produced from the 2"–4" drooping male flowers (catkins) in early spring. The pollen may be an issue for hay fever sufferers, and the catkins may clog drains and downspouts when they drop. The resulting fruit is an acorn, which matures in autumn of the year it is formed, as in all species of the white oak group. The acorns may be a maintenance issue on walkways or in well-manicured lawns. They are palatable to humans and wildlife.

Young trees produce a deep taproot, making it difficult to transplant and requiring root pruning when grown in a nursery. It is best to transplant a young tree, balled and burlapped, in the early spring.

A mature white oak, at least 150 years old.

Q. bicolor, the swamp white oak (zones 4–8), is a similar species that is found in swamps and along streams. It is much more adaptable to wet soils but tolerates dry soils as well. The leaves are round lobed, but not nearly as deeply incised as on white oak. The swamp white oak has an oval form in maturity, with upper branches ascending and lower branches descending. It does not have the massive branching of the white oak.

There are many pests listed for white oak. Although a number of these pests can be serious, most cultivated specimens thrive with minimum care once the tree is established. Deer readily browse foliage and twigs in reach, and seedlings are frequently killed through deer browsing.

COMPANION PLANTS – In nature, the white oak associates with sugar maple, white pine, and cucumber tree, as well as other oaks and hickories. The deep roots of white oak allow underplanting with shade-loving plants such as Florida leucothoe, native azaleas, rhododendrons, and Virginia sweetspire.

WILDLIFE – Oaks are very valuable plants for wildlife. They are host to hundreds of butterfly and moth larvae—more than any other tree. The acorns are a favorite food of birds, small mammals, and deer.

CULTIVATED VARIETIES – Cultivated varieties are not readily available.

'Fastigiata' – A very narrow and upright form. Currently it is very difficult to locate in nurseries.

Quercus coccinea

Scarlet Oak

ATTRIBUTES/USE IN LANDSCAPE – The scarlet oak is a handsome, popular, large tree with a rounded, dense growth habit. The brilliant red autumn foliage is very attractive and provides excellent color late into the fall season. Scarlet oak adapts well to a variety of growing conditions. They are appreciated as street trees, in parking lot buffer strips and median strips, as shade trees in lawns, and in reclamation sites. Oaks are excellent for wildlife.

SEASONS OF INTEREST

WINTER	SPRING	SUMMER	AUTUMN

FORM – The scarlet oak is a large deciduous tree, 60'–75' tall × 40'–50' spread. When grown in full sun, the form is very symmetrical, dense, and rounded to sometimes elliptical. The habit is very consistent

USDA Zones: 5–8		
SUN	**MOISTURE**	**pH**
Full sun	Dry to moist	4–7

among individuals. Growth rate is medium, with growth rate and form best in full sun.

COLOR – The leaves turn a brilliant scarlet in autumn. It is the finest oak for autumn color, and trees hold most of their leaves into the fall. The medium to dark green leaves emerge in spring and cast a moderately heavy shade throughout the summer. They are oval with deeply incised bristle-tipped lobes, to 8" in length and 5" wide. The bark, smooth when young, becomes rough and fissured. It is very dark brown, appearing almost black when wet.

The bright, persistent autumn foliage.

A large scarlet oak in full sun.

Scarlet oaks at Mt. Cuba Center, Delaware.

TEXTURE – Medium in summer and winter, with well-balanced branches.

CULTURE – The scarlet oak is a beautiful and relatively easily grown, large tree. It is native from southern New England south to northern Georgia and west to the Mississippi River. It is not common on the southern coastal plain.

Scarlet oak grows best in an acidic soil but will tolerate soils with a neutral pH. It tolerates many soil types ranging from sand to clay, but the fastest growth will occur in moist alluvial soils. Scarlet oak survives urban conditions very well, thriving in many difficult situations. It is tolerant of drought and moderately tolerant of both soil and aerosol salt. The wood of scarlet oak is strong and resists wind and breakage from heavy loads of ice and snow.

The oaks are a wind-pollinated species, with copious amounts of pollen produced from the 2"–4" drooping male flowers (catkins) in early spring. The pollen may be an issue for hay fever sufferers, and the catkins may clog drains and downspouts when they drop. The resulting fruit is an acorn, which matures in two years in all species of the red oak group. The acorns are a favorite wildlife food, but they may be a maintenance issue on walkways or in well-manicured lawns.

Scarlet oak can be difficult to transplant. Plant only nursery-grown specimens, preferably, in the spring.

Q. rubra, northern red oak (zones 4–8), is very similar to scarlet oak in appearance, though the leaves are not as deeply incised and it lacks the brilliant autumn foliage color. The northern red oak is slightly faster growing and easier to transplant, but otherwise its culture and attributes are the same.

Q. falcata, southern red oak (zones 6–9), is similar in growth habit, culture, and attributes to scarlet oak but is more tolerant of the heat and humidity of the southern coastal plain. It is also more tolerant of periodic flooding, and slightly more shade tolerant. The autumn color is a less attractive brownish red. In *Gardening with Native Plants of the South*, Wasowski, 1994, recommends *Quercus shumardii*, the Shumard red oak (zones 5–9), for the coastal plain and better tolerance of limestone soils.

There are many pests listed for oaks. Although some of these pests can be serious, most cultivated specimens thrive with minimum care once the tree is established. Deer may sometimes browse the foliage.

COMPANION PLANTS – Scarlet oak combines well with black gum, bald cypress, pond cypress, Darlington oak, willow oak, southern magnolia, sweetbay, American holly, yaupon holly, hophornbeam, inkberry, winterberry, spicebush, Virginia sweetspire, southern wax myrtle, groundsel bush, and titi.

WILDLIFE – Like all oaks, scarlet oak supports hundreds of butterfly and moth larvae. Many species of mammals and birds feed on the acorns. The foliage may be browsed by deer but is not preferred.

CULTIVATED VARIETIES – Cultivated varieties are not available commercially.

Quercus hemisphaerica

Darlington Oak

ATTRIBUTES/USE IN LANDSCAPE – The Darlington oak is a beautiful, easily grown, evergreen, medium to large shade tree. It is fast growing and popular in the South and mid-Atlantic. The Darlington oak is appreciated for its evergreen foliage; dense rounded form; and ability to grow in a variety of conditions including dry, compacted, and poorly drained soils. It makes a superb specimen for lawns, bioretention areas, parks, highway plantings, median strips, and golf courses. Oaks are excellent for wildlife.

SEASONS OF INTEREST

| WINTER | SPRING | SUMMER | AUTUMN |

FORM – The Darlington oak is a medium to large tree with a dense oval to round form. Ultimately, after many years, it may reach 50'–85' tall with a

USDA Zones: 7–10		
SUN	**MOISTURE**	**pH**
Full sun	Dry to wet, well drained	4–7

50' spread. When grown in full sun, with no competition, the form is consistently rounded. It is fast growing, and its life span of 75–125 years is shorter than many other oaks.

COLOR – The lustrous dark green leaves are evergreen to semi-deciduous and linear, 4" long × ½" wide. They emerge in spring and cast a heavy shade. The acorns are up to ½" long.

TEXTURE – Medium fine in summer; medium fine in winter.

CULTURE – The Darlington oak is native to the coastal plain area of the southeast United States

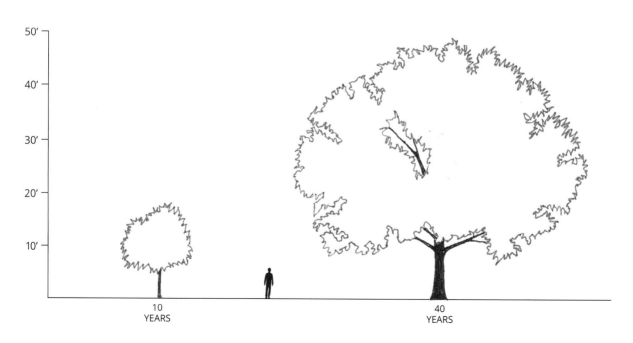

50'

40'

30'

20'

10'

10
YEARS

40
YEARS

ABOVE: *A 25-year-old Darlington oak in full sun in Washington, DC.*
LEFT: *Foliage close-up.*

from southern North Carolina to Florida and west to Texas.

Darlington oak is easy to transplant and grows rapidly to make a fine, rounded, dense specimen. It grows best in an acidic soil. It tolerates many soil types ranging from sand to clay, but the fastest growth will occur in moist alluvial soils. It is tolerant of drought and both soil and aerosol salt. The leaves are sometimes damaged in the cold winters of 7a.

The branches are not as strong as in some other oak species. But in my Maryland garden, Darlington oak has shown remarkable resistance to breakage

A 75-year-old Darlington oak in part shade at the US National Arboretum, Washington, DC.

from the full sweep of winter winds to ensure that the leaves remain undamaged. Although this species has survived –14°F in my zone 7 garden with no dieback, the leaves turned brown at temperatures of 0°F or below.

Like other oaks, this tree may produce copious amounts of pollen from the 2"–4" drooping male flowers (catkins) in early spring. The pollen may be an issue for hay fever sufferers, and the catkins may clog drains and downspouts when they drop. The resulting fruit is an acorn, which matures in two years in all species of the red oak group. The acorns are a favorite wildlife food, but they may be a maintenance issue on walkways or in well-manicured lawns.

Q. laurifolia, laurel oak, is a very similar species that is found in swamps and along streams. The leaves are similar in shape, but this species is consistently more deciduous than Darlington oak.

There are few serious pests listed for Darlington oak. Most cultivated specimens thrive with minimum care once the tree is established. Deer are not usually an issue.

COMPANION PLANTS – Native azaleas, Virginia sweetspire, spicebush, winterberry, and oakleaf hydrangea may be grown with Darlington oak. The shallow roots and dense branching can make it difficult to grow turf beneath this tree.

WILDLIFE – Many species of mammals and birds feed on the acorns, including deer. Oaks host hundreds of larvae for birds to feed upon.

CULTIVATED VARIETIES – Named varieties are generally not available in nurseries.

under heavy loads of snow and ice. Due to its dense branching and foliage, it is not uncommon for this species to uproot in high winds when grown in wet soils. This is less likely when grown in drier, well-drained soils. In the northern part of the range for Darlington oak, it is best to plant in areas protected

Quercus phellos

Willow Oak

ATTRIBUTES/USE IN LANDSCAPE – The willow oak is a handsome, popular, large shade tree with an attractive rounded, dense habit and narrow, willowlike leaves. It survives urban conditions very well, thriving in almost impossible situations, and is one of the most adaptable native trees. Willow oaks are appreciated as street trees, in parking lots and median strips, in sidewalk tree pits, as shade trees in lawns, in reclamation sites, and in rain gardens. Unfortunately, willow oak is only hardy from zone 6 southward. The oaks are excellent plants for wildlife.

SEASONS OF INTEREST

WINTER	SPRING	SUMMER	AUTUMN

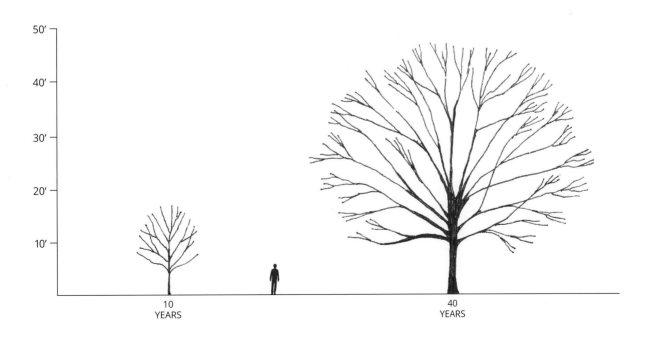

FORM – Willow oak is a large tree with a rounded, dense growth habit, 60'–75' (90') × 55'–70' spread.

USDA Zones: 6–9		
SUN	**MOISTURE**	**pH**
Full sun	Dry to wet	4–6.5

The branching is well balanced, terminating in thin, fine twigs. Trunks can grow to be 3'–4' in diameter. When grown in full sun, the form is especially symmetrical, rounded to sometimes elliptical. It has a fast growth rate and can live more than 200 years.

COLOR – The medium to dark green leaves, which are linear and resemble a willow leaf rather than the typical oak leaf, up to 5" long and 1" wide, emerge in spring. The leaves turn yellowish brown in fall and, unlike some other oak species, willow oak drops all of its leaves, even from the lower branches. The bark, smooth when young, becomes rough and fissured. It is very dark brown, appearing almost black when wet. The acorns are ¼"–½" long.

ABOVE: *A mature willow oak.*
LEFT: *Willow oak autumn foliage.*

TEXTURE – Medium fine. Willow oak casts a moderately heavy shade through summer.

CULTURE – The willow oak's native range is throughout much of the coastal plain of the mid-Atlantic and southeastern United States.

The willow oak is both beautiful and easy to grow. It grows well in poorly drained heavy clay as well as dry, sandy soils, with fastest growth occurring in alluvial soils. Willow oak is not very tolerant of shade. It is highly tolerant of drought and both aerosol and soil salt, but it is not tolerant of high pH. Acid soils are required. As mentioned above, willow oak does well in urban situations. Even though the growth rate is rapid, the wood of willow oak is strong and resists breakage from wind and heavy loads of ice and snow.

Willow oak is not difficult to transplant, but it seems to survive better in the northern part of its range (USDA zones 7a and north) if it is transplanted in the spring. In the South, spring and autumn transplanting are equally acceptable. The roots of willow oak tend to be shallower than many other oaks.

Like other oaks, the willow oak may produce copious amounts of pollen from the 2"–4" drooping male flowers (catkins) in early spring. The pollen may be an issue for hay fever sufferers, and the catkins may clog drains and downspouts when they drop. The resulting fruit is an acorn, which matures in two years in all species of the red oak group. The acorns are a favorite wildlife food, but they may be a maintenance issue on walkways or in well-manicured lawns.

There are many pests listed for willow oak. Although some of these pests can, at times, be serious, most cultivated specimens thrive with minimum care once the tree is established. Willow oaks in a heavily trafficked parkway median strip near Washington, DC, survived defoliation by gypsy moths with few lasting adverse effects. The foliage may be browsed by deer but is not preferred.

COMPANION PLANTS – Companion plants include black gum, bald cypress, pond cypress, Darlington oak, willow oak, American holly, southern magnolia,

A 15-year-old willow oak as a street tree in a dense urban environment.

sweetbay magnolia, yaupon holly, inkberry, winterberry holly, wax myrtle, spicebush, Virginia sweetspire, groundsel bush, and titi.

WILDLIFE – Many species of mammals and birds feed on the acorns, including deer. The oaks support hundreds of insect larvae for native birds.

CULTIVATED VARIETIES

'Hightower' – Develops a straight central leader, grows taller than wide, 55'–65' × 30'–45'.

Quercus virginiana

Live Oak

ATTRIBUTES/USE IN LANDSCAPE – The live oak is a handsome, large, evergreen oak, popular in the South. It is notable for its picturesque and wide-spreading habit, evergreen foliage, and tolerance for a variety of environments including poorly drained soils and even saltwater flooding. It makes a superb specimen for lawns, parks, highway plantings, lining entrance drives, median strips, parking lot islands, and golf courses.

SEASONS OF INTEREST

WINTER	SPRING	SUMMER	AUTUMN

FORM – The live oak is a large, evergreen tree with a dense, round to wide-spreading form 35'–45' (80') × 55'–75' spread. It has a very large trunk and horizontal, undulating branches. Several very old and massive trees have limbs that serpentine along the

USDA Zones: 7–10		
SUN	**MOISTURE**	**pH**
Full sun to full shade in all seasons	Dry to wet, well drained	4–7

ground for 100' in all directions. Live oak grows lower and wider in the northern part of its range. In some areas of Zone 8 and further south, trees may be festooned in copious amounts of Spanish moss (*Tillandsia usneoides*), especially in low-lying areas near the coast. Live oak is moderately fast growing and quite long-lived, to over 1,000 years.

COLOR – The lustrous dark to gray-green leaves are linear, to 4" long × 1½" wide and "evergreen," with some variation in leaf margin. Live oaks hold their leaves for one year. In some locations they may drop all of their older leaves in spring before the new leaves have fully

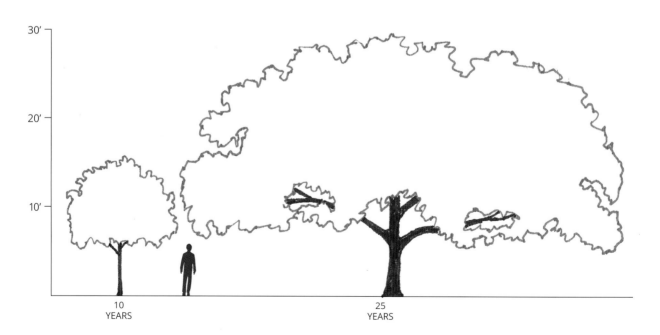

ABOVE: *A 35-year-old live oak.*
RIGHT: *Foliage and fruit close-up.*

expanded. They are sometimes damaged in cold winters in zone 7. The narrow acorns are up to 1".

TEXTURE – Medium fine in all seasons. The tree casts a heavy shade.

CULTURE – The live oak is a beautiful and easily grown, large shade tree. It is native to the coastal plain area of the southeast United States from southeastern Virginia to Florida and west to Texas.

Live oak grows best in an acidic soil. It tolerates many soil types ranging from sand to clay, but the fastest growth will occur in moist, alluvial soils. It is tolerant of drought and both soil and aerosol salt. In the northern part of the area where it can be grown, cold and exposure to cold winds may turn the foliage brown. This occurs from time to time even in some areas where it is native.

It is easy to transplant and grows fairly rapidly (more slowly to the north) to make a fine, rounded to spreading, dense specimen. The branches are among

the strongest of any tree, and it has shown remarkable resistance to breakage from hurricane-force winds and heavy accumulations of ice.

All oaks are wind-pollinated species, and copious amounts of pollen are produced from the 2"–4" drooping male flowers (catkins) in early spring. The pollen may be an issue for hay fever sufferers, and the catkins may clog drains and downspouts when they drop. The resulting fruit is an acorn, which matures in one year in all species of the white oak group. The acorns are a favorite wildlife food, they but may be a maintenance issue on walkways or in well-manicured lawns.

There are many serious pests listed for live oak, but most cultivated specimens thrive with minimum care once the tree is established. Deer are usually not an issue for live oak.

ABOVE: *A 300-year-old live oak tree, North Carolina.*
LEFT: *A 4-year-old planting of live oaks.*

COMPANION PLANTS – Companion plants include southern magnolia, sweetbay, Darlington oak, laurel oak, black gum, American holly, yaupon, inkberry, winterberry, bald cypress, pond cypress, wax myrtle, groundsel bush, and titi.

WILDLIFE – Many species of mammals and birds feed on the acorns. Oaks host hundreds of butterfly and moth larvae. Deer readily feast on the acorns.

CULTIVATED VARIETIES – Varieties are not available in commerce at this writing.

Taxodium distichum

Bald Cypress

ATTRIBUTES/USE IN LANDSCAPE – The bald cypress is a stately, large, deciduous conifer appreciated as a specimen and in groupings; or in rain gardens, riverine swamps, parks, and large properties. It can be used to reduce flood damage, control erosion, and provide a trap for sediment and pollutants. Bald cypress can be a street tree where there are no overhead lines.

SEASONS OF INTEREST

WINTER	SPRING	SUMMER	AUTUMN
See form below			

FORM – Bald cypress is a tall, moderately fast-growing tree, 70'–100' or more with a trunk diameter of 3'–5'. The pyramidal form of young trees (less than 150 years old) resembles a narrow crowned evergreen. In maturity, the tree is rather flat topped and spreading. Fluted, buttressed trunks develop with

USDA Zones: 5–8		
SUN	**MOISTURE**	**pH**
Full sun	Dry to wet	5.5–6.8

maturity in compacted or wet soil. A very long-lived tree, bald cypress can live well past 1,000 years.

COLOR – The narrow, ¾" leaves are arranged spirally on deciduous branchlets, giving the appearance of a light green, pinnately compound leaf in spring. The medium green summer color turns an attractive coppery tan in autumn before dropping. The tan 1" cones mature in autumn. In winter the reddish brown, fibrous bark creates compelling interest.

TEXTURE – Fine in summer and autumn, medium in winter.

CULTURE – Bald cypress's name refers to this tree's early leaf drop in autumn. The bald cypress is a true obligate wetland species, reproducing naturally only on wet soils. It is native along rivers and in swamps from southern Delaware to Florida, west to Texas, and north along the Mississippi to southern Illinois.

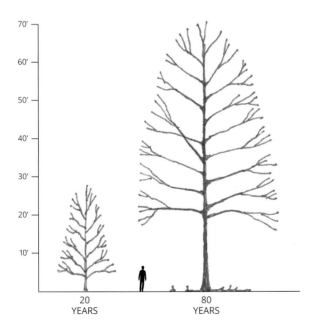

The young, summer cones with foliage.

Bald cypress in winter.

A mature specimen, about 85 years old.

Bald cypress will withstand very dry, compacted soils, as well as soils that are flooded for long periods of time. It tolerates heat, wind, cold, and urban conditions very well. It grows most rapidly in rich, wet to moist soil high in organic matter, but it will grow almost as well in heavy clay, sand, gravelly soils or, as mentioned above, compacted urban soils. Two 19th-century specimens at the National Museum of Natural History on the National Mall, in Washington, DC, survive despite several feet of heavy clay fill over their roots along with compaction by fifty million pedestrian tourists each year.

When bald cypress is grown in saturated soils, and sometimes in very compacted soils, the roots produce "knees." They are not produced in well-drained, average garden soils.

The wood is lightweight, strong, and very resistant to rot. The tree is remarkably resistant to high winds, even when growing in saturated soils. I have seen bald cypress trees standing as lone survivors after Hurricane Hugo (1989) devastated many bottom-land forests in South Carolina. As a deciduous tree, it resists breakage from the ice and snow that can cause damage to evergreen conifers in the North. The feathery foliage is arranged along small twigs that are themselves deciduous.

The root system of bald cypress is moderately shallow, allowing for relatively easy transplanting. The roots will be somewhat deeper when planted in well-drained soils with little or no hardpan. That said, I have transplanted many 5'–6' trees bare rooted with an impressive success rate even when the young trees had developed a deeper root system. Spring transplanting is preferable in the colder parts of zone 6 and all of zone 5.

Pond cypress, *T. ascendens*, differs from bald

A bald cypress with a fluted, buttressed trunk and "knees" in wet soils.

cypress in its smaller stature, fewer knees, and needles that are pressed flat to the branchlets. In nature, the range of the pond cypress does not extend as far north as bald cypress. It is almost always found growing in shallow, acid, and still water depressions.

Very few pests cause serious damage. The cypress twig gall midge may cause unsightly but not serious problems in some years. Deer are not usually a problem.

COMPANION PLANTS – In nature, bald cypress is usually found in pure stands (in standing water) or in association with sweet gum, black gum, red maple, loblolly pine, American snowbell, and dwarf palmetto. It combines well with many other plants. In the Deep South, it is usually festooned with Spanish moss and its older branches covered with resurrection fern. The feathery foliage casts a light shade that allows many herbaceous perennials and shrubs to thrive beneath its branches.

WILDLIFE – Seeds are eaten by wild turkeys, evening grosbeaks, squirrels, waterfowl including wood ducks, and wading birds. Yellow-throated warblers forage in the Spanish moss when it is present. Treetops provide nesting sites for the bald eagle, osprey, heron, and egret. It is the host plant for the bald cypress sphinx moth.

CULTIVATED VARIETIES – Select for form.

'**Shawnee Brave**' – 80' × 20', narrow fastigiated growth.
'**Monarch of Illinois**' – 90' × 70', wide-spreading branches.

Thuja occidentalis

Arborvitae, Northern White Cedar

ATTRIBUTES/USE IN LANDSCAPE – The arborvitae is an attractive, versatile, colorful, dense, evergreen conifer for specimen, hedging, screening, rain gardens, rooftop and windbreak use. It may be used for large residences, parks, and golf courses. Many popular varieties are available in sizes and forms suitable for smaller-scale projects.

SEASONS OF INTEREST

WINTER SPRING SUMMER AUTUMN

FORM – The arborvitae is a large, generally pyramidal, evergreen tree, 20'–40' (70') tall × 10'–20'. It usually develops a single leader, providing protection from some storm damage, and has a dense growth habit, particularly when grown in full sun. Arborvitae develops a picturesque form as it opens with age. While the species varies in nature,

USDA Zones: 3–7		
SUN	**MOISTURE**	**pH**
Full to part shade in all seasons	Dry to wet	4.5–7.2

cultivated varieties offer specific, reliable forms and sizes including columnar, pyramidal, spreading, and dwarf. It is typically a slow-growing tree but is encouraged in moist soils with ample sun exposure. A long-lived tree, it has reached 1,500 years in remote locations.

COLOR – The species is a rich green to blue-green in summer but can be yellow-green to brownish in winter, depending on site conditions. The attractive

Arborvitae foliage.

40'

30'

20'

10'

10 YEARS   40 YEARS

terminal, scale-like leaves are in broad, flat sprays. The foliage is a darker green on top and a pale yellow-green below. Cultivated varieties offer more reliable coloring through the seasons. The fibrous bark of the arborvitae is gray-brown to gray, with shallow furrows, sometimes revealing a reddish bark beneath.

TEXTURE – Fine.

CULTURE –The familiar arborvitae's native range extends south from eastern Canada through Maine and our New England states and west into Minnesota. Sporadic populations occur in the Appalachians from Pennsylvania to Tennessee.

While the tree grows well in the cooler areas of the South, it is much less vigorous in the humid coastal plain from 7b southward. Arborvitae has more drought tolerance than *Chamaecyparis thyoides*, the Atlantic white cedar. The arborvitae grows well to zone 5, generally the northern limit of this book, but in zones 3 and 4, it should be protected from winter sun and wind.

As noted above, full sun is preferred, but it will grow very slowly in partial sun to shade. Heavy clay soils, almost pure sand, gravelly soils, moderately dry soils, and wet soils are tolerated, including moderate drought. Circumneutral to acid soils are tolerated as well. Arborvitae is moderately tolerant of soil salt, but the foliage is sensitive to aerosol salt related to seashore and roads.

The arborvitae takes shearing well, but like evergreens generally, does not rejuvenate well from old wood. Prune before new growth emerges in the spring. Snow and ice loads are tolerated fairly well due to the plant's central leader.

The arborvitae is fairly easy to transplant, but success rates can decline with age.

Deer browse can be a serious problem for arborvitaes, but it has few disease and insect pests. Bag

A 40-year-old arborvitae.

worms can be an issue, but trees usually recover from their damage. Scale insects may become more of an issue with increased use of more members of the Cupressaceae family.

COMPANION PLANTS – Arborvitae is often planted as a single species and combines well with turf.

WILDLIFE – Arborvitae provides good nesting and roosting cover for many species of birds. It also provides pollinator support. Again, deer frequently browse the foliage.

CULTIVATED VARIETIES – Select for size, growth rate and form, foliage color and texture.

'Bobozam' (**'Mr. Bowling Ball'**) – 2'–3' by same. A globe form with fine-textured, gray-green foliage.

'Degroot's Spire' – 15'–20' × 4'–5'. Medium green foliage in a spiral rather than flat arrangement of species. Red-brown in winter.

'Emerald' – 10'–15' (20') × 3'–4'. Bright green through winter. Cold-hardy, drought tolerant.

'Golden Globe' – 2'–4' by same. A dense, globe-shaped dwarf. Yellow foliage in flat sprays.

'Hetz Midget' – 3'–4' by same. A popular globe-shaped dwarf. Good bluish green foliage.

'Little Gem' – 1'–3' × 2'–6'. A broad globe-shaped dwarf. Dark green foliage with some winter color change.

'Lutea' – 25'–30' × 12'–15'. A narrow cone-shaped form. A good yellow variety.

'Nigra' – 20'–30' × 5'–10'. Conical form. Dark green foliage throughout the year.

'Rheingold' – 3'–5' tall by same. Gold foliage turning a bronze-gold in winter.

'Techny' (**'Mission'**) – 10'–15' × 4'–6'. Dark green foliage throughout the seasons. A popular hedge plant.

'Yellow Ribbon' – 8'–10' × 2'–3'. Young foliage is yellowish orange maturing to medium green. May be susceptible to ice and snow damage and winter discoloration to green-brown.

'Emerald' at 15 years.

Aesculus parviflora

Bottlebrush Buckeye

ATTRIBUTES/USE IN LANDSCAPE – The bottlebrush buckeye is a large, distinctive, deciduous shrub known for its unique habit, with showy, early-summer flowering and attractive, unique summer and autumn foliage. It can be spectacular as a specimen when given plenty of room. Bottlebrush buckeye is valuable for park, large residential, golf course, and highway plantings. It is a good plant for wildlife.

USDA Zones: 4–8 (9)		
SUN	**MOISTURE**	**pH**
Part shade to full shade	Moist	5.5–7.5

SEASONS OF INTEREST

WINTER   SPRING   SUMMER   AUTUMN

FORM – The bottlebrush buckeye is a handsome and unique plant, spreading into a large mound of vertical branches, rising from suckers. While growth on old wood can be slow, new growth is fast, with rapid spreading in ideal conditions, to 8'–12' tall × 8'–15' wide or more. Spread may be controlled by removal of suckers. Some older stems may attain almost small tree proportions.

COLOR – Showy, large, profuse, terminal, white flowers bloom for about two weeks in late spring to early summer. The flowers are arranged on large erect panicles in clusters, 8"–12" long × 2"–4" wide. The palmately compound leaves have five to seven 3"–8" leaflets plus a 3"–5" petiole. They emerge bronze, turning to a medium to dark green above and pubescent gray below. In autumn, the foliage can turn a bright yellow before leaf drop, but it is not common. Strong autumn leaf color is more likely where the day and nighttime temperature gradient is larger. In winter, the gray-brown mature stems are revealed.

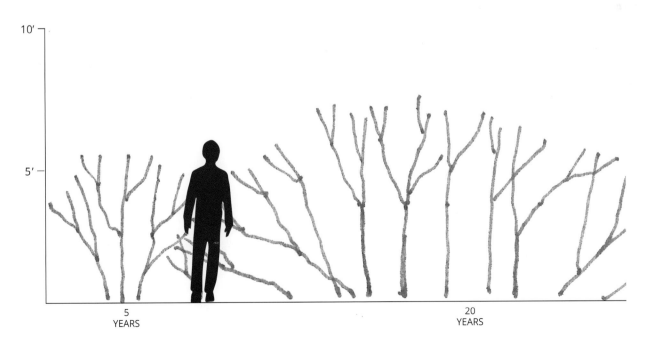

10'

5'

5
YEARS

20
YEARS

TEXTURE – Medium coarse summer and winter.

CULTURE – The bottlebrush buckeye is native to rich woodlands in southern South Carolina, Georgia, Alabama, and northern Florida.

Easily grown in rich, moist and wet soils, it does not tolerate saturated soils. It will tolerate clay and salt. It also tolerates drought, though foliage may scorch.

In a very deep shade setting, the habit is rangy, flowering will be reduced, and autumn coloring is

LEFT: *A mature specimen thriving under a blue Atlas cedar.*
BELOW: *A 7-year-old plant in summer with inkberry.*

A single flower panicle illuminated in morning sun.

Bottlebrush buckeye in autumn.

less likely. It may be pruned to rejuvenate. Bottlebrush buckeye is low maintenance as leaves, flowers, and nuts fall to the ground beneath the plant. The fruit has little ornamental value.

A. parviflora var. *serotina* is a larger, naturally occurring variety. It can reach 20' tall with larger, 30" inflorescences. It blooms about three weeks later in mid- to late summer.

It is tolerant of pollution and rarely bothered seriously by insect pests, disease, or deer.

COMPANION PLANTS – Bottlebrush buckeye is best alone as a large spreading specimen.

WILDLIFE – This is an excellent plant for wildlife. It provides cover, nesting sites, and food for birds and butterfly larvae. It is also an excellent pollen and nectar producer. The buckeyes are eaten by mammals, but all parts of the plants are poisonous to humans and cattle.

CULTIVATED VARIETIES – Varieties offer choices in flowering time.

A. parviflora var. *serotina* 'Rogers' – Blooms in late summer, with longer, more drooping inflorescences.

Agarista populifolia

Florida Leucothoe, Pipestem, Tall Fetterbush

ATTRIBUTES/USE IN LANDSCAPE – Florida leucothoe is an attractive, medium-sized, broad-leaved evergreen shrub known for its shade tolerance and late-spring flowering. It is effective as a specimen and for informal mass plantings and screening. Florida leucothoe provides valuable, understory vegetation in highly shaded residential and park locations.

SEASONS OF INTEREST

| WINTER | SPRING | SUMMER | AUTUMN |

FORM – The form is arching, multi-stemmed, and irregular, reaching 8'–12' tall × 6'–10' wide. The glossy, dense foliage and many tall, arching stems can create an effective screen element in shade.

USDA Zones: 6b–8 (9)		
SUN	**MOISTURE**	**pH**
Part shade to shade	Moist	5.5–7.5

COLOR – Glossy, rich green foliage with red-tinged new foliage. The small, profuse, creamy, fragrant, bell-shaped flowers bloom along the branches for about two weeks in late spring to early summer.

TEXTURE – Medium.

CULTURE – Florida leucothoe is native to a few areas in the states of South Carolina, Georgia, and Florida.

Florida leucothoe prefers well-drained, cool, moist, acid soils, high in organic content, but it is tolerant of moderate drought, especially when grown in shade. It is intolerant of wind and salt.

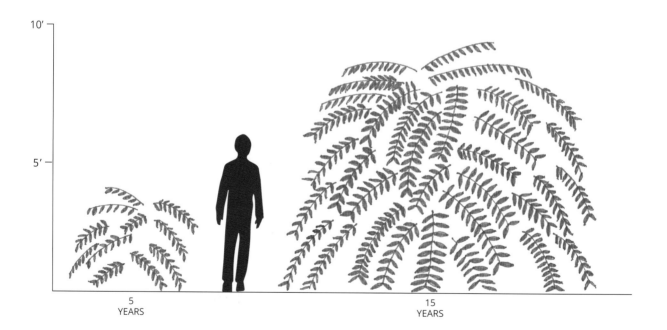

5 YEARS / 15 YEARS

TOP, LEFT: *Florida leucothoe.*
ABOVE AND LEFT: *The late-spring flowers.*

The habit is denser and flowering is better in part shade. The stems are hollow, and pruning is useful to remove dead stems and form the desired shape. Previously known as *Leucothoe populifolia*, it resembles *Leucothoe* spp. but is more closely related to *Pieris*.

It is rarely bothered seriously by insect pests and is rarely browsed by deer.

COMPANION PLANTS – Florida leucothoe combines well with eastern white pine, sweetbay magnolia, rhododendrons, and azaleas.

WILDLIFE – Florida leucothoe's fragrant flowers attract pollinators, and its foliage provides evergreen understory for year-round wildlife habitat.

CULTIVATED VARIETIES

'Taylor's Treasure' ('Leprechaun') – A dwarf variety, 4' × 4', with smaller foliage, is said to tolerate full sun in a moist location.

Aralia spinosa

Devil's Walking Stick

ATTRIBUTES/USE IN LANDSCAPE – Devil's walking stick is a unique and striking large shrub to small tree. Its large, showy white bloom in late summer is followed by a showy fruit display in autumn. Devil's walking stick tolerates a wide range of growing conditions. Very large, terminal, compound leaves give an interesting fine texture and tropical appearance. Devil's walking stick can be used as a specimen; in large elevated planters and roof gardens; at the back of a border; and along roadsides, ponds, and woodland edges. Its spiny stems are not appropriate for lining walkways but can create an effective barrier or living fence.

SEASONS OF INTEREST

WINTER	SPRING	SUMMER	AUTUMN

FORM – Devil's walking stick is a large, multi-stemmed shrub, occasionally a tree, with stout, spined

USDA Zones: 5–9		
SUN	**MOISTURE**	**pH**
Full sun to part shade	Dry to moist	5.5–7.1

stems and branches, 10'–20' (30') × 10'–20'. The plant naturally forms a dense thicket of upright stems with limited branching. The few horizontal branches and large leaves occur toward the end of stems, giving the plant an umbrella-like shape. Devil's walking stick spreads horizontally through rhizomes and suckering and should be contained or given plenty of room. The stems reach a maximum diameter of about 8". The form is generally similar to sumac. Growth is slow to moderate, generally, but new shoots grow rapidly.

COLOR – The very large, dark, bluish green, bi- to tripinnately compound leaves are similar in size to the Kentucky coffee tree, 30" × 30" to 48" × 48", with 2"–4" long, serrated leaflets. Leaf out is late in the season. The attractive, very showy, creamy white, 12" × 12" to 24" × 24", terminal, fleecy flower

The showy, summer flowers in late summer.

20'		
10'		
	5 YEARS	15 YEARS

Devil's walking stick in autumn, as a small tree.

panicles rise upright above the leaves in late summer and are especially effective when viewed from the side or above. The autumn leaf color is usually reddish or purplish but can be yellow. The profuse, showy clusters of purple-black, berrylike fruit, with persistent red to purple petioles, contribute to an attractive autumn display. The stems are brown, rough, and covered with numerous short spines.

TEXTURE – Coarse in winter, fine in leaf.

TOP: *The showy fruit developing in early autumn.*
BOTTOM: *Autumn fruit and foliage.*

CULTURE – Devil's walking stick is a relatively common native from Delaware and Pennsylvania west to Indiana and the Mississippi River Valley. It spreads south into northern Florida and the Gulf States.

Devil's walking stick is a hardy plant. While it prefers moist, deep loam, it grows well in heavy clay and rocky soils. It also tolerates drought, heat, and seasonal flooding. Part shade is preferred, with some direct sun required for flowering and best foliage color. The plants grow more slowly and densely in relatively poor soil. It is tolerant of salt.

The small, sharp spines are arranged radially and randomly around stems and on branches. They can cause painful injury, hence its usefulness as a barrier plant. Even the leaf petioles are prickly.

Suckers can be removed to confine spread or maintain as a single-trunked tree. The plant is best confined unless it is used in a large naturalized setting. Selective pruning or cutting to the ground can be used to rejuvenate the plant. Handling of the bark and roots may cause brief contact dermatitis, and the raw berries are mildly toxic.

There are few serious pests or diseases associated with this plant. The leaves may be browsed by deer in some locations but not in others.

COMPANION PLANTS – Devil's walking stick associates in nature with eastern red cedar, sumac, and chokeberry. In cultivation, it is generally used as a single specimen.

WILDLIFE – Devil's walking stick has good wildlife value. The flowers appeal to many pollinators including bees, the tiger swallowtail butterfly, and other insects. The fruit is enjoyed by many bird species and mammals.

CULTIVATED VARIETIES – The species is available in commerce, but cultivars are not available at this writing.

Aronia arbutifolia

Red Chokeberry

ATTRIBUTES/USE IN LANDSCAPE – Red chokeberry is an ornamental and in many cases an underused, medium-sized, multi-season shrub noted for its profuse white flowers and berries, superior autumn color, and colorful bark. It is tolerant of many soil conditions. Red chokeberry is effective in the back of the shrub border; for massing, naturalizing, and erosion control along ponds and streams; and in domestic landscapes, parks, rain gardens and rooftops. This is an excellent plant for wildlife but should be used in areas without a deer population.

SEASONS OF INTEREST

WINTER   SPRING   SUMMER   AUTUMN

FORM – The slow-growing red chokeberry has multiple erect, slender stems that spread to a somewhat rounded crown, 6'–12' × 3'–6'. Older plants may

USDA Zones: 4–9		
SUN	**MOISTURE**	**pH**
Full sun to part shade	Dry to wet	5.1–6.5

spread widely if not restrained in containers or planters. The lower stems are often sparsely foliated.

COLOR – The finely serrated elliptical, oval, or obovate leaves are up to 3½" long × 1¾". They emerge a shiny, medium green and darken through the season, turning a brilliant orange to red in autumn. In spring, showy, dense, domed 1"–2" clusters of small, white apple-blossom-like flowers appear. The bright red, ¼", fleshy fruit clusters underscore the showy autumn foliage and persist into winter.

TEXTURE – Medium in all seasons.

CULTURE – Red chokeberries are found from New York and coastal Massachusetts south along the East Coast and through the Appalachians to northern Florida. Chokeberries are common in some parts of their range.

Red chokeberry in spring.

10'

5'

5
YEARS

15
YEARS

Red chokeberry fruits in late summer to early autumn.

They grow well in moist to wet, well-drained soils, but they tolerate dry sandy soils and poorly drained soils as well. The chokeberries tolerate drought, salt, and soil compaction. Flowering and fruit production are best in full sun. As with most species that occur naturally over such a broad range, there are variations in growth and autumn color and, one would expect, in cold hardiness.

Chokeberries can become leggy with age, which may require renewal pruning. The fruits are edible but, as their name implies, they are very tart. *Aronia* has also been known as *Pyrus arbutifolia* and *Photinia pyrifolia*.

Aronia melanocarpa, black chokeberry, is a closely related plant, occurring naturally in more northerly climates, from Maine to Minnesota, south through New Jersey, and from Pennsylvania into the Appalachians. Its purple-black fruit dries and drops rather than persisting on the plant. The black chokeberry is shorter, has less showy flowers, is dense in habit, and has more full foliage on the lower stem. Its leaves have brilliant purple-red autumn color. Where the two plants coexist in nature, there are naturally occurring hybrids. The black chokeberry is used in wetland reclamation.

There are few diseases and insects that pose problems. But in some areas, like many other members of the rose family, the chokeberries can prove irresistible to deer, and deer may do considerable damage.

COMPANION PLANTS – In nature chokeberries associate with river birch, bald cypress, sweet gum, swamp azalea, inkberry, and ferns.

WILDLIFE – The chokeberry flowers attract butterflies and other pollinators. Birds eat the profuse berries in late winter and enjoy the dozens of caterpillars

The showy autumn foliage.

the plant hosts in warmer months. Mammals enjoy the berries too. As mentioned earlier, deer find chokeberries irresistible.

CULTIVATED VARIETIES

A. arbutifolia 'Brilliantissima' – This variety is more dense and compact, 6'–8' × 3'–4', than the species. Its leaves are glossier and more brilliant in autumn, and it produces larger, brighter fruit and is suitable for specimen use. The cultivar is widely available.

A. melanocarpa 'Elata' – A more vigorous and less suckering variety with larger flowers, foliage, and fruit.

Baccharis halimifolia

Groundsel Bush, Saltbush, High-Tide Bush, Sea Myrtle

ATTRIBUTES/USE IN LANDSCAPE – The groundsel bush is an attractive deciduous to partially evergreen shrub with showy silver seeds in autumn. It is appreciated for its autumn seed display, along with its high tolerance of salt, dry and wet sites, and other difficult soil conditions. Use as a specimen, in a dry border, in rain and rooftop gardens, in buffer strips, around parking areas, and for massing and naturalizing in seaside and roadside plantings.

SEASONS OF INTEREST

WINTER	SPRING	SUMMER	AUTUMN

FORM – Groundsel bush is an open, multi-stemmed, rigid, upright shrub, typically about 6'–12' tall with equal spread. It can be a nice small tree. The growth rate is moderate to fast (young stems). They are short-lived, to about 50 years.

USDA Zones: 4–9		
SUN	**MOISTURE**	**pH**
Full sun	Dry to wet	7–8.5

COLOR – The oval to elliptical leaves are a gray-green to a bright, medium green, 2"–4" long by nearly half as wide. The leaves may be entire or deeply serrate toward the apex. The small, white late-summer flowers are prolific but visually insignificant on both sexes. But, on female plants, they are followed by a very showy, silvery white seed display in autumn. The bark is also silvery before aging to gray.

TEXTURE – Fine in leaf and seed display, with rough, shredded bark.

CULTURE – The groundsel bush is native primarily to the coastal plain from Massachusetts south to Florida and west to Texas.

The groundsel prefers moist, well-drained soil,

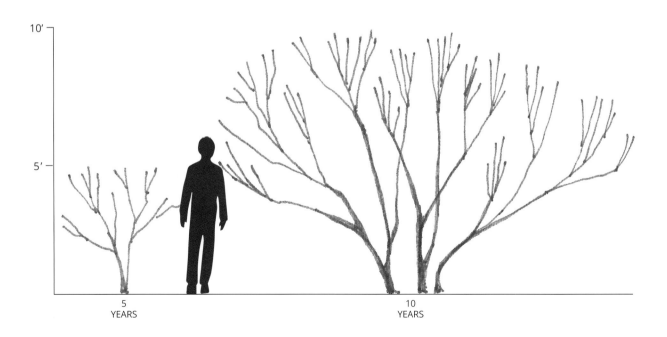

ABOVE: *A groundsel specimen in a busy park.*
LEFT: *A close-up of groundsel in autumn.*

but it is tolerant of drought, heat, and periodic tidal saltwater inundation. It does not tolerate clay soils or full shade. It is weak wooded and can suffer storm damage, so it is best in a natural setting rather than a formal landscape.

The groundsel is most likely to be partially evergreen in zones 8b–9. For fruiting on female plants, male plants must be in the area. Groundsel bush naturalizes in disturbed areas and along

Groundsel and sumac in a roadside border.

Groundsel in a salt marsh.

highway edges where road salt has accumulated in the soil. It can be pruned for renovation, improved form, and to remove dead twigs.

Few disease and insect pests bother the groundsel. Deer do not favor the groundsel.

COMPANION PLANTS – In nature, groundsel bush associates with live oak, beautyberry, yaupon, southern wax myrtle, and titi. It combines well with sumac spp.

WILDLIFE – Groundsel bush provides shelter for wildlife and supports migrating monarch butterflies. Birds sometimes eat the seeds. The leaves are toxic to livestock.

CULTIVATED VARIETIES – Varieties are not available at this writing.

Callicarpa americana

American Beautyberry

ATTRIBUTES/USE IN LANDSCAPE – American beautyberry is a medium-sized, deciduous shrub valued for its showy berry display and adaptable culture, particularly its shade tolerance. It is useful for massing and naturalizing, as a woodland border, along water's edge, in rain gardens, and rooftops. It is moderately tolerant of airborne and soil salt. American beautyberry is a good plant for wildlife.

SEASONS OF INTEREST

WINTER   SPRING   SUMMER   AUTUMN

FORM – A shrub reaching 3'–6' (8') by the same width or more, with a loose, open, arching structure.

COLOR – The green, serrated, pubescent, elliptical leaves, 3"–6" by half as wide, turn a yellow-green in autumn. The delicate, light pink to white flowers

USDA Zones: (6) 7–11		
SUN	**MOISTURE**	**pH**
Full sun to full shade	Dry to wet	4.8–6b

occur in spring. Beautyberry is noted for showy, profuse clusters of small, bright, purple berries along the stems, at the base of the opposite leaves. The fruit can persist through early autumn leaf fall and into late winter. There are also white- and pink-berried forms. The stems and bark are light gray.

TEXTURE – Medium.

CULTURE – American beautyberry is native to moist, sandy, acid soils of the coastal plain from Maryland through Florida and west to Texas.

Beautyberry prefers an acid, organic, rich, moist soil. Sand or sandy loam seems to suit it best, but it tolerates clay soils. It also tolerates strongly acidic to neutral soils and occasional flooding or drought.

The most profuse berries and dense form occur in full sun. It prefers part shade, but in moist soil it grows equally well in part shade or sun. Plants in shade will be taller, with sparser foliage generally, particularly at the base. Beautyberry is said to bloom

10'

5'

5
YEARS

15
YEARS

Beautyberry flower.

ABOVE: *Pink-berried form.*
ABOVE, RIGHT: *Young beautyberry.*
RIGHT: *Purple-berried form.*

and produce more berries when several are planted together. When sheltered from winter winds, beauty-berry will sustain less cold damage in the northern zones of its range.

Beautyberry will take hard pruning, even to the ground. During a hard freeze (zone 6), it may die back completely, but it will emerge again in spring. It may be pruned to improve form in early spring; berries are produced on new growth. It is easily transplanted.

C. americana var. *lactea* is a naturally occurring form with white fruit and flowers.

Beautyberry is rarely bothered by disease or insect pests. The leaves contain a compound that repels mosquitoes. Foliage is sometimes browsed by deer, but due to its rough pubescence it is usually not preferred.

COMPANION PLANTS – In nature beautyberry occurs with oak, white pine, sweet gum, black gum, hickory, and flowering dogwood, as well as summer-sweet and southern bayberry.

WILDLIFE – The flowers attract insects, including butterflies, and it is a larval food source. Beautyberry fruit is an autumn and winter food source for many bird species, small mammals, and deer. It provides wildlife cover as well.

CULTIVATED VARIETIES

'Welch's Pink' – A showy pink-berried variety. It is smaller than the species, to 6'.

Calycanthus floridus

Common Sweetshrub, Carolina Allspice, Strawberry Bush

ATTRIBUTES/USE IN LANDSCAPE – The common sweetshrub is a medium-sized deciduous shrub valued for its superb fragrance and adaptable culture. It is useful as a specimen, informal hedge, woodland border, and for massing, naturalizing, and in rain and rooftop gardens. The fragrance is especially effective near outdoor living spaces. Cultivars provide good yellow autumn foliage.

SEASONS OF INTEREST

WINTER	SPRING	SUMMER	AUTUMN

FORM – Sweetshrub grows to 6'–10' × 6'–12', with a dense, upright habit. In nature, it forms colonies through suckering. It has a slow to medium growth rate and is a potentially long-lived plant.

COLOR – The medium green, 2"–6", elliptical to

USDA Zones: 4–9		
SUN	**MOISTURE**	**pH**
Full sun to part shade	Dry to moist	4.8–7

oval, serrated, fuzzy leaves turn yellow in autumn and persist late into the season. The signature bloom is a 2" lotus-shaped, red to maroon flower, blooming for several weeks in mid-spring to early summer. The attractive, sweet fragrance of the bloom is extremely variable, but there are cultivated varieties with exceptional, reliable fragrance. The leaves and fruits are also fragrant, extending the season for the sweet aroma. The stems are aromatic when crushed. The dark, dry, 3" fruits can persist into winter.

TEXTURE – Medium.

CULTURE – Sweetshrub naturally occurs from Pennsylvania south to the Florida panhandle, but

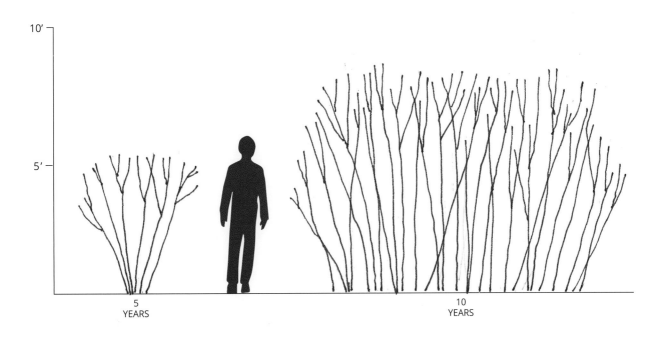

ABOVE: *A lightly pruned sweetshrub in landscape.*
RIGHT: *Sweetshrub in spring.*

it is most common in the Appalachians from West Virginia through Alabama.

Sweetshrub is tolerant of a wide range of soils, including heavy clay and poorly drained soil, but it prefers a rich, well-drained loam. Flowering and a dense form are best in full sun with moist soils. It also grows well in part shade. Plants in more shade will be taller with fewer flowers and sparser foliage generally, particularly at the base. Sweetshrub has a low tolerance for salt.

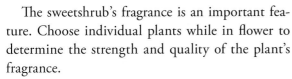

Sweetshrub in autumn.

The fragrant, mid-spring to early summer flower.

The sweetshrub's fragrance is an important feature. Choose individual plants while in flower to determine the strength and quality of the plant's fragrance.

Sweetshrub transplants easily and can be pruned as required for shaping, after flowering. Root suckers are easily removed to prevent the plant from spreading.

It is rarely bothered by insect pests or disease and is infrequently browsed by deer.

COMPANION PLANTS – In nature sweetshrub associates with cucumber tree, cinnamon clethra, spicebush, and native azaleas. In cultivation, sweetshrub combines well with Virginia sweetspire, fothergilla, ornamental grasses, and ferns.

WILDLIFE – Sweetshrub provides food for caterpillars and pollen for bees. It provides cover for small mammals and birds.

CULTIVATED VARIETIES – Choose for fragrance, autumn color, and leaf finish.

'Athens' – Yellow bloom. Glossy, dark green leaves turn golden yellow in autumn. A Michael Dirr introduction.

'Edith Wilder' – Both the sweet, strong fragrance and the clear yellow autumn color are excellent. The habit is rounded.

'Michael Lindsey' – Good, sweet fragrance, glossy leaves, and good yellow autumn color.

Cephalanthus occidentalis

Buttonbush

ATTRIBUTES/USE IN LANDSCAPE – Buttonbush is a medium-sized, deciduous shrub with fragrant, showy, midsummer, spherical flower clusters. It is valued for its adaptability to many conditions, particularly wet soils. Use for naturalizing and stabilization, in moist to wet soil, along streams and ponds. Buttonbush is an excellent choice for rain gardens. It is also good for wildlife.

USDA Zones: 4–10		
SUN	**MOISTURE**	**pH**
Sun to part shade	Moist to wet	5–7

SEASONS OF INTEREST

WINTER SPRING SUMMER AUTUMN

FORM – Buttonbush is an 8'–15' tall and wide, medium to large shrub or, rarely, a small tree. It is generally smaller in its northern range. The growth rate is medium, and it is rather short-lived.

COLOR – The showy, fuzzy, 1½" balls of creamy white flowers bloom for several weeks in early to midsummer. Buttonbush is slow to leaf out in the spring. The 3"–6" leathery leaves are a bright, shiny medium to light green with reddish vein and prominent red midrib on the undersurface. Dark, reddish brown, hard, spherical, ¾" ball-like fruit follows the flowers and persists through winter. The good autumn foliage color can be yellow with a bronze or burgundy red tone. The bark is gray-brown and becomes scaled and ridged with age.

TEXTURE – Medium.

CULTURE – Buttonbush is native to both the East and West Coasts, but it is most common from New England south to Florida, and west to the Mississippi River valley. It grows in moist to wet, acid to neutral soils of the swamps and coastal areas.

In cultivation, it prefers an acid, organic, rich, moist to wet soil. It will tolerate heavy clay soils and standing water. Sandy loam or clay soils seem to suit it best. Buttonbush does not tolerate long periods of drought or dry sandy soils, but it does tolerate

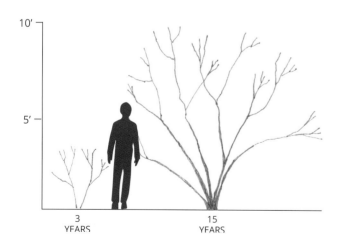

10'

5'

3
YEARS

15
YEARS

The flowers appeal to many pollinators.

moderate drought. The growth rate is slower in drier soils and soils that are permanently flooded. It is also tolerant of salt. Flowering is reduced as shade increases, but otherwise it is generally tolerant of light to moderate shade. Buttonbush takes pruning well for shaping or rejuvenation.

Buttonbush is rarely bothered by deer, insect pests, or disease.

COMPANION PLANTS — In nature and cultivation, buttonbush may associate with sweet gum, red maple, American holly, bald and pond cypresses,

TOP: *Buttonbush.*
BOTTOM: *The flowers persist for several weeks.*

The early-autumn foliage and fruit of buttonbush.

sweetbay magnolia, viburnum, summersweet, Virginia sweetspire, winterberry, spicebush, and swamp azalea.

WILDLIFE – The flowers are particularly abundant in nectar and are often covered with many bees, butterflies, other insects, and hummingbirds. It is a larval host, and the persistent nutlike seeds are eaten by birds and small mammals. Buttonbush provides cover for fish, birds, and mammals.

CULTIVATED VARIETIES – Select for size, bloom, and autumn color.

'**Sputnik**' – Larger, pinkish white flower clusters with a more enduring bloom than the species.
'**Sugar Shack**' – A compact, up to 4', specimen with reddish new growth and burgundy autumn foliage color.

Clethra acuminata

Cinnamon Clethra, Mountain Pepperbush

ATTRIBUTES/USE IN LANDSCAPE – Cinnamon clethra is a tall, deciduous shrub or small tree with handsome, peeling bark, midsummer flowering, and good golden yellow fall color. Cinnamon clethra is taller than summersweet and is more tolerant of dry soils. It is grown especially for its showy bark, most apparent in winter. Use in groupings, shrub borders, and the woodland understory.

USDA Zones: 5–8		
SUN	**MOISTURE**	**pH**
Part shade to shade	Dry to moist	4.5–6.5

soil. The trunk can grow to 3" diameter, but it is usually less in cultivation.

COLOR – The colorful, pinkish gold to cinnamon red, peeling bark of cinnamon clethra is its most distinctive feature. Light green leaves emerge in late spring, becoming a dark, glossy green as the season moves on. The leaves are larger than summersweet, 6"–8" and oval, obovate, or lanceolate in shape. Abundant, showy, small, lightly fragrant, ivory flowers on terminal 2"–6" racemes appear in early summer and remain for three to four weeks. The mild fragrance is sweet. Autumn color begins with a golden yellow and becomes a golden brown. The dark brown seed capsules may persist into winter.

SEASONS OF INTEREST

WINTER   SPRING   SUMMER   AUTUMN

FORM – Cinnamon clethra is a medium-sized, sparsely multi-stemmed, rounded, deciduous shrub or an upright, open small tree to 12'–20' by half as wide. It is stoloniferous with horizontal spreading, but is easily controlled. Faster growth occurs in moist

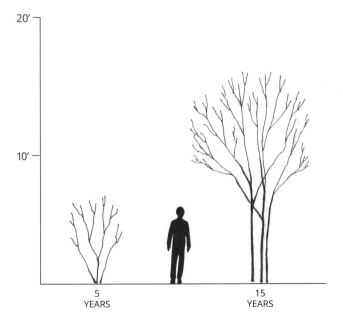

The abundant, early-summer flowers of cinnamon clethra at Mt. Cuba Center, Delaware.

The autumn foliage of cinnamon clethra at Mt. Cuba Center, Delaware.

The distinctive, namesake bark of cinnamon clethra.

TEXTURE – Medium in all seasons.

CULTURE – Cinnamon clethra is native to the Appalachians from southwestern Pennsylvania to northern Alabama and Georgia, at a higher elevation than summersweet, which is a plant of the southeastern coastal plain. It is considered endangered in some areas including the states of Pennsylvania and Alabama.

Cinnamon clethra varies from summersweet in several ways. Cinnamon clethra is more intolerant of the combination of high summer temperatures, high humidity, and occasional drought of the coastal plain. It also has a low tolerance for salt. Cinnamon clethra is larger overall. It is taller with a coarser and more open habit, larger leaves, and larger but less prolific and less fragrant flower panicles. It usually blooms a couple of weeks earlier than summersweet. Cinnamon clethra tolerates drier soils, but not wet soils.

Cinnamon clethra can be difficult to transplant. Choose container-grown nursery stock.

It is rarely bothered by insect pests or disease and is very deer resistant.

COMPANION PLANTS – In nature, it is often found growing with sugar maple, sweetbay magnolia, spicebush, and smooth hydrangea. Cinnamon clethra combines well and thrives in the same growing conditions as native azaleas, ferns, ginger, and other native perennials.

WILDLIFE – The flowers attract hummingbirds and numerous species of bees and butterflies. Birds eat the seeds. Deer do not favor cinnamon clethra but may browse the summer foliage.

CULTIVATED VARIETIES – There are no cultivated varieties in the trade at this time.

Clethra alnifolia

Summersweet, Sweet Pepperbush

ATTRIBUTES/USE IN LANDSCAPE – Summersweet is an intensely fragrant, summer-blooming shrub with good to excellent, yellow fall color. The upright racemes of white to pale pink flowers are produced in summer, long after most spring-flowering plants are finished. It is notable for good flowering in light to moderate shade. Use in groupings, shrub borders, seashore plantings, rain gardens and the understory. Summersweet is a good plant for stabilizing the tops of stream and pond banks. It can be clipped into a formal hedge or pruned back if it becomes rangy.

USDA Zones: 4–9		
SUN	**MOISTURE**	**pH**
Full sun to full shade	Moist to wet	4.5–6.5

SEASONS OF INTEREST

WINTER   SPRING   SUMMER   AUTUMN

FORM – Summersweet is a medium-sized, multi-stemmed, neat, upright and somewhat rounded deciduous shrub to 8' tall × 9' wide in the wild. It is stoloniferous with horizontal spreading, but easily controlled. It is fast growing in moist soil.

COLOR – Fresh, light green leaves emerge in late spring, becoming a dark, glossy green as the season moves on. Profuse, small, fragrant, ivory flowers on terminal 2"–6" racemes appear in midsummer and remain for three to four weeks. Some cultivars provide pink flowers. The notable fragrance is sweet and

10'

5'

5
YEARS

15
YEARS

Summersweet is often covered with butterflies in summer.

The autumn foliage of summersweet.

peppery. Autumn color begins with a golden yellow and becomes a golden brown. Dark brown seed capsules may persist into winter.

TEXTURE – Medium in all seasons.

CULTURE – Summersweet is native from Nova Scotia southward through the eastern states and along the Gulf States to Texas.

Summersweet prefers an acid, organic, rich, moist soil. Sand or sandy loam seems to suit it best, but it tolerates clay soils. Shallow rooted, it spreads by stolons from the base, forming thickets of 5'–6' stems in cultivation. Flowering is reduced in full shade. In moist soil, it grows equally well in part shade or sun. Plants retain foliage further down the stem when grown in full sun. Plants in shade will be taller, with sparser foliage generally, particularly at the base. It is fairly salt tolerant. Although tolerant of occasional drought, hot and dry positions should be avoided; planted near downspouts, it will thrive.

Over such a wide range, varying degrees of hardiness and insect and disease resistance are to be expected. Obtain plants that are native to, or clones proven to succeed in, the geographic region where they are to be used in the landscape. I have seen winter damage in mid-Atlantic gardens when the plants are sourced from more southern regions. The foliage on these southern plants has remained green until frozen in early winter, while the leaves on locally sourced plants turn yellow in autumn and drop in early to mid-autumn.

Summersweet is rarely bothered by insect pests or disease. Deer will occasionally browse the summer foliage.

COMPANION PLANTS – In nature, summersweet is usually found growing with blueberries, native azaleas, spicebush, winterberry holly, and other understory plants that thrive in moist soil and shade. Common overstory associates include bald cypress, Atlantic white cedar, pines, red maple, and American beech. It also combines well and thrives in the same growing conditions as southern magnolia, American holly, Virginia sweetspire, oakleaf hydrangea, and needle palm.

A summersweet variety.

Summersweet species.

WILDLIFE – The flowers are especially attractive to hummingbirds and many species of bees and butterflies.

CULTIVATED VARIETIES – Select for variations in size, bloom color, and bloom time.

'Anne Bidwell' – 5'–8' × 4'–6'. Larger white flowers, usually flowering later than the species. A more compact plant than the species. Bred in Massachusetts.

'Caleb' ('Vanilla Spice') – 3'–6' tall by same. Largest flower panicles at 10"–12". Individual flowers are also larger. Yellow-brown autumn color. Bred in Michigan.

'Crystalina' ('Sugartina') – 3' × 5'. Compact and dense with dark green foliage. 'Crystalina' was bred in North Carolina.

'Hummingbird' – 2'–4' × 3'–5'. Shorter, more compact growth. Good golden yellow autumn color. Bred in Georgia.

'Pink Spires' – 3'–8' × 4'–6', with light pink flowers. A northern selection.

'Ruby Spice' – 4'–6'. Red flower buds open to rose-pink flowers that do not fade. The darkest pink variety. Cold-hardy. Bred in Connecticut.

'September Beauty' – 4'–6' × 3'–4'. Generally more compact, with a profuse, notably later bloom than the species. Upright, white flowers. Bred in New Jersey.

'Sixteen Candles' – 4'–5' × 2'–3'. A very compact form. Upright white racemes. Bred in Georgia.

'Tom's Compact' – 3½' × 3½'. Very compact, dense, and non-suckering. Leaves emerge dark green. Bred in New Jersey.

TOP: *'Sixteen Candles'*.
BOTTOM: *'Ruby Spice'*.

Comptonia peregrina

Sweet Fern

ATTRIBUTES/USE IN LANDSCAPE – Sweet fern is a low, deciduous shrub with notable attractive, fragrant foliage. It is very tolerant of dry, sandy, sterile, acidic soils. Use for informal borders, massing, and naturalizing at the seashore or woodland edge. Sweet fern is good for erosion control and slope stabilization, along highways, on rooftops, and as a groundcover. It is salt tolerant.

USDA Zones: 2–6b		
SUN	**MOISTURE**	**pH**
Full sun to part shade	Dry to moist	4.5–6.5

TEXTURE – Medium to fine in leaf. Medium in winter.

SEASONS OF INTEREST

WINTER   SPRING   SUMMER   AUTUMN

FORM – Sweet fern is an upright, 3'–4' × 4'–8', spreading, colonizing, rounded to flat-topped shrub.

COLOR – Sweet fern is an attractive addition to the landscape. The simple elongated leaves, with a variety of shades of green, resemble narrow fern fronds. They are up to 4" long × ½" wide with 20 or more rounded lobes. The foliage emerges light green and matures to dark green, often with multiple shades on the plant at the same time. In autumn the foliage is green or has a bronze tone, before dropping. The foliage is especially fragrant when crushed.

CULTURE – Native east of the Mississippi from New Brunswick to the higher elevations in southern Georgia and west to Minnesota and Indiana.

Its rate of growth vertically is slow to moderate, but the horizontal spread may be fairly rapid. The shrub readily forms colonies. In nature, it is found in dry, sandy, acid soil, but it grows best in full sun in moist to dry, well-drained soils. It is very drought tolerant. It is difficult to grow in zone 7 and farther south.

Sweet fern's fragrance resembles the bayberry, another member of the Myricaceae family. Like bayberry, it is a pioneer species, with nitrogen-fixing ability, improving soil for later succession plants. In rich soils, it may not compete well with other plants. Install container-grown plants in spring or fall. The flower is an insignificant catkin, with female catkins developing into burrlike seed capsules.

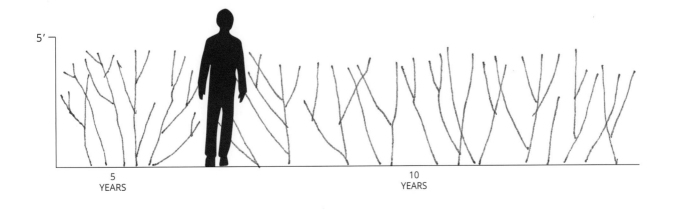

5'

5
YEARS

10
YEARS

There are no serious diseases or insect problems, and it is rarely browsed by deer.

COMPANION PLANTS – In nature, sweet fern may be found with creeping juniper, northern bayberry, and fragrant sumac.

WILDLIFE – Sweet fern attracts butterflies and other pollinators. It supports 64 species of Lepidoptera larvae, including the gray hairstreak butterfly. Birds eat the seeds.

CULTIVATED VARIETIES – Cultivated varieties are not available in the trade at this writing.

ABOVE: *Autumn foliage.*
TOP, LEFT: *Sweet fern spring foliage.*
TOP, RIGHT: *Sweet fern in summer.*

Cornus sericea

Red Twig Dogwood, Red Osier Dogwood

ATTRIBUTES/USE IN LANDSCAPE – Red twig dogwood is a medium-sized, multi-season deciduous shrub whose bright red (or yellow) stems are excellent for winter interest. Use in a moist shrub border, rain gardens, rooftops, massing, and for the woodland edge. Good for erosion control and slope stabilization and along streams. It is effective for residential, park, highway, and golf course projects. It is an excellent plant for wildlife.

USDA Zones: 3–7		
SUN	**MOISTURE**	**pH**
Full sun to part shade	Moist to wet	6.1–8.5

COLOR – Red twig dogwood is an exceptionally attractive addition to the winter landscape. The bright red (see yellow varieties) young stems are striking against snow and evergreens. The simple ovate to elongated leaves are 2"–5" long × 1"–2½" wide. The glossy foliage emerges light green, maturing to dark green, often with multiple shades on the plant at the same time. The autumn foliage is not reliably showy but can be an orange-red to purple-red before dropping. The attractive, small flowers are gathered in upright, flat, white clusters. The white berries are more striking but are quickly eaten by birds.

SEASONS OF INTEREST

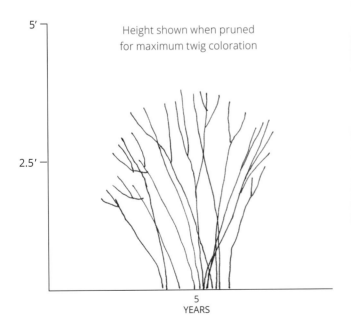

WINTER — *See below* SPRING SUMMER AUTUMN

FORM – Red twig dogwood is 6'–10' tall by same width and more, spreading by stolons to form an upright, rounded shrub. It is a fast-growing plant.

Height shown when pruned for maximum twig coloration

5'

2.5'

5
YEARS

Red twig dogwood in winter, at Tyler Arboretum, Pennsylvania.

ABOVE: *Red twig dogwood summer foliage and form.*
LEFT: *The white berries in late summer.*

TEXTURE – Medium.

CULTURE – Red twig dogwood is native to moist and wet swamps and bogs in the northern United States and in the east from New York across to Michigan including areas of the Appalachians into Virginia. Red twig dogwood was formerly known as *C. stolonifera*.

The red twig dogwood prefers rich, moist to wet soils in nature but can tolerate occasional drought. It also tolerates soils high in clay to high in sand. The best twig and autumn colors, as well as dense habit, will be in full sun, where a moist soil is most important. Red twig dogwood is tolerant of soil salt.

Pruning is not required, but stems under two years old have the best color and vigor. If pruning takes place in late autumn following leaf drop, the plant's colorful stems are shown to their best advantage. Prune stems over two years old to the ground (but not more than one-third of the plant), leaving the most colorful one- and two-year-old stems. New growth during the following growing season will be the primary show for the next winter. Keep in mind that pruning out older stems will reduce flowering and fruiting.

Red twig dogwood suffers in the hot, humid summer climates south of zone 7. *C. amomum*, silky dogwood, zones 4–8, is a more southerly dogwood shrub with less brilliant stem color and dark blue fruits. *C. racemosa*, gray dogwood, zones 3–8, with white fruit, is also good farther south and is more tolerant of dry soils in full sun.

The dogwood shrubs can be affected by powdery mildew and leaf spot in late summer. Dogwood sawfly may be an issue in some locations.

COMPANION PLANTS – In nature, red twig dogwood is usually found in wet clay loams with spicebush, arrowwood and blackhaw viburnum, red maple, sweet gum, black gum, and pin oak. In cultivation, it combines well and thrives in the same growing conditions as buttonbush, Virginia sweetspire, titi, and ferns including Christmas, cinnamon, and New York ferns.

WILDLIFE – The red twig dogwood attracts butterflies and other pollinators. Birds and mammals eat the fruit. Deer may browse, but it is generally not a preferred plant.

CULTIVATED VARIETIES – Choose for stem and leaf color and more compact habit.

A yellow twig variety

'**Alleman's Compact**' – Leaves hold up well in summer. More compact growth, to 6' tall.
'**Cardinal**' – Especially red, orange stems.
'**Farrow**' ('**Arctic Fire**') – Compact, to 4' tall by same width. Dense and less spreading.
'**Flaviramea**' – Attractive yellow to yellow-green stems. Creamy white leaf margins. Autumn color may be yellow.
'**Kelseyi**' – Compact, red, dwarf form. 24"–30" tall and wide.
'**Neil Z**' ('**Pucker Up!**') – A more compact form, 3'–4' by same. The leaves have a glossy finish and are "puckered."
'**Silver and Gold**' – Creamy white leaf margins with yellow stems and autumn color.

A variegated foliage form.

Croton alabamensis

Alabama Croton

ATTRIBUTES/USE IN LANDSCAPE – Alabama croton is an uncommon and valuable shrub noted for unique, attractive, deciduous to semievergreen, aromatic foliage. The bright green leaves, which have a distinct, shiny silver underside, turn a brilliant orange in autumn. Use as an understory shrub or specimen in woodlands, shrub borders, rain gardens, planters, buffer strips around parking areas, and for massing and naturalizing in part shade to shade in moderately dry to wet soils. It tolerates moderate drought and some flooding.

SEASONS OF INTEREST

WINTER   SPRING   SUMMER   AUTUMN

FORM – Alabama croton is an open, loose, upright understory shrub, typically about 5'–10' tall with equal spread. It may be multi-stemmed and may form thickets through layering.

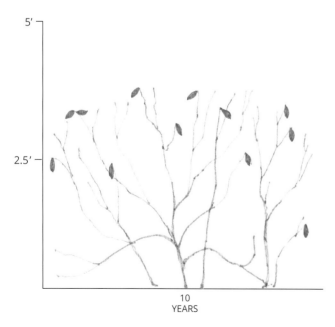

USDA Zones: 6–8		
SUN	**MOISTURE**	**pH**
Part shade to shade	Moist	6–8

COLOR – The new, bright green leaves emerge in early spring with very shiny, silver undersides that flash in a breeze. The leaves, 2"–4" long by nearly half as wide, are oval to elliptical. In autumn, the semievergreen or deciduous leaves turn a brilliant orange starting low on the stems and progressing to the tip. Some leaves may remain in winter and curl to expose their silver underside. The early-spring flowers are insignificant. The bark is also silvery before aging to gray. The fragrance of the leaves, when crushed, is often described as like an apple.

TEXTURE – Medium.

The brilliant autumn foliage of our native croton at Mt. Cuba Center, Delaware.

Alabama croton summer foliage.

The interesting, small, late-winter flower of the native croton.

CULTURE – In nature the Alabama croton is found only in a few small areas in Alabama, Tennessee, and Texas. It is available from specialty nurseries in the trade.

In cultivation the croton prefers moist, well-drained soils with high organic content, in part shade, but it is moderately tolerant of drought and flooding. It is intolerant of wind.

Pruning may be helpful for improved vigor and shaping the plant.

Croton has no serious pests or diseases. Deer do not favor it.

COMPANION PLANTS – Croton combines well with other shade-tolerant shrubs including buttonbush, winterberry holly, spicebush, fothergilla, titi, herbaceous wildflowers, ground covers, and ferns. It does especially well in the shade and wind protection of overhead pines.

WILDLIFE – The seeds are eaten by birds.

CULTIVATED VARIETIES – No varieties are available in the trade.

Cyrilla racemiflora

Titi, Swamp Cyrilla, Leatherwood

ATTRIBUTES/USE IN LANDSCAPE – The titi (rhymes with bye-bye) is a large, semievergreen shrub or small tree, with fragrant, attractive flowers and glossy green foliage. It is useful for naturalizing, as an informal hedge, as a woodland border, in rain gardens, and along streams and water.

USDA Zones: 6–11		
SUN	**MOISTURE**	**pH**
Full sun to full shade	Dry to wet	6.8–7.2

SEASONS OF INTEREST

WINTER	SPRING	SUMMER	AUTUMN

COLOR – Creamy white, profuse, semi-pendulous racemes of flowers, 2"–4" long, appear in a whorled spray below new leaves in late spring to early summer. Their racemes, with small fruit capsules, remain into winter. The 3"–6" leathery leaves are a bright, shiny, medium green. While titi is more evergreen in the South, in the northern part of its range the leaves turn orange to bright red in autumn, progressing up the stem, with the older leaves turning first. This effect is most attractive when viewed in close proximity. Where leaves persist, retention may vary from winter to winter. The smooth, tan bark becomes scaly with age.

FORM – Titi is a large shrub or small tree, usually about 12' tall by the same width. The shrub can have one to a few primary stems, up to 6' diameter, and spreads by root suckers. The titi's upright, contorted, wide-spreading branches form a dense, rounded crown. It is taller and narrow in warmer climates. It is long-lived and has a medium growth rate.

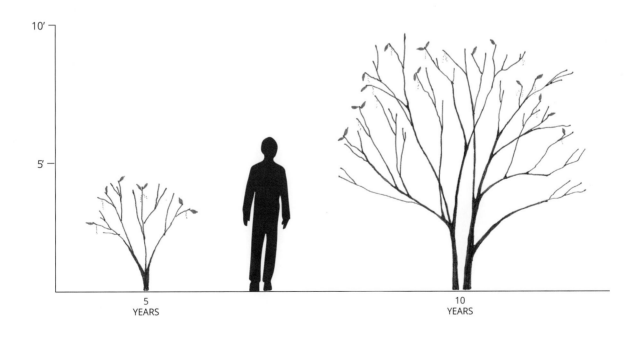

10'

5'

5
YEARS

10
YEARS

ABOVE: *Young titi in bloom.*

LEFT: *The late-spring to early-summer flowers of the titi.*

TEXTURE – Medium in summer and winter.

CULTURE – Titi is native to moist, sandy, acid soils of the swamps and coastal areas from Virginia to northern Florida. In fact, its range extends along the coast of the Atlantic into the southern hemisphere.

Titi prefers an acid, organic, rich, moist soil. Sand or sandy loam seems to suit it best, but it is tolerant of clay soils, drought and salt. Shallow rooted, it spreads by root suckers from the base, forming thickets of 5'–6' stems. Flowering is reduced in full shade. In moist

Titi in autumn at Mt. Cuba Center, Delaware.

soil, it grows equally well in part shade or sun. Plants retain foliage further down the stem when grown in full sun. Plants in shade will be taller, with sparser foliage, particularly at the base.

Titi is rarely bothered by insect pests or disease. Sapsuckers will sometimes damage the bark in the winter. Deer may browse.

COMPANION PLANTS – In nature and cultivation, titi may associate with black gum, sweet gum, American holly, yaupon, sweetbay magnolia, inkberry, sweetshrub, Virginia sweetspire, spicebush, winterberry holly, and ferns.

WILDLIFE – Titi provides cover for birds, mammals, and aquatic life. The nectar is attractive to bees, and it supports insect larvae.

CULTIVATED VARIETIES – Varieties are not readily available at this time.

Fothergilla spp.

Dwarf or Coastal Fothergilla and Large or Mountain Fothergilla

ATTRIBUTES/USE IN LANDSCAPE – Both fothergillas are handsome, underused, multi-seasonal shrubs. They are noted for their attractive, neat form, showy flowers, and usually excellent autumn foliage. They are appreciated in rain gardens, rooftops, and as a shrub border in formal and informal settings.

SEASONS OF INTEREST

WINTER	SPRING	SUMMER	AUTUMN

FORM – *Fothergilla gardenii* or dwarf fothergilla is a small, dense, upright to rounded shrub, with some plants spreading through suckering, typically about 3' tall and nearly as wide. *Fothergilla major*, large fothergilla, can reach 15' but generally are 6'–10' tall, with equivalent width. They are slow growing with a moderate life span.

COLOR – In spring, showy, profuse, upright, creamy white, plump flower spikes bloom before leaf out, and they last for several weeks. In the dwarf fothergilla the spikes are 1"–2" tall and precede the beginning of leaf out. Large fothergilla blooms can reach 2"–4"

USDA Zones: 5–8		
SUN	**MOISTURE**	**pH**
Full sun to part shade	Moist	5.5–7

and are concurrent with leaf out. The leaves emerge a medium green, turning a matte green to blue-green. The light gray undersides are pubescent. The leaf shape resembles the leaf of fothergilla's family member witch hazel. Leaves of the dwarf fothergilla measure 1"–2½" long, while the large fothergillas grow 2"–4" long. The exceptional autumn color is late developing with brilliant yellow, orange, and red

The showy, spring flowers with emerging foliage.

5'

Dwarf Fothergilla

Large Fothergilla

A large fothergilla, in autumn, Annapolis, MD.

Large fothergilla in spring.

leaves. Multiple colors can be on one leaf. The flowers are honey scented.

TEXTURE – Medium in all seasons.

CULTURE – The fothergillas are uncommon in nature and deserve a more prominent position in cultivation. Dwarf fothergilla is native to the coastal plain from North Carolina to the panhandle of Florida, growing in swampy areas where it may be inundated or face periods of drought. Large fothergilla is a plant of the southern Appalachians, from Virginia to Alabama, where it occurs at 1,500' and above.

The fothergillas grow best in a moist, rich, acid soil with good drainage and bloom best in full sun. They are also salt tolerant. The large fothergilla is more tolerant of dry conditions, especially in shade. The terrific autumn color is almost always reliable, and it is best in full sun.

There are few diseases and insects that pose problems. It is usually not preferred by deer.

COMPANION PLANTS – In nature and cultivation fothergillas associate well with white oak, shagbark hickory, loblolly and Virginia pines, cucumber tree, common witch hazel, clethra, oakleaf hydrangea, American beautyberry, native azaleas (with some shade), spicebush, and Virginia sweetspire.

WILDLIFE – The flowers attract butterflies and other pollinators. The inconspicuous seeds are eaten by birds and small mammals.

ABOVE: *Another example of brilliant autumn foliage.*
RIGHT: *A "blue"-leaved fothergilla variety with oakleaf hydrangea.*

CULTIVATED VARIETIES – Cultivars offer variation in growth habit, summer foliage, and autumn coloration. There are also hybrid crosses between the two species.

'**Harold Epstein**' – A small plant, 1' tall × 1½' wide. Excellent autumn color.

'**Suzanne**' – Compact at 2½' tall × 3' wide. Strong orange-red autumn color. Bred by Michael Dirr.

'**Windy City**' – Upright habit at 3'–4' by same width. Superb autumn coloring in the North.

'**Mount Airy**' – 5'–6' upright habit. Dark blue foliage with superb, consistent yellow-orange-red autumn color, abundant flowers, and vigorous constitution. Bred by Michael Dirr.

Hamamelis vernalis

Vernal Witch Hazel, Ozark Witch Hazel

ATTRIBUTES/USE IN LANDSCAPE – Vernal witch hazel is an underused multi-season shrub noted for its small, very fragrant early- to late-winter flowers and its bright yellow autumn color. Use as a tall understory shrub in woodlands, shrub borders, and hedges; and for massing, naturalizing, rain gardens, and erosion control. It is good for wildlife.

SEASONS OF INTEREST

WINTER	SPRING	SUMMER	AUTUMN

FORM – Vernal witch hazel is a tall, dense, upright to rounded shrub typically about 6' to 8' tall, but may reach 12' to 15'. It may spread by underground stolons to form a wide thicket of stems. Vernal witch hazel tends to be relatively short-lived, about 30–50 years. The growth rate is usually medium, but it may be fast growing in moist, well-drained, rich soil, and slow in drier soils.

USDA Zones: 5–8		
SUN	**MOISTURE**	**pH**
Full sun to part shade	Moderately dry to wet	6–6.5

COLOR – The 4"–6" leaves are medium green and obovate with a slightly scalloped edge. In early to midwinter, the plant develops small, up to 1", four-petaled, extremely fragrant, bright orange to yellow flowers, with red centers. The flowers are unharmed by cold temperatures. The autumn color is almost always a bright yellow. Unfortunately, many individuals and some varieties hold on to dead leaves throughout the winter. Therefore, the best use of vernal witch hazel is at the back of a border or as an understory plant, where the fragrance of its small flowers may be enjoyed but its potentially unsightly dead winter foliage is obscured from view. See below for varieties that drop leaves in winter.

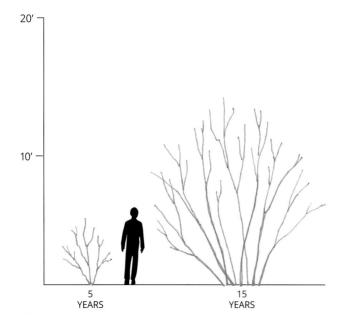

The fragrant winter flowers of vernal witch hazel.

Autumn foliage on mature vernal witch hazel.

Autumn foliage on a young plant.

TEXTURE – Medium in all seasons.

CULTURE – Vernal witch hazel is native to the Ozark Plateau in Missouri, Arkansas, and Oklahoma. In its native habitat, it is usually found growing near streams at the base of rocky slopes.

The best growth occurs in organic, rich, well-drained, moist soil, but it grows almost as well in dry soil. In cultivation, vernal witch hazel is tolerant of gravelly and sandy soils and clay soils as long as drainage is adequate. It is also tolerant of periodic flooding. Although tolerant of drought, some leaf scorch may occur during severe drought. Vernal witch hazel is not salt tolerant.

As with other winter-flowering witch hazels, the four strap-like petals curl up on very cold days and unfurl as the weather warms. Flowering is best on plants growing in full sun, while plants growing in partial shade are usually larger in stature. The flowers are most fragrant on warmer days. It is not unusual to detect the fragrance of a larger plant from a distance of over 100 feet on a good day. The best time to prune is in spring after flowering has occurred. Please see our *H. virginiana* article for comparisons with *H. vernalis*.

H. vernalis f. *carnea* syn. is a naturally occurring variety with pink to red flowers. Vernal witch hazel has been crossed with the Japanese (*H. japonica*) and Chinese (*H. mollis*) witch hazel to produce many of the most popular cultivated varieties of witch hazels in the garden.

Leaf gall aphids and a few other pests may be found on Ozark witch hazel, but they do not do significant harm to the plant. Vernal witch hazel is rarely browsed by deer.

COMPANION PLANTS – In nature and cultivation, vernal witch hazel may associate with willow oak, sweet gum, river birch, sycamore, oakleaf hydrangea, summersweet, spicebush, fothergilla, Virginia sweetspire, and winterberry.

WILDLIFE – The flowers attract bees during a time of year (depending on the local climate) when other sources of pollen are rare or do not exist. The seeds are eaten by birds and small mammals. It supports butterfly and moth larvae.

CULTIVATED VARIETIES – Choose for flower color and winter leaf drop.

'Autumn Embers' – Blue-green foliage with orange flowers. The autumn foliage is a mix of yellow with orange and yellow.
'Squib' – Bright yellow flowers, stems may be bare in winter.

Hamamelis virginiana

Common Witch Hazel

ATTRIBUTES/USE IN LANDSCAPE – Common witch hazel is an underused, multi-season shrub or small tree, noted for its small, very fragrant, mid- to late-autumn flowers and its bright yellow autumn foliage. It is appreciated in shrub borders, rain gardens, planters, buffer strips around parking areas, and for massing and naturalizing. Common witch hazel tolerates moderate drought and some flooding.

USDA Zones: 3–8		
SUN	**MOISTURE**	**pH**
Full sun to part shade	Dry to moist	5–7

SEASONS OF INTEREST

WINTER	SPRING	SUMMER	AUTUMN

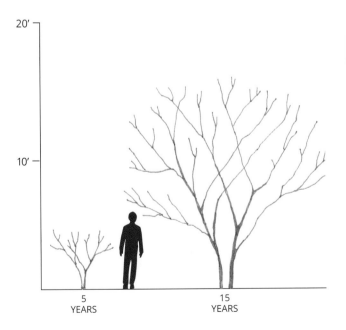

FORM – Common witch hazel is a tall, open, upright shrub or small tree to typically about 15'–20' (35') tall with equal spread. It is relatively long-lived, generally 75–100 years. The growth rate is usually moderate, but it is fast in moist, well-drained, rich soil and slow in drier soils. Plants grown in shade will be taller and much less dense than those growing in full sun.

COLOR – The aromatic, medium to dark green leaves, about 3"–5" long, are obovate with a lightly scalloped edge. In mid- to late autumn, small, fragrant, ½–⅔", four-petaled, yellow flowers are borne close to the stems. In many locations, it is the last native shrub to flower in the season. The flowers are usually on the plant after leaf drop, but they may appear at the same time the foliage is turning its golden yellow autumn color. As with other witch hazels, the four strap-like petals curl up on very cold days and unfurl as the weather warms.

5 YEARS

15 YEARS

A mature specimen of common witch hazel, Grove Street Cemetery, New Haven, Connecticut.

The common witch hazel in autumn.

TEXTURE – Coarse in summer, medium in winter.

CULTURE – Common witch hazel is native to an extensive area from the Canadian Maritimes westward to Wisconsin, and south to the panhandle of Florida.

It grows well in both acid and moderately alkaline soils. It is tolerant of salt. Common witch hazel grows best when it is planted in organic, rich, well-drained but moist soil. In cultivation, witch hazel is tolerant of clay with adequate drainage, as well as gravelly and sandy soils. While it is tolerant of drought, some leaf scorch may occur during severe drought. Flowering is most prolific on plants in full sun. The best time to prune is in spring after flowering. Common witch hazel's bark contains

beneficial chemicals that are used extensively by herbalists to treat many different maladies.

The common witch hazel is taller and has a more treelike structure than vernal witch hazel. Its yellow autumn flowering is also earlier than the orange-red winter flowering of the vernal witch hazel. Additionally, common witch hazel does not hold its leaves throughout the winter.

Leaf gall aphids and a few other pests may be found on witch hazel, but they do not do significant harm to the plant. It is seldom browsed by deer.

COMPANION PLANTS – In nature, common witch hazel associates with American holly, sugar maple, striped maple, flowering dogwood, and pinxterbloom azalea. It combines well with other shade-tolerant shrubs including winterberry holly, spicebush, Virginia sweetspire, summersweet, and fothergilla, as well as herbaceous wildflowers, ground covers, and ferns.

WILDLIFE – The flowers attract bees during a time of year (depending on the local climate) when other sources of pollen are rare or do not exist. The seeds are eaten by birds and small mammals. It supports butterfly and moth larvae.

CULTIVATED VARIETIES – Cultivars may provide for a showier floral display, flower color variation, and smaller-scale plants.

'Harvest Moon' – Showy, abundant yellow flowers in late autumn, to about 18' tall. Flowers open after leaf drop.
'Little Suzie' – A very compact form at 4'–5' tall by same width. Abundant flowers.
'Mohonk Red' – 15'–20' by same width. The flowers are red with yellow at petal tip.

Hydrangea arborescens

Smooth Hydrangea, Wild Hydrangea, Sevenbark

ATTRIBUTES/USE IN LANDSCAPE – The smooth hydrangea is a handsome, medium-height deciduous shrub with showy, extended, midsummer bloom and attractive dark foliage. It is effective in massing and foundation plantings, the foreground of a shrub border, woodland edge, and rooftop gardens; and as a hedge in residential, campus, park, and golf course projects. The cultivated varieties may be used as specimen plants.

SEASONS OF INTEREST

	USDA Zones: 3–9	
SUN	**MOISTURE**	**pH**
Full sun to part shade	Dry to wet	5.5–7

WINTER	SPRING	SUMMER	AUTUMN

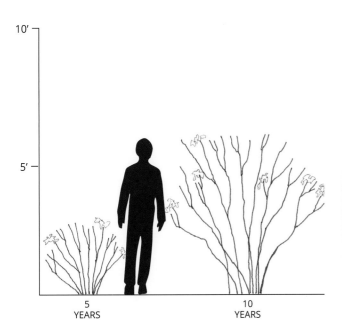

FORM – The smooth hydrangea is a medium-sized, multi-stemmed, dense, upright and mounded shrub, reaching 3'–6' × 3'–9'. It is stoloniferous and will form thickets. Smooth hydrangea is fast growing and moderately long-lived, to 30–40 years.

COLOR – The ovate, serrated leaves, 4"–8" long, are dark green above and lighter below. In mid- to late summer, showy, flat-topped white flower heads (corymbs) are effective for two months. In the wild, subtle 3"–6" corymbs are usually a cluster of non-showy, small fertile flowers surrounded by a single row of larger white sterile flowers. The named cultivated varieties are much larger and showier than the species. The thin bark of mature stems peels in successive layers to reveal cinnamon brown inner bark. The dried flowers can remain through winter.

TEXTURE – Coarse in all seasons.

CULTURE – Native to woodlands of southern New York and south through the Appalachian Mountains into Alabama and Georgia, west into Arkansas.

Smooth hydrangea grows best in moist, loamy

The fertile and infertile flowers of the smooth hydrangea species.

Smooth hydrangeas in summer.

soils, but it will tolerate clay soils. It is tolerant of dry and wet soils but not prolonged drought or prolonged flooding. It may be grown in full sun to full shade, but it prefers shade in drier soils and full sun in more moist soils. Smooth hydrangea, like all hydrangeas, generally performs well with protection from afternoon sun, but it flowers best with more sun. It tolerates erosion as well. Smooth hydrangea is slightly tolerant of salt, but less tolerant than some other hydrangea species.

The persistent flowering of the smooth hydrangea follows the bloom of oakleaf hydrangea. The smooth hydrangea flowers on new wood, so the plant can be pruned within 6" of the soil in late autumn through late winter for a more rounded form. When pruned, it is effective in the front of the border; if not pruned, its stem grows more woody and works well mid-border. The seed heads and dried, dark sterile florets remain through winter if not pruned back. *H. arborescens* subsp. *radiata* has particularly attractive leaves with a silvery white underside and has good drought tolerance.

There are few diseases and insects that pose problems. Deer sometimes browse the foliage.

COMPANION PLANTS – In nature, it may be found in association with American holly, other evergreens, sugar maples, white oaks, sourwood, Carolina silver bell, spicebush, and other plants that thrive in moist soil and shade. Smooth hydrangea combines well and thrives in the same growing conditions as Virginia sweetspire, summersweet, fothergilla, chokeberry, and others.

WILDLIFE – The flowers provide midsummer pollen and nectar for pollinators. It is a host plant for the hydrangea sphinx moth and dozens of other caterpillars.

CULTIVATED VARIETIES – The cultivars offer more flowering options and may be used as specimens.

The prominent flowers of 'Annabelle' in a South Carolina garden.

'**Annabelle**' – This variety has much larger, heavier, more-rounded flower corymbs, 8"–12" across, with mainly sterile flowers. Showy and profuse blooms appear in early summer for two months, and may repeat bloom in autumn. Very popular and widely available in garden centers. 'Annabelle' is sterile and does not provide pollen and nectar.

'**Dardom**' ('**White Dome**') – This variety has 6"–10" rounded corymbs (domes) with fertile flowers surrounded by large sterile flowers.

'**Grandiflora**' – Another widely available variety with large, rounded, showy and profuse corymbs, 6"–8" across.

'**NCHA1**' (**Invincibelle™ Spirit**) – A more compact, pink variety growing 3'–4' by same. Large globular corymbs up to 6"–8".

'**Samantha**' – A particularly attractive cultivar of *H. arborescens* subsp. *radiata*.

Hydrangea quercifolia

Oakleaf Hydrangea

ATTRIBUTES/USE IN LANDSCAPE – The oakleaf hydrangea is an exquisite, boldly textured shrub. It is noted for its foliage; showy, white, persistent flowers; and good autumn color. Oakleaf hydrangea is useful for massing, the back of a border, or as a hedge.

USDA Zones: 5–8		
SUN	**MOISTURE**	**pH**
Full sun to part shade	Moist	5.5–7.5

SEASONS OF INTEREST

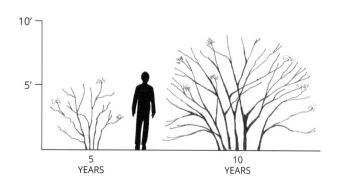

WINTER   SPRING   SUMMER   AUTUMN

FORM – Oakleaf hydrangea is a handsome, medium-sized, multi-stemmed, mounding shrub, reaching 8' × 8' in warmer climates. It is stoloniferous and will form thickets.

COLOR – The distinctly lobed, 3"–8" leaves are a medium to dark green. In late spring to early summer, large, showy, upright, chalky white flower panicles are displayed. The flowers emerge as light green buds and become white, fading through pink and green and finally to tan and brown at the end of the summer. The small, dried, dark florets remain through the winter. The autumn leaf color includes shades of purple to red and reddish orange. In winter, mature stems peel to reveal attractive cinnamon brown inner bark.

TEXTURE – Coarse in all seasons. The leaves are larger on plants grown in the shade.

CULTURE – Oakleaf hydrangea is native to woodlands of Georgia, Florida, Alabama, and Mississippi.

The oakleaf hydrangea can be grown in sun to full shade, but it prefers shade if growing in dry, sandy soils. It grows best in moist, loamy soils but will tolerate clay soils. Oakleaf hydrangea is more tolerant of drier soils than other hydrangeas. It prefers a slightly acid soil (pH 5.5–6.5) but tolerates slightly alkaline soils (pH 7–7.5) and is tolerant of salt.

The height, spread, leaf size, and autumn foliage color vary with growing conditions. The hairy foliage is thinner and larger in shade (up to 12") than it is when grown in sun (4"–8"). Flower size and fall color can vary with sun exposure. The panicles of flowers will be shorter and more numerous in the sun. A

The showy persistent bloom.

10'

5'

5 YEARS   10 YEARS

ABOVE: *A large plant in spring.*
RIGHT: *A more compact variety.*

plant of the same cultivated variety may have purple autumn foliage when grown in full sun but may be reddish orange grown in shade. When well situated it can reach heights of 6'–8' and irregularly spread to widths over 8'. In the North (zones 5–6a), plants are smaller, and stems may be winter killed, requiring some pruning and removing the flower buds. Even so, it remains valuable for its foliage.

There are usually both fertile and sterile flowers within the upright panicles. The sterile flowers are showier, and in some cases have multiple florets and appear double. The most showy, cultivated varieties have a large percentage of sterile flowers. Flower buds for the following season are produced in midsummer. Any needed pruning should be performed immediately after flowering to prevent the loss of flower buds. The flowers can be cut and—if hung upside down in a shaded, dry, and well-ventilated area—preserved in their natural color.

There are few diseases and insects that pose problems. Deer frequently browse this species.

COMPANION PLANTS – In nature, it is usually found in association with spicebush, possum haw holly, inkberry, arrowwood viburnum, American snowbell, and other understory plants that thrive in

ABOVE: *'Alice' in flower.*
RIGHT: *The pink sepals of 'Alice'.*

moist soil and shade. It combines well and thrives in the same growing conditions as bald cypress, southern magnolia, fothergilla, summersweet, winterberry holly, needle palm, Virginia sweetspire, and others.

WILDLIFE – The flowers provide pollen for native bees. Seeds are eaten by some songbirds, game birds, and mammals.

ABOVE: *The often stunning autumn foliage.*
RIGHT: *The colorful, peeling bark is a nice winter feature.*

CULTIVATED VARIETIES – Cultivars offer more compact forms and showier floral displays.

'Alice' – 8' × 8' (12'). A vigorous variety with large, arching flower panicles, to 1' and more. A Michael Dirr introduction.

'Pee Wee' – 2'–4' tall and wide, a smaller variety similar to 'Sikes Dwarf'.

'Sikes Dwarf' – 3' × 4', dwarf, mounded with smaller leaves and panicles, 3"–4", than the species. It is less spreading and more densely foliaged. Showy, mostly sterile flowers. Can be grown in large containers.

'Snowflake' – 7'–8' tall and wide, with "double" flowers lasting over a long period in the summer.

'Snow Queen' – 6' × 6' with large, erect panicles of mostly sterile "single" flowers.

Hypericum frondosum

Golden St. John's Wort

ATTRIBUTES/USE IN LANDSCAPE – Golden St. John's wort is an attractive, small and deciduous to semievergreen to evergreen shrub with a showy, extended midsummer bloom, blue-green foliage, attractive peeling bark, and a wide soil tolerance.

This plant is effective in the foreground of a shrub border, as a tall ground cover, for massing, at the woodland edge, as a low hedge, in rain and rooftop gardens, and for erosion control. St. John's wort is useful for many types of projects including residential, parks, campuses, and golf courses.

SEASONS OF INTEREST

WINTER	SPRING	SUMMER	AUTUMN

FORM – Golden St. John's wort is a small, multi-stemmed, dense, rounded shrub, reaching 3'–4'. The growth rate is medium and it is rather short-lived.

USDA Zones: 5–8		
SUN	**MOISTURE**	**pH**
Full sun to part shade	Dry to moist	5.5–8

COLOR – Showy, bright yellow 1"–1¾" single flowers in midsummer, persisting for a month to six weeks, have prominent pincushion-like stamens. The blue-green, oblong leaves are 1"–2" long and about a third as wide. The flowers are followed by persistent ½" red-brown seed capsules. In some areas, where deciduous, the autumn leaves can be orange, red, or purple.

TEXTURE – Medium in leaf, fine in winter.

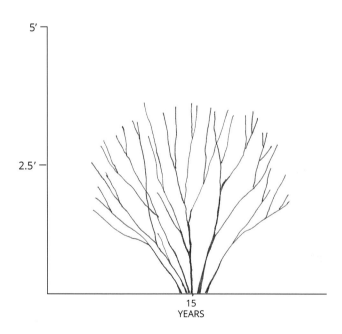

The attractive, bright, yellow St. John's wort flower.

ABOVE: *St. John's wort in summer.*
LEFT: *Autumn foliage.*

CULTURE – Golden St. John's wort is native in the east in scattered populations through the southern Appalachians.

Golden St. John's wort grows best in full sun and well-drained sandy loams, but it is tolerant of drought, poor and alkaline soils, and salt. It tolerates erosion as well. Golden St. John's wort prefers some shade in the more southern parts of its range.

There are several native *Hypericum* species available in nurseries, including the following, all of which are denser and have a finer texture than Golden St. John's wort. *H. kalmianum*, Kalm's St. John's wort (zones 4–7), is native primarily to the shore area of Lake Michigan in the United States. It is 2'–3' tall by same, with narrow, dark green, willowlike leaves, 1"–2" long, and ½"–1" flowers. *H. prolificum*, shrubby St. John's wort (zones 4–8), is native from New York to Iowa and south to Louisiana. It is 3'–6' tall by same, spreading with age, with ¾" flowers and 1½"–3" narrow, bright green leaves. *H. densiflorum*, the dense St. John's wort (zones 6–8), is similar in size to the former, with ½" flowers.

The St. John's worts may be evergreen in warmer climates, and further north leaves may shrivel and remain into winter. They may be pruned for shaping within 6" of the ground in late autumn through late winter. The name refers to the plant being said to begin bloom on St. John's Day in late June.

There are few diseases and insects that pose problems, and St. John's wort is not a preferred plant for deer in most areas.

COMPANION PLANTS – In nature, it may be found in association with oaks, hickories, eastern red cedar, American beautybush, fragrant sumac, and native azaleas.

Golden St. John's wort combines well and thrives in the same growing conditions as the oakleaf hydrangea.

WILDLIFE – The flowers provide excellent midsummer pollen for pollinators, including honeybees, butterflies, and hummingbirds. It is a host plant for gray hairstreak butterfly larvae.

CULTIVATED VARIETIES

'**Sunburst**' – Lower growing than the species, up to 3' tall, with a larger, 1"–2" flower.

Ilex glabra

Inkberry, Gallberry

ATTRIBUTES/USE IN LANDSCAPE – An evergreen holly shrub valued for its clean habit; attractive, fine foliage; and tolerance of wet sites. Inkberry is used as an accent plant and for shrub borders, screening, massing, hedging, rain and rooftop gardens, naturalizing, erosion control, and along waterways in residential, park, and other projects.

SEASONS OF INTEREST

WINTER	SPRING	SUMMER	AUTUMN
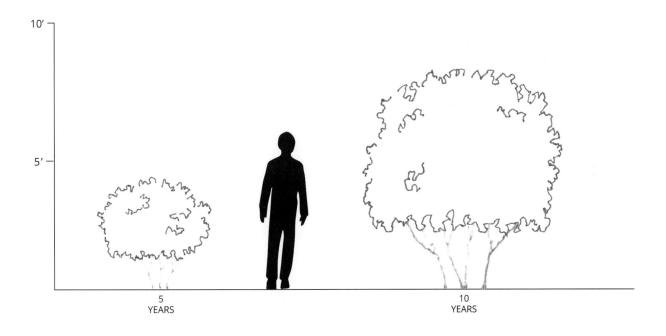			

FORM – Inkberry is an upright, rounded, multi-stemmed plant, often with sparse foliage on lower stems. In the wild, it can grow 6'–12' tall and slightly wider, with a lanky, open habit, spreading through stolons. In cultivation, due to horticultural practices, it is usually shorter with a denser habit. Inkberry is generally a smaller plant in the

USDA Zones: (4) 5–9		
SUN	**MOISTURE**	**pH**
Full sun to part shade	Dry to wet	4.5–6.5

North. The growth rate is moderate but can be enhanced with nutrition and water. Inkberry is long-lived. See cultivars below for improved form and fruit color.

COLOR – 1"–2" leaves are a glossy, dark green above and lighter below; they are elliptical to oblanceolate in shape. In the North, they may have a purplish cast through the winter. The inconspicuous white flowers are followed by a black, rarely white, ⅜" drupe fruit on female plants in autumn. The berries persist into winter until the birds enjoy them. The white fruit has more visual impact than the black.

TEXTURE – Medium fine.

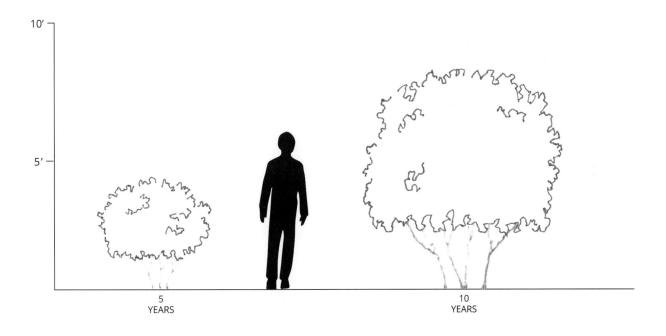

ABOVE: *'Shamrock' planting, about 12 years old, at Mt. Cuba.*
RIGHT: *Fruit on 'Shamrock'.*

CULTURE – Inkberry is native along the coastal plain from Nova Scotia south to Florida and Texas, where it can form large thickets in wet woodlands and along stream borders.

A rich, moist, well-drained, acid soil in full sun is best for vigor and form, but it will grow in almost any soil. It will tolerate wet, heavy soils and is tolerant of moderate drought and periodic flooding. While it is tolerant of shade, its habit is much more lanky.

Inkberry responds well to pruning and shearing. Pruning is not required, but plants may be pruned back hard in late winter to achieve the desired effect. Winter storm damage may require pruning in the North.

The sexes are separate, so at least one male plant

must be present for female plants to produce berries. Variety *leucocarpa* is a naturally occurring white-berried form. *I. coriacea* is a more southern form (zones 7–9) with larger leaves and better heat tolerance.

The inkberry tolerates salt, soil compaction,

Inkberry with oakleaf hydrangea.

The species in a garden landscape.

erosion, wet soil, and air pollution. There are few insect and disease pests. Deer do not favor it but may browse in winter. It tolerates rabbits.

COMPANION PLANTS – In nature, inkberry is often associated with red maple, bald cypress, sweetbay magnolia, buttonbush, and winterberry. It combines well and thrives in the same growing conditions as sweetbay magnolia, titi, clethra, itea, spicebush, and wax myrtle.

WILDLIFE – Inkberry is a pollen and nectar source for native bees. The berries on female plants provide abundant fruit for many different species of birds. Inkberry provides year-round wildlife cover.

CULTIVATED VARIETIES – The cultivated varieties provide variation in form as well as retention of good

lower foliage and winter color. For berries, a male is required.

'Compacta' – 3'–4' × 4'–6'. Female and heavy fruiting. A more rounded leaf with olive-green color in winter. Good lower foliage retention.

'Ivory Queen' – White fruit and good lower foliage retention.

'Chamzin' ('Nordic') – A compact, dense, male cultivar, 3'–4' by same. Very cold-hardy with dark green leaves and good color retention in winter. It is also less likely to sucker than the species. Good lower branch leaf retention.

'Shamrock' – A compact, rounded, dense habit, female cultivar, 5'–6' by same. The leaves are more lanceolate for a finer texture. Good leaf retention on lower branches. Less suckering than the species.

Ilex verticillata

Winterberry

ATTRIBUTES/USE IN LANDSCAPE – Winterberry is a deciduous shrub holly notable for its profusion of small red berries on female plants from mid-autumn through winter. It is used for borders, massing, hedging, rain gardens, erosion control, and along stream banks, where it forms thickets. Winterberry is excellent in the early-winter garden with a background of evergreens or snow. The branches are frequently used in holiday decorations.

SEASONS OF INTEREST

WINTER	SPRING	SUMMER	AUTUMN

FORM – Winterberry is a deciduous, upright, multi-stemmed plant in youth, becoming more open with age. In cultivation, it grows 6'–8' tall with 10' spreads and a more dense habit. The growth rate is slow to medium but can be enhanced with nutrition and water. Winterberry can be pruned to shape.

COLOR – Profuse, showy, ¼"–½", red berries on bare branches are revealed with leaf drop, at first

USDA Zones: 5–8		
SUN	**MOISTURE**	**pH**
Full sun to full shade	Dry to wet	4.5–6.5

freeze, in autumn and winter. 3"–6" leaves are a lustrous dark green.

TEXTURE – Fine in winter, medium in summer.

CULTURE – Winterberry holly is also known as black alder, fever bush, and coralberry, among others. It is native east of the Mississippi, occurring in wet woods and swamps, where it may spread to form thickets. It is also native to upland, drier sites, where it is usually seen as a dense shrub. When a species is native over such a wide area, use cultivated varieties proven to be hardy and thriving locally.

A soil rich in organic matter suits winterberry best. It will tolerate wet, heavy soils and periodic flooding, but is also tolerant of moderate drought. It is slightly salt tolerant. Berries are produced most abundantly when plants are grown in full sun, but an adequate crop of berries may be expected on plants

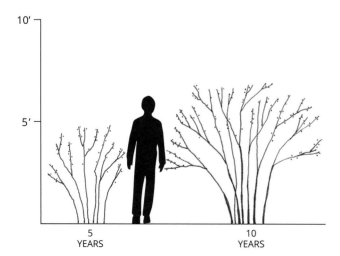

A group of pruned winterberry in the landscape.

End of summer with berries.

grown in partial shade. Fruits on some plants may be damaged and turn dark below 20°F. The 1½"–4" leaves tend to be wider on later-blooming plants.

The sexes are separate, so at least one male plant must be present for female plants to produce berries.

There are few insect and disease pests. While some consider winterberry deer resistant, in my experience, deer will frequently browse the leaves in certain locales.

COMPANION PLANTS – In nature, winterberry holly is usually found in association with silky dogwood, spicebush, possum haw, inkberry, arrowwood viburnum, and other understory plants that thrive in moist soil and shade. It combines well and thrives in the same growing conditions as bald cypress, southern magnolia, summersweet, oakleaf hydrangea, Virginia sweetspire, and needle palm.

WILDLIFE – The berries provide winter fodder for many different species of birds; they seem to prefer the red fruit. Winterberry is a pollen source for bees and supports insect larvae.

CULTIVATED VARIETIES – The many named cultivated varieties provide variation in form, size,

TOP: *'Winter Red' in winter.*

BOTTOM: *The autumn foliage and berries before leaf drop.*

berry color, leaf color, finish, and retention. For best berry production, coordinate female and male bloom times. The earlier-blooming varieties tend to bloom a week to a month earlier than the later-blooming plants. There are hybrids between this native species and Asiatic species. Male cultivar listings follow female cultivars.

Earlier-blooming varieties:

'Afterglow' – 3'–6' tall and wide. Vivid, orange-red fruit in a showy display often persisting until spring. Attractive, lustrous, 3" dark green leaves turn yellow bronze in autumn. A compact, rounded habit, smaller and denser than other cultivars and slow growing.

'Spriber' (Berry Nice) – 6'–8' tall and wide. An upright, rounded habit. Profuse dark red fruit, with good retention. Lustrous dark green foliage is mildew resistant.

'Chrysocarpa' (f. *chrysocarpa*) – 6'–10' × 5'–10'. A rounded vase shape with weeping branches, true yellow fruit, not as profuse or long-lasting as some red-berry types. Early leaf drop.

'Earlibright' – 6'–7' × 4'. Columnar habit, fastigiate branching. Large, orange-red fruit, early developing.

'Jolly Red' – 7'–10' × 8'–10' red fruit, abundant. An older variety.

'Red Sprite' ('Compacta', 'Macrocarpa', 'Nana') – 2'–4' tall and wide. A popular, compact, rounded form. Large, abundant red fruit, often persisting to early spring. Glossy medium green leaves drop early.

'Shaver' – 5' × 3'. Compact, upright habit, large, persistent red fruit in early autumn becomes a rich orange in winter. Smaller, 2½", glossy light green leaves.

'Jim Dandy' – 3'–6' × 4'–8'. Early-flowering dwarf male. No berries. Slow-growing, dense, upright, rounded form. Glossy green leaves fade to a purplish green and then yellow before drop. Long blooming period.

Later-blooming varieties:

'Sunset' – 8' × 9'. Vigorous spreading habit. Large, early coloring, reddish orange to dark red berries, arranged singly or two to five on a short branch. Profuse berry production.

'Winter Gold' – 7' × 8'. An upright, rounded habit. Showy, bright orange-yellow (also called peach or apricot) berries. Lustrous medium green leaves.

ABOVE: *A pruned winterberry in late autumn."*
LEFT: *A new installation of winterberry in a rain garden."*
BELOW: *'Winter Gold' in early autumn."*

'**Winter Red**' – 6'–8' tall and wide. An upright, rounded habit. Large, profuse, bright red fruit persisting throughout the winter and often to early spring. Lustrous dark green leaves.

'**Southern Gentleman**' – 6'–8' tall and wide. Late-flowering male. No berries.

Ilex vomitoria

Yaupon Holly

ATTRIBUTES/USE IN LANDSCAPE – The yaupon is an evergreen, large shrub or small tree. It is valued for its attractive form, foliage, and berries. It grows well under a variety of conditions and takes pruning and shearing well. Yaupon is useful as a specimen plant and for screening, hedging, rooftop, and rain gardens, in residential, park, commercial, and naturalizing and seaside projects. Yaupon is an excellent plant for wildlife.

SEASONS OF INTEREST

| WINTER | SPRING | SUMMER | AUTUMN |

FORM – Yaupon is an upright, multi-stemmed large shrub or small tree. There is considerable natural variation within the species. In the wild, yaupon

USDA Zones: 7–9		
SUN	**MOISTURE**	**pH**
Full sun to full shade	Dry to wet	3.5–6.5

grows 12'–20' (25') tall with an equal amount of spread, with a loose, open habit, spreading slowly through stolons. The growth rate is medium to fast. There are many cultivated varieties with varied, reliable growth habits ranging from spreading dense dwarfs to narrow, upright, and weeping.

COLOR – The ½"–2" leaves are a shiny, leathery dark green and have a nearly smooth margin with small rounded teeth. They are oval to oblong in shape. The new leaves have a reddish cast. The inconspicuous, fragrant white flowers are followed

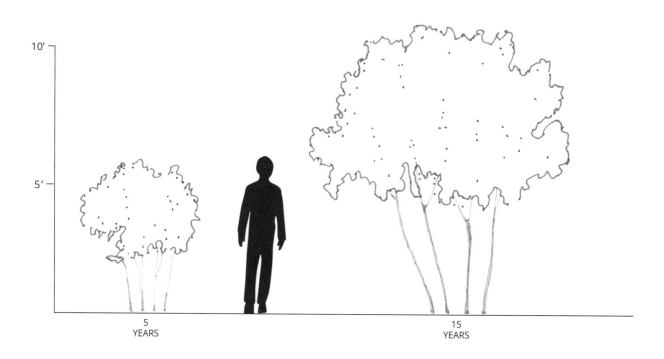

10'

5'

5
YEARS

15
YEARS

A species form of yaupon.

by showy, profuse, ¼" red (rarely yellow) berries on female plants in autumn. The berries persist through the winter or beyond. The berries are sought after as winter food for many species of birds. The light gray bark contrasts nicely with the evergreen foliage.

TEXTURE – Medium fine.

CULTURE – Yaupon is native along the coastal plain from Virginia south to Florida and Texas, where it grows in many habitats including both wet and dry soils.

A pendulous variety of yaupon holly.

the yaupon's growth rate responds well to nutrients and rich soils.

Yaupon is tolerant of moderate drought and periodic flooding, and very tolerant of both soil and atmospheric salt, soil compaction, erosion, wet soil, and air pollution. It is very resistant to nematodes that affect other shrubs, particularly Japanese holly, *Ilex crenata*, in the South.

There are few insect and disease pests. Deer do not favor yaupon.

COMPANION PLANTS – In nature, yaupon is often associated with live oak, post oak, American holly, and winterberry. It combines well and thrives in the same growing conditions as sweetbay magnolia, titi, summersweet, Virginia sweetspire, spicebush, and wax myrtle.

'Schilling's Dwarf' as a ground cover in a parking island.

Full sun is best for berry production on female plants. Yaupon tolerates both sandy soils and heavy clay. It is tolerant of shade, but its habit is much more open in the shade than when grown in full sun.

Like all hollies, the sexes are separate, so a male plant must be present for female plants to produce berries.

Yaupon responds well to pruning and shearing. Pruning is not required, but plants may be pruned to achieve the desired landscape effect. It may even be used for topiary and espalier. Like other hollies,

The 'Nana' variety left unpruned.

WILDLIFE – The berries on female plants provide abundant fruit for many species of birds and small mammals. Yaupon provides year-round wildlife cover and is a larval host.

CULTIVATED VARIETIES – The cultivated varieties provide variation in form, foliage, and berry production. For berries, a male is required for every eight females.

'**Schilling's Dwarf**' – 3'–4' by same, male; a dense, symmetrical mound. Fine textured with smaller leaves, ½"–1½" long. It is excellent as a formal, low, sheared hedge.

'**Nana**' – A female, dwarf form similar to 'Schilling's Dwarf'.

'**Pride of Houston**' – Female with good berry production. The form is upright and more uniform, growing to about 15' tall × 8' wide.

The 'Will Fleming' in a southern landscape.

'**Will Fleming**' – A very narrow, upright form with a tendency to flop, requiring support or selective pruning. Male cultivar.

'**Pendula**' – 15'–20' × 6'–12', a distinct, irregular form, occurring naturally (zones 8b–9a+), with cultivated varieties of its own. There are female and male forms.

Illicium floridanum

Florida Anise Tree

ATTRIBUTES/USE IN LANDSCAPE – The Florida anise tree is a tall, aromatic, evergreen shrub for shade, with attractive flowers and glossy foliage. Use as a specimen or dense screen, for naturalizing, as a woodland border, in rain gardens, and along streams and other bodies of water.

SEASONS OF INTEREST

| WINTER | SPRING | SUMMER | AUTUMN |

FORM – Florida anise tree is a large shrub or, in the South, a small tree from 6'–20' depending on location. It is usually a large shrub, up to 8' × 8', with close branching. The branching habit and evergreen foliage combine to make a dense screen in shady locations. It will usually produce sprouts from the roots and can form dense thickets, particularly in

USDA Zones: 6b–11		
SUN	**MOISTURE**	**pH**
Full shade	Dry to wet	5–6.5

naturalized plantings. It has a medium growth rate and is long-lived.

COLOR – The medium green, 2"–8" lanceolate leaves are pale below with red leaf stalks. They are very fragrant when bruised, with a scent similar to anise, hence the common name. The unique and profuse, 1"–2" diameter single flowers are usually maroon and are borne in the axils of new leaves in late spring; they are usually hidden in the foliage, but they make their presence known by emitting a foul smell sometimes described as "wet dog." The brown fruit is 1"–1½", star shaped and interesting, but not particularly attractive.

TEXTURE – Medium in summer and winter.

10'

5'

| 5 | 10 |
| YEARS | YEARS |

ABOVE: *Florida anise tree in spring, Mt. Cuba Center, Delaware.*
RIGHT: *The unique, late-spring flowers.*

CULTURE – Florida anise tree is native to moist, sandy, acid soils of the swamps near the Gulf of Mexico coastal areas from the panhandle of Florida westward to Louisiana. While it is native to such a warm climate, I have not seen it damaged in my southern Maryland garden, even in temperatures to –10°F. In this location, adjacent plants provide some winter shade and wind protection. It should be perfectly hardy in zone 6b.

Organic, rich, moist soil and shade suit it best.

Florida anise tree in a woodland.

Florida anise tree is one of the finest native shrubs for shade. The foliage tends to yellow in full sun. It is tolerant of drought and wind in shady locations and is rarely bothered by insect pests or disease. The branches bounce back after heavy loads of ice and snow and are rarely broken.

It seldom needs pruning but can be sheared.

Although the common name is derived from the leaves having an anise fragrance, the leaves of *Illicium* are toxic.

I. parviflorum, yellow anise tree, is a close relative and a better performer in the Deep South, especially in more sunny locations. The greenish yellow flowers are smaller than Florida anise tree. The leaves are lighter green, stiffer, more rounded at the apex, and possess a distinctive licorice aroma when bruised.

Florida anise tree has no serious insect or disease issues. Deer will not browse the foliage due to the spicy fragrance.

COMPANION PLANTS – Florida anise tree combines well with shade-loving wildflowers, herbaceous perennials, and shrubs, including southern magnolia, yaupon, *Rhododendron* spp., Virginia sweetspire, spicebush, winterberry, inkberry, needle palm, and dwarf palmetto.

WILDLIFE – Florida anise tree provides cover for birds, mammals, and aquatic life. Its pollen is attractive to bees.

CULTIVATED VARIETIES – Select for flower color, cold hardiness, and foliage color.

'Alba' – White flowers.
'Halley's Comet' – Similar to the species, but improved cold hardiness (zone 6a) and faster growth. Larger blossoms.
'Shady Lady' – Foliage margins are white, with light pink flowers.
'Pink Frost' – Leaves with cream margins and green centers; leaves are rose tinted in cold weather; flowers are maroon red.

Itea virginica

Virginia Sweetspire

ATTRIBUTES/USE IN LANDSCAPE – The Virginia sweetspire is a small- to medium-sized, deciduous to "evergreen" shrub. Where deciduous, the leaves have a long-lasting, attractive autumn color. The showy, profuse, lightly fragrant, white flowers bloom in early summer at a time when other shrubs may not be blooming. Use as a specimen and for informal borders, rain gardens, rooftops, massing, naturalizing in a moist or wet area, stream and pondside stabilization, or as a woodland edge in residential, park, commercial, or highway use. Varieties are more readily available than the wild species.

USDA Zones: 5–8		
SUN	**MOISTURE**	**pH**
Full sun to full shade	Dry to wet	4.5–6.5

SEASONS OF INTEREST

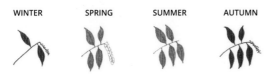

WINTER   SPRING   SUMMER   AUTUMN

FORM – Virginia sweetspire is an erect but informal spreading, arching, multi-stemmed mound, readily forming colonies. The wild species is about 3' × 3' in the North but can reach 10' × 10' in the South. The stems branch primarily at their ends. In moist, sunny conditions, itea spreads by easily controlled suckering and may become wider than tall. 'Henry's Garnet' is 3'–4' tall × 4'–6' wide.

COLOR – White, lightly fragrant flowers appear in early summer for two weeks. They are produced on 3"–6" terminal, curving or pendulous racemes on the wild variety. The flowers resemble a bottlebrush and make an attractive addition to the landscape. Leaves are medium to dark green and, where deciduous, the persistent leaves are red-purple, orange, and yellow when grown in shade and a beautiful burgundy red when grown in full sun. The medium green, oblong leaves are totally deciduous to the north and increasingly evergreen to the south. 'Henry's Garnet' turns a red-purple fall color. The shiny red-purple leaf stems are appealing in the winter.

TEXTURE – Medium in all seasons.

CULTURE – Virginia sweetspire is native to the southeastern states as far north as Pennsylvania and New Jersey.

    Its rate of growth vertically is slow, but the horizontal spread may be fairly rapid. The shrub readily forms colonies. In the more southern area of its range, the rapid spread of the species and cultivated varieties may be considered objectionable. In nature, it is found in sandy, wet, acid soil, but

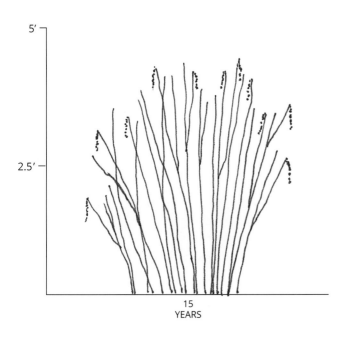

5'

2.5'

15
YEARS

TOP: *'Henry's Garnet' in bloom.*
ABOVE: *Flowers with pollinator.*
LEFT: *'Henry's Garnet' as a specimen in the landscape.*

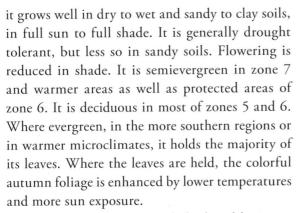

The stems and foliage of the species in winter.

'Henry's Garnet' in autumn.

it grows well in dry to wet and sandy to clay soils, in full sun to full shade. It is generally drought tolerant, but less so in sandy soils. Flowering is reduced in shade. It is semievergreen in zone 7 and warmer areas as well as protected areas of zone 6. It is deciduous in most of zones 5 and 6. Where evergreen, in the more southern regions or in warmer microclimates, it holds the majority of its leaves. Where the leaves are held, the colorful autumn foliage is enhanced by lower temperatures and more sun exposure.

Virginia sweetspire is rarely bothered by insect pests or disease. Deer rarely cause serious damage by browsing. Even if severely browsed, the plants usually recover rapidly.

COMPANION PLANTS – In nature, Virginia sweetspire can be found with bald cypress, river birch, sweetbay magnolia, inkberry, winterberry holly, swamp azalea, summersweet, and other plants that thrive in moist soil and shade. It combines well and thrives in the same growing conditions as southern magnolia, oakleaf hydrangea, and needle palm.

WILDLIFE – Virginia sweetspire attracts butterflies and other pollinators. Birds eat the seeds.

CULTIVATED VARIETIES – Virginia sweetspire has become more well-known since the introduction of 'Henry's Garnet' in the 1980s.

'Henry's Garnet' – The most commercially available form. Compact growth habit with lustrous bronzed to dark green foliage. The flowers are showier than the species, and the autumn foliage is an excellent red-purple. 3'–4' tall × 4'–6' wide.

'Sprich' ('Little Henry') – A more compact form, 2'–4' tall.

Juniperus horizontalis

Creeping Juniper

ATTRIBUTES/USE IN LANDSCAPE – Creeping juniper is a popular, low, woody, evergreen shrub, noted for its aromatic foliage and ability to thrive in hot, dry situations. It is used primarily as a ground cover, edging plant, on top of walls, on steep slopes, on rooftops, and in rock gardens and parking area buffer strips. Creeping juniper has a high tolerance for salt and is a good plant for wildlife.

SEASONS OF INTEREST

WINTER	SPRING	SUMMER	AUTUMN

FORM – Creeping juniper is a procumbent, low-growing, mat-forming, irregular shrub. It is variable in nature, but it typically grows up to 1' tall, spreading 5'–10'. The growth rate is slow, to 10' diameter in 10 years, and they are long-lived.

COLOR – The evergreen foliage is medium green to blue-green with a glaucous, blue, waxy bloom in summer. Creeping juniper turns purplish or burgundy in late autumn and winter. The foliage consists of either a juvenile needlelike form or an adult scalelike form, borne on branchlets along the long, horizontal, rooting stems. The foliage and stems are aromatic. The ¼" gray-blue berries (actually fleshy seed cones) occur on female plants but

USDA Zones: 3–9		
SUN	**MOISTURE**	**pH**
Full sun	Dry to moist, well drained	5–8.5

are not especially ornamental. The varieties seem to produce less fruit.

TEXTURE – Fine.

CULTURE – Creeping juniper is native in the eastern United States from the coast of Maine south to Long

The fine texture of creeping juniper is a useful design element.

2.5'

5
YEARS

10
YEARS

The 'Wiltonii' variety.

Island, scattered sites in New York, and along the coast of Lake Michigan.

Creeping juniper does best in full sun and a well-drained soil. It grows well in both acid and moderately alkaline soils and in moderately dry to moist soils. It will tolerate extreme drought and air pollution. Creeping juniper thrives in both clay and gravelly or sandy soils as long as drainage is adequate. It is intolerant of shade, poorly drained soils, and flooding. Stems will root when in contact with the ground, enhancing its ability to stabilize slopes. Creeping juniper takes pruning well.

Insects and diseases are occasionally a problem, especially in areas of high humidity and in partial shade. Spider mites may be a problem when plants are stressed. Deer may browse in winter.

COMPANION PLANTS – Companions include sweet fern, sumacs, native grasses, and drought-tolerant perennials.

WILDLIFE – The berrylike cones, when present, on female plants are relished by many species of birds and small mammals. The plant provides a habitat for birds and small mammals. It is a larval host.

CULTIVATED VARIETIES – Choose varieties for consistent form and color.

'**Bar Harbor**' – 9"–12" × 6'–7' wide. Gray-blue foliage becomes purplish in winter. Usually male.

'**Mother Lode**' – Feathery, bright gold in summer turning a yellow-orange in autumn, then tinged with purple in winter.

'**Prince of Wales**' – 3"–6" × 3'–6'. Medium green to green-blue with a silvery-purple-tinged winter coloring. Female.

'**Wiltonii**' ('**Blue Rug**') – 4"–6" × 6'–8', quite prostrate, with silver-blue summer foliage. The winter foliage has a purplish tinge.

Lindera benzoin

Spicebush

ATTRIBUTES/USE IN LANDSCAPE – The spicebush is an underused, multi-season shrub noted for its very early, fragrant, yellow flowers, bright red berries (drupes), and excellent yellow autumn color. It is useful as an understory shrub, in shrub borders, rain and rooftop gardens, and for massing and naturalizing in sun to shade with moderately dry to wet soils. All parts emit a spicy fragrance when bruised. Spicebush has high value for wildlife.

SEASONS OF INTEREST

WINTER	SPRING	SUMMER	AUTUMN

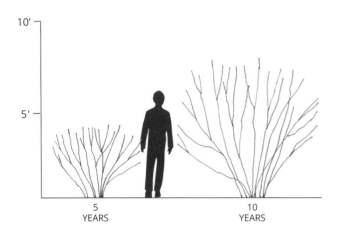

FORM – The spicebush is a medium to tall, dense, upright to rounded shrub typically about 6'–8' (18'–20') tall and nearly as wide. The growth rate is usually medium, but it is fast in moist, well-drained, rich soil, and slower in drier soils. Spicebush can live to about 50 years.

COLOR – The 3"–5" long leaves are medium green and have a very spicy fragrance when bruised or brushed. In spring, showy, profuse small clusters of

USDA Zones: 4–8		
SUN	**MOISTURE**	**pH**
Full sun to full shade in all seasons	Moist to wet	6–6.5

sweetly fragrant, bright yellow flowers bloom. The bloom brightens woodlands before most plants have begun to grow. The sexes are separate, with showier flowers, in slightly larger clusters, on male plants. The flowers on female plants are followed by ½" glossy, oval drupes, which ripen to scarlet red. Although the drupes are relatively short-lived (birds devour them) and are partially obscured by the foliage at a distance, they are remarkably attractive when viewed close-up. The autumn foliage color is a bright yellow. The color is consistent on almost all plants of this species and in almost every year.

TEXTURE – Medium in all seasons.

A male spicebush in early spring.

ABOVE: *Autumn foliage on large plant at woodland edge.*
RIGHT: *Early-spring flowers.*

CULTURE – Spicebush is native to moist woodlands over much of the eastern half of the United States. In colonial times, woodlands with quantities of spice-bush were sought out because large numbers of this plant could indicate a very rich soil.

Although such rich, moist soils produce the fastest growth, spicebush can also grow well in sandy soils, and it tolerates moderate drought. A slightly acid soil suits it best. Spicebush is tolerant of clay soils, periodic flooding, and salt.

Flowering is best when planted with some sun. The foliage may drop early in dry seasons when planted in sandy soils. Plants grow best when planted from containers, as the coarse, fibrous root system is sometimes slow to establish. The leaves and twigs are used to make a spicy tea.

There are few diseases and insects that pose prob-lems for spicebush. It is sometimes browsed by deer, but usually not a favorite. In fact, spicebush can

Young plant form in autumn.

Spicebush autumn fruit on a female plant.

become dominant in favorable locations where more deer-palatable plants are companions.

COMPANION PLANTS – The spicebush naturally grows with white oak, sugar maple, red maple, sweet gum, shagbark hickory, American holly, eastern redbud, flowering dogwood, smooth hydrangea, Virginia sweetspire, ferns, and others.

WILDLIFE – The flowers attract butterflies and other pollinators. The drupes provide food for birds and small mammals. Spicebush is the host plant for the spicebush swallowtail and other larvae.

CULTIVATED VARIETIES

'Xanthocarpa' – Orange-yellow fruit.
'Rubra' – Reddish flowers in large clusters; a male variety.

Morella cerifera

Southern Wax Myrtle, Southern Bayberry

ATTRIBUTES/USE IN LANDSCAPE – Southern wax myrtle is an attractive, evergreen tall shrub or small tree. It is valued for its dense and fragrant foliage, fast growth, and good response to pruning. The southern wax myrtle is tolerant of salt and many soil conditions. It is useful as a fast-growing screen and filler, for hedging and massing, in rain and seaside gardens, and as erosion control along stream banks, where it forms thickets. Southern wax myrtle works well for residential, city, highway, and conservation plantings. It is good for wildlife.

SEASONS OF INTEREST

WINTER	SPRING	SUMMER	AUTUMN

FORM – Southern wax myrtle is an evergreen, upright, open, often multi-stemmed, dense tall shrub or small tree reaching 15'–20' (30') tall by the same width. Trunks can be up to 10" in diameter. It has

USDA Zones: 7–10		
SUN	**MOISTURE**	**pH**
Full sun to part shade	Dry to wet	4.5–6.5

a very fast growth rate, even 3' per year, and takes pruning well. It is rather short-lived.

COLOR – The evergreen leaves are light olive green, 2"–4" long, ¼"–⅜" wide, narrow, oblanceolate, with small, rounded serration at tip margins. On female plants, the ⅛" pale blue-gray, wax-covered berries are clustered profusely along the stem. The berries mature in summer and autumn and may persist into the following spring. The leaves and berries are aromatic when bruised. The attractive bark is light gray, thin, and smooth. The fragrance of the foliage is pleasantly spicy when bruised or brushed.

TEXTURE – Medium fine.

CULTURE – Southern wax myrtle is native, and common, in many habitats from the coast of New Jersey south through Florida and into Texas and

New growth and mature foliage.

A sheared southern wax myrtle.

South America. Plants in moist to wet sites tend to form thickets and be larger than those grown in drier sites. It was formerly known as *Myrica cerifera*.

Southern wax myrtle prefers a moist site in full sun, where berry production is most abundant. It is tolerant of soil and aerosol salt, drought, flooding, heat, and compaction. The sexes are generally separate, so at least one male plant must be present for female plants to produce berries.

Wax myrtles' fast growth and short life span may require them to be replanted every decade or so. The *Morella* spp. take pruning and frequent shearing well. They are nitrogen fixing and useful for restoration projects. In zone 7 winters, the leaves of southern wax myrtle may be burned in a cold, windy location during abnormal cold spells. Wax myrtle is frequently damaged by high winds, snow, and ice, especially when it is allowed to grow to large sizes.

M. pensylvanica, northern bayberry, is a related, more northern species (zones 3b–7). It is smaller (6'–12' by same) and more deciduous, although semi-evergreen in the warmer parts of zone 6. The shiny green leaves are broader and more oval, 1½"–4" × ½"–1½", for a more medium-textured plant. In winter the habit and profuse ⅕" berries are revealed, to good advantage. It prefers dry to moist soils and does not tolerate prolonged flooding.

Morella spp. have few insect and disease pests. Deer do not readily browse. However, I have noticed that nursery specimens of southern wax myrtle are more frequently browsed than older, naturally occurring plants, especially during the first year in the garden. *M. cerifera* var. *pumila* is a naturally occurring dwarf variety.

COMPANION PLANTS – Southern wax myrtle associates with longleaf pine, sweetbay, yaupon, inkberry, beautyberry, chokeberry, and swamp azalea.

WILDLIFE – The fruit is eaten by many species of birds. It provides cover and nesting sites for birds and mammals. It is also a host plant for caterpillars and a pollen and nectar provider.

CULTIVATED VARIETIES

'Fairfax' – 4'–5' tall with lighter green leaves.
'Willowleaf' – 5'–6' by same. Very narrow, shiny green leaves.

Species pruned as hedge.

A large naturalized grouping of the wax myrtle species.

Philadelphus inodorus

Scentless Mock Orange

ATTRIBUTES/USE IN LANDSCAPE – Our native mock orange is an ornamental flowering shrub noted for its profuse white flowers. It is tolerant of many soil conditions, particularly drought. Mock orange is effective as a barrier, for slope stabilization, naturalization, shrub borders, and at the woodland edge. It is primarily used in residential landscapes and parks. It is not salt tolerant.

SEASONS OF INTEREST

WINTER	SPRING	SUMMER	AUTUMN

FORM – Mock orange is a dense, medium-sized shrub, 6'–12' by same, with multiple erect, slender stems, arching in maturity to a somewhat rounded crown. This plant is fast growing.

USDA Zones: (5) 6–8		
SUN	**MOISTURE**	**pH**
Full sun to part shade	Dry to moist	5.5–8

COLOR – The most ornamental feature of the native mock orange is the showy, profuse, mid- to late spring flowering display. The pretty 1¾" flowers have four white petals surrounding orange anthers. Usually in clusters of three, they are arranged along new growth. The thin, medium to dark green, obovate leaves are 2½"–3" long and drop in mid-autumn. The brown stems develop a paperlike, peeling, orange-brown to gray-brown bark as they age. The flowers are not fragrant.

TEXTURE – Medium fine in summer, fine in winter.

CULTURE – This mock orange is found in scattered sites, especially forest edges and disturbed areas,

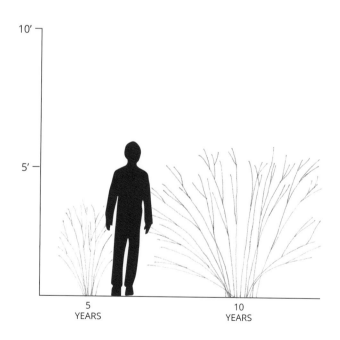

The scentless mock orange flowers.

An unpruned mock orange in spring.

mostly in the southern Appalachians, from Kentucky and North Carolina south to northern Florida and the Gulf States.

The mock orange grows best in full sun and moist soil, but it will flower well in part shade, and it tolerates occasional drought. It enjoys rich, well-drained soils best. With tough, flexible stems, it tolerates wind, snow, and ice well. It will volunteer where it is well suited. Mock orange may be pruned back by a third after flowering. Dead canes can be removed at any time.

Deer do not prefer mock orange, and there are few diseases and insects that pose problems.

COMPANION PLANTS – In nature, this mock orange associates with red and sugar maples, cucumber tree, redbud, native hydrangeas, and bottlebrush buckeye. It combines well with chokeberry, sweetshrub, and the viburnums.

WILDLIFE – Mock orange's pollinators include native bees. The seeds are eaten by some birds.

CULTIVATED VARIETIES – None available in the trade.

Rhapidophyllum hystrix

Needle Palm

ATTRIBUTES/USE IN LANDSCAPE – The needle palm is one of our most cold-hardy palms. It makes a striking evergreen accent and an excellent understory plant. Needle palm is useful in a grouping, border, or container. It is a very effective plant for winter foliage interest, especially in dense shade and in regions where palms do not usually thrive due to cold temperatures. The needle palm is low maintenance, but the sharp, recessed needles require some caution when working around the plant.

SEASONS OF INTEREST

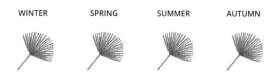

| WINTER | SPRING | SUMMER | AUTUMN |

FORM – Needle palm is a slow-growing, dense fan palm. It ultimately reaches 6'–8' (10') tall with equal spread. Tightly packed stems form a crown that can reach 4' in height on a very old plant. Each

USDA Zones: (5) 6–11		
SUN	**MOISTURE**	**pH**
Summer: partial sun to shade Winter: shade	Moist but withstands dry shade	3.5–6

stem carries about twelve 4'–6' palmate leaves. As the stems mature, slender spines or "needles" grow beneath the leaves on the stubby crown. It suckers freely, and the multiple stems can form an impenetrable thicket over many years.

COLOR – The evergreen leaves have a lustrous dark green upper surface and a dull grayish green color beneath. The flowers and fruit are inconspicuous.

TEXTURE – Coarse in all seasons.

CULTURE – Needle palm is native along coastal

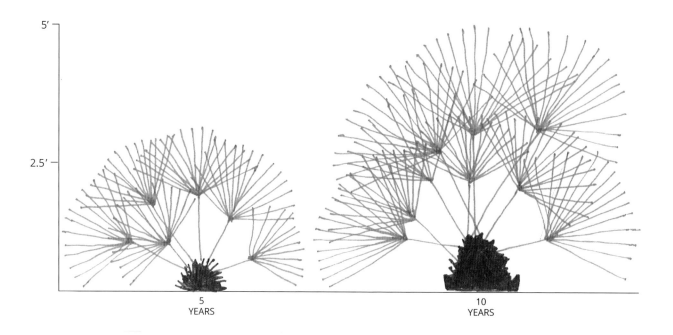

5'

2.5'

| 5 YEARS | 10 YEARS |

A young needle palm as an accent in the garden.

areas of the southeast from South Carolina to Alabama, where it is found along streams and wooded hillsides. It is listed as endangered in its native range. The plant is becoming more available from nurseries and should never be collected in the wild.

Needle palm contributes a tropical feel to landscapes that may be covered in snow many times during the winter. Even though it is native to a mild climate area, the plant is documented as surviving –12°F, with some literature stating that it will survive –20°F. It has been successfully grown in parts of Rhode Island as well as Ohio. Plants growing under pines that are pruned clear of branches for the first 15' are rarely damaged at all in winters that remain above –5°F. A word of caution in assuming the cold-hardiness ratings for needle palms: High summer temperatures are required to gain this degree of winter cold tolerance. Winter shade and protection from harsh winter winds is also preferable, at least for the first several years in the colder

areas. There are splendid specimens in Washington, DC, and in the Philadelphia area. Several specimens planted at the US Botanic Garden in Washington, DC, survive (although more yellow-green in color) harsh winter winds and sun, along with winter road treatment on Independence Avenue. Once established, needle palm is drought tolerant and salt tolerant.

In colder zones (5–7), it is advisable to plant container-grown specimens, in the spring, in order to give the plant an entire summer growing season to become established before the onset of winter. Further south (zone 8), plants may be dug at the nursery and are best transplanted in the heat of summer. In these southern areas, most of the foliage and roots may be removed and the plant may be set slightly deeper than previously grown. Suckers can be planted with success.

The species is usually free from insect and disease pests. It is never or rarely browsed by deer.

Needle palm in the shade of a southern magnolia in Maryland.

COMPANION PLANTS – Combines well with summersweet, oakleaf hydrangea, Virginia sweetspire, winterberry holly, native azaleas, and many other understory plants. It thrives when planted beneath pines and is one of the few plants that will thrive in the dense shade and root competition of southern magnolia.

WILDLIFE – We are not aware of significant relationships.

CULTIVATED VARIETIES – Currently, there are no named cultivated varieties.

Rhododendron calendulaceum

Flame Azalea

ATTRIBUTES/USE IN LANDSCAPE – The flame azalea is one of the most attractive shrubs. It is notable for its large, showy, colorful, mid-spring flowers. The flowers appear before the leaves are fully developed. Use as a shrub border, rain gardens, and for massing and naturalizing.

SEASONS OF INTEREST

WINTER	SPRING	SUMMER	AUTUMN

FORM – The flame azalea is a deciduous, upright, loose open shrub, 6'–12' tall and spread.

COLOR – The flowers are very showy, large, and funnel shaped, 1½"–2½", appearing in terminal clusters of five or more in mid-spring. The color varies from plant to plant and can be clear brilliant

USDA Zones: 4–8		
SUN	**MOISTURE**	**pH**
Full sun to part shade	Moist, well drained	4.5–6.5

yellow, apricot, orange, or brilliant red. The dull, medium green summer foliage turns subdued shades of orange and red in autumn. The 1½"–3" leaves are clustered toward the ends of branches.

TEXTURE – Medium fine in all seasons.

CULTURE – The flame azalea is native to the Appalachian Mountains from southern Pennsylvania and southeast Ohio southward to northern Georgia and Alabama. It is usually found in open areas, or "balds," where it forms thickets that provide unparalleled beauty when in flower.

As with most ericaceous plants, flame azalea prefers acid soils. It is tolerant of drought, but will not tolerate poor drainage, compacted soils, or heavy clay soils. In cultivation, well-drained, organic, rich, acid soils suit this species best. The best flowers are produced when grown in full morning and late-afternoon sun, with high shade during midday. Flame azalea is relatively intolerant of salt.

R. bakeri, Cumberland azalea, is a similar species, blooming slightly later than flame azalea, with orange-red flowers.

The flame azalea is rarely bothered by pests, although azalea sawfly can damage new foliage in the spring. Foliage is sometimes browsed by deer.

COMPANION PLANTS – The flame azalea combines well with oaks, hickories, pines, sourwood, Catawba rhododendron, spicebush, Florida anise tree, and others.

10'

5'

5 YEARS	10 YEARS

ABOVE: *The species, along the Appalachian Trail, Roan Highlands, in North Carolina and Tennessee.*
RIGHT: *The brilliant flame azalea flowers in spring.*

WILDLIFE – The flowers attract butterflies and other pollinators, especially bumblebees. Foliage is sometimes browsed by deer.

CULTIVATED VARIETIES

'**Cherokee**' – Apricot flowers.
'**Golden Yellow Flame**' – Large yellow flowers with a gold blotch.
'**Golden Sunset Flame**' – Flowers are a blend of yellow, gold, and orange.
'**Smokey Mountaineer**' – A compact growth habit with bright orange-red flowers and a good red autumn foliage color.
'**Wahsega**' – Excellent dark red flowers.

Rhododendron catawbiense

Catawba Rhododendron

ATTRIBUTES/USE IN LANDSCAPE – The Catawba rhododendron is a handsome, evergreen, large multi-stemmed shrub noted for its showy lavender to white flowers in mid- to late spring and its lustrous olive-green evergreen foliage. It is useful as a specimen, in mixed shrub borders, and for massing and naturalizing. This species and its hybrid progeny are some of the most successful evergreen rhododendrons for the eastern garden. They are tolerant of sites that would normally not be suitable to the majority of rhododendron species and cultivars.

SEASONS OF INTEREST

WINTER	SPRING	SUMMER	AUTUMN

FORM – Catawba rhododendron is a mounding evergreen, wide-spreading, dense shrub 8'–15' tall and up to 20' wide. It spreads to such widths by

USDA Zones: 4–8		
SUN	**MOISTURE**	**pH**
Full sun to full shade	Moist	4.5–6.5

natural layering (rooting) of the branches touching the ground. The branches are stout and irregular. It has a moderate growth rate and can live 75–100 years.

COLOR – In late spring or early summer, lavender to sometimes white flowers bloom in showy, globular terminal clusters (trusses) 5"–6", lasting about two weeks. The 3"–6" elliptical to oblong, lustrous, thick green to olive-green leaves remain on the plant for two seasons, usually dropping in late spring of the second year.

TEXTURE – Medium to coarse in all seasons.

CULTURE – Catawba rhododendron is one of the most adaptable rhododendrons in cultivation. Native

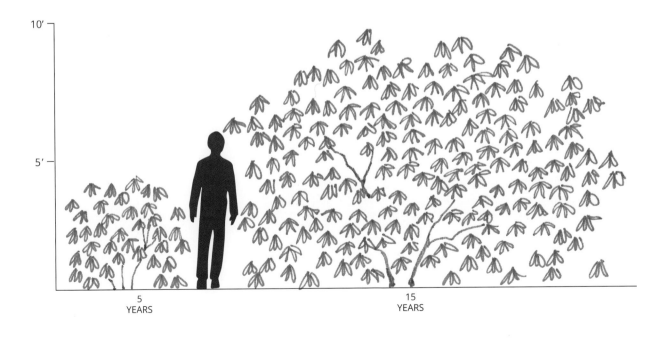

'Roseum Elegans'.

to the higher elevations of the southern Appalachian Mountains from West Virginia through Alabama, Catawba rhododendron is sometimes found growing in pure stands on treeless, open "balds," exposed to full sun and drying winds.

A well-drained, acid, organic, rich, sandy loam soil suits it best. Rhododendrons will not survive poorly drained, heavy, or wet soils. Catawba rhododendron is much more tolerant of heavier soils than most other rhododendron species. Partial shade suits it best in hot, humid coastal areas, but

it also survives in full sun. It flowers in partial shade. The foliage will usually be slightly smaller, more cupped, and a lighter green when grown in full sun as opposed to partial shade. It is sensitive to salt and soil compaction.

Catawba rhododendron has been used extensively for its cold hardiness and tolerance of harsher environments than most rhododendrons. It has also been used in breeding programs to create easier-to-grow cultivars with varying flower color.

In areas of poor air circulation, the flowers may

fall victim to azalea petal blight in especially rainy seasons. Rhododendron may be browsed, and damaged, by deer when other sources of food are scarce in winter.

COMPANION PLANTS – Catawba rhododendron associates with oak and pine spp. and native azaleas.

WILDLIFE – The flowers attract butterflies and other pollinators. Hummingbirds are attracted to the nectar.

CULTIVATED VARIETIES – Varieties provide many choices for bloom color.

'**Album**' – A vigorous, naturally occurring variety with white flowers with a yellow blotch, 6' tall.
'**Roseum Elegans**' – A very tough variety, common in the nursery trade. The lilac-purple flowers are borne in mid-May to early June. (One word of caution—the flower color does not combine well with red brick.) Not far from my house in Maryland, in a lawn at the top of a slope next to a busy highway, is a specimen of 'Roseum Elegans'. The plant is in full sun, a clay loam soil, with grass growing right up to the trunk. It is never watered, and it is exposed to drying

Spring bloom.

winter winds as well as salt spray from ice-melting materials used in the winter on the highway. This plant blooms heavily each year, and surprisingly, it looks indifferent to the abuse it must endure.

Rhododendron periclymenoides

Pinxterbloom Azalea

ATTRIBUTES/USE IN LANDSCAPE – The pinxterbloom azalea is a tall, native, multi-stemmed shrub noted for its early to mid-spring, lavender-pink or sometimes white, slightly fragrant flowers. It is one of the easier native azalea species to grow in cultivation. Use as a shrub border, rain garden, and for massing and naturalizing.

SEASONS OF INTEREST

WINTER	SPRING	SUMMER	AUTUMN

FORM – The pinxterbloom azalea is a deciduous upright, loose, dense, suckering shrub. It varies in size but can be up to 6'–10' tall with a spread of 6'–8'.

COLOR – The flowers, 1"–1½", are funnel shaped, lavender-pink or white, appearing in terminal clusters

USDA Zones: 4–9		
SUN	**MOISTURE**	**pH**
Part shade, especially in warmer areas	Moist, well drained	4.5–6.5

in spring preceding the foliage. The leaves are dark green and oblong to elliptical in shape, 2½" × 1". Leaves sometimes may turn a subdued yellow, orange, or red in the autumn, but usually they are not very colorful.

TEXTURE – Medium fine in all seasons.

CULTURE – The pinxterbloom azalea's native habitats are moist woods and at the margins of swamps from southern New England south to South Carolina and Tennessee. It was formerly known as *R. nudiflorum*.

The pinxterbloom grows best in moisture-retentive but well-drained, organic, rich, acid soil. It is tolerant of moderate droughts and sandy and rocky soils. As with most ericaceous plants, pinxterbloom azalea

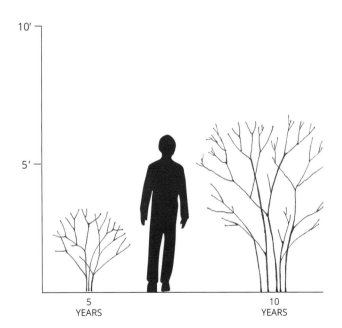

A pollinator appreciating the pinxterbloom.

Pinxterbloom in a natural setting.

prefers acid soils. It will not tolerate poor drainage, compacted soils, or heavy clay soils. The best flowers are produced when grown in full morning sun, with high shade during the hottest time of the day. It is relatively intolerant of salt.

Azalea sawfly can damage new foliage in the spring, and the foliage is sometimes browsed by deer.

COMPANION PLANTS – The pinxterbloom azalea grows and combines well with oaks, hickories, magnolias, pines, hydrangea, hollies, Virginia sweetspire, Florida leucothoe, summersweet, and ferns.

WILDLIFE – The flowers attract butterflies and other pollinators, especially hummingbirds, and many caterpillars.

CULTIVATED VARIETIES – Cultivated varieties are not readily available in the trade at this writing.

Rhododendron prunifolium

Plumleaf Azalea

ATTRIBUTES/USE IN LANDSCAPE – The plumleaf azalea is a tall, native, multi-stemmed shrub noted for its very late, summer-blooming red flowers. The plumleaf azalea is useful in the shrub border, rain garden, and for massing and naturalizing.

SEASONS OF INTEREST

WINTER	SPRING	SUMMER	AUTUMN

FORM – The plumleaf azalea is a deciduous, upright, loose, open shrub, up to 8'–18' tall with a spread of 6'–8'.

COLOR – The flowers, 1½"–2", are tubular in shape, orange to deep red, appearing in terminal clusters in late July and early August. The plumleaf azalea and the white-flowering *R. viscosum* var. *serrulatum* are usually the latest-blooming native azaleas. Flowers

USDA Zones: 5–9		
SUN	**MOISTURE**	**pH**
Part shade	Moist, well drained	4.5–6.5

persist longer when grown in areas with afternoon shade. The buds for the next season are usually formed before the flowers of the current season open. The foliage is dark green and, as the common name implies, very similar in size and shape to the leaves of a plum tree. The 2½" × 1" leaves can turn a subdued yellow, orange, or red in autumn, but usually they are not very colorful.

TEXTURE – Medium fine in all seasons.

CULTURE – The plumleaf azalea grows naturally in a limited area at the base of ravines and along streams in Georgia (where it is listed as endangered due to logging practices) and Alabama. Removal of the plant from the wild is not suggested and may be illegal.

As with most ericaceous plants, plumleaf azalea prefers acid soils. It is tolerant of drought and heat, but it will not tolerate poor drainage, compacted soils, or heavy clay soils. In cultivation, well-drained, organic, rich, acid soils suit this species best. The best flowers are produced when grown in full morning sun, with high shade during the hottest time of the day. It is relatively intolerant of salt.

Plumleaf azalea is rarely bothered by pests, although azalea sawfly can damage new foliage in the spring. Foliage is sometimes browsed by deer.

COMPANION PLANTS – The plumleaf azalea occurs naturally and combines well with oaks, hickories, magnolias, pines, native hydrangea and

ABOVE: *Pollinators find the plumleaf azalea very attractive.*
RIGHT, TOP: *The species, Calloway Gardens, Georgia.*
RIGHT, BOTTOM: *The brilliant, midsummer flowers.*

hollies, Virginia sweetspire, Florida leucothoe, summersweet, and ferns.

WILDLIFE – The flowers attract butterflies and other pollinators, especially hummingbirds, and dozens of caterpillars.

CULTIVATED VARIETIES

'**Pine Prunifolium**' – Especially attractive dark red flowers in summer.

'**Lewis Shortt**' – Superior dark red flowers in summer.

'**Cherry Bomb**' – Selected for large orange-red flowers in summer.

'**Coral Glow**' – Unusual pink-orange flowers in summer.

'**Peach Glow**' – Pink-orange flowers in midsummer.

Rhododendron viscosum

Swamp Azalea

ATTRIBUTES/USE IN LANDSCAPE – The swamp azalea is an attractive, underused, multi-stemmed shrub noted for showy, creamy white, extremely fragrant, tubular flowers in late spring to early summer. The lustrous green summer foliage turns an excellent vibrant red autumn color. Use as a shrub border, rain garden, and for massing and naturalizing.

SEASONS OF INTEREST

WINTER	SPRING	SUMMER	AUTUMN

FORM – Swamp azalea is a deciduous, upright, loose open shrub, 3'–8' (15') tall. It spreads slowly by suckering.

COLOR – In very late spring or early summer, 1¼" × 2" sticky white tubular flowers are borne in terminal clusters, persisting for two weeks or more. The leaves, up to 2½" long, are a lustrous dark green that can turn a brilliant red in the autumn. The flowers are exceedingly fragrant. Cultivars offer pink-flowering

USDA Zones: 5–8		
SUN	**MOISTURE**	**pH**
Full sun to part shade	Moist	4.5–6.5

options. It is one of the latest-blooming deciduous (native) azaleas.

TEXTURE – Fine in all seasons.

CULTURE – The swamp azalea occurs naturally along the coastal plain of the East Coast from Maine to Mississippi, excluding some of the Florida peninsula. It grows in swampy areas, where it may experience periodic flooding or periods of drought.

The native azaleas are all tolerant of partial shade, but flowering occurs best in full sun. They will not survive poorly drained heavy or wet soils.

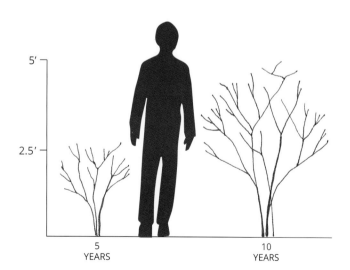

The very fragrant, late-spring to early-summer flowers.

ABOVE: *Swamp azalea in late spring to early summer.*

Autumn foliage.

Even though this shrub is native to swampy areas and subject to short periodic flooding, the soil where it grows is almost exclusively sandy with very rapid drainage. Swamp azalea is usually found growing on small rises above the marsh, known as hummocks. The shallow roots are supplied with oxygen as soon as any short-lived floodwaters recede. In cultivation, well-drained, organic, rich, acid soils suit this species best. When growing in such soils, swamp azalea tolerates moderate drought. It is sensitive to salt.

R. atlanticum, coast azalea, is another swamp-inhabiting native azalea. It is found along the coastal plain from New Jersey and Pennsylvania south to Georgia. Coast azalea has very fragrant white tubular flowers in mid-spring. Coast azalea reaches 3' tall and spreads by underground stolons to form clumps. The leaves on coast azalea are bluish green.

R. viscosum var. *serrulatum* (*R. serrulatum*), sweet azalea, is very similar in appearance and cultural requirements to swamp azalea. The white, usually slightly less fragrant flowers appear in very late summer after the flower buds for the following year have appeared. Along with some plumleaf azaleas, swamp azalea is one of the last native azaleas to flower.

Swamp azalea is rarely bothered by pests, although azalea sawfly can damage new foliage in the spring. Foliage is sometimes browsed by deer, but it is not preferred.

COMPANION PLANTS – Swamp azalea associates with bald cypress, loblolly pine, arborvitae, red maple, sweetbay magnolia, ilex glabra, summersweet, Virginia sweetspire, titi, and winterberry.

WILDLIFE – The flowers attract butterflies and other pollinators. Hummingbirds are attracted to the nectar. Our deciduous azaleas support dozens of species of caterpillars.

CULTIVATED VARIETIES – Choose for flower and foliage color variations.

'Delaware Blue' – Fragrant clusters of white flowers in early summer. The foliage has a powder blue color.
'Pink and Sweet' – Purplish pink flowers have a golden flare in the throat and a spicy, sweet fragrance. Striking blossoms are set off by deep green foliage that turns red each fall.
'Lollipop' – Clear pink flowers with a wonderful vanilla scent.
'Parade' – Bright pink flowers are very fragrant in summer.

Rhus aromatica

Fragrant Sumac

ATTRIBUTES/USE IN LANDSCAPE – The fragrant sumac is a low, sprawling, colony-forming shrub noted for its glossy, dark green, aromatic summer foliage; attractive red berry clusters on female plants; excellent autumn colors; and ability to thrive in hot, dry situations. It is useful in shrub borders, as a ground cover, for steep slope stabilization, parking buffer strips, rooftop gardens, and for massing and naturalizing. Fragrant sumac is an excellent plant for wildlife.

SEASONS OF INTEREST

WINTER	SPRING	SUMMER	AUTUMN

FORM – Fragrant sumac is a low-growing, dense, irregular shrub. It is variable in nature, but typically 2'–6' tall, spreading to 8'. The growth rate is slow to moderate.

COLOR – The small, pale yellow flowers on terminal clusters, to 1", appear in early spring, before leaf out. The tan, immature male catkins may hang on into the winter. The leaves are medium to dark to blue-green and glossy on the upper surface. The three leaflets, 1"–1½", are coarsely toothed. The ¼" fuzzy red berries hang in dense, 1½" clusters. They ripen in

5'

3 YEARS	10 YEARS

USDA Zones: 4–9		
SUN	**MOISTURE**	**pH**
Full sun to part shade	Dry to moist	5–7

early autumn and can persist throughout the winter, when they darken. The autumn foliage colors are orange, red, and purple, with best color in lighter soils.

TEXTURE – Medium.

CULTURE – Populations of fragrant sumac occur in the eastern United States from southern Maine to Florida.

'Gro-Low' as a ground cover in part shade.

'Gro-Low' summer foliage.

'Gro-Low' in early autumn.

Fragrant sumac is intolerant of dense overhead shade. Although it will grow well in a shady location, full sunlight for at least eight hours per day during the growing season will produce the best results. Fruit production and autumn foliage coloration is best when planted in full sun.

Fragrant sumac grows well in both acid and moderately alkaline soils and in moderately dry to moist soils. It will tolerate extreme drought. In cultivation, fragrant sumac is tolerant of difficult sandy and gravelly soils and clay soils as long as drainage is adequate. It is very salt tolerant.

Stems will root in contact with the ground, enhancing its ability to stabilize slopes. It may be pruned to the ground to reinvigorate or maintain dense structure. The aromatic foliage may cause contact dermatitis in some people when they touch the plant.

Fragrant sumac is free from serious pests and disease. It is rarely browsed by deer.

The attractive summer foliage.

Early-spring flowers and emerging foliage.

The fragrant sumac species in mid- to late autumn.

WILDLIFE – The flowers support butterflies and other pollinators, especially honeybees and wild bees. The round, fleshy fruits on the female plants are relished by many species of birds and small mammals. Fragrant sumac supports dozens of species of butterfly larvae.

CULTIVATED VARIETIES

'Gro-Low' – 1½'–2' tall × 6'–8' wide. A female clone with glossier foliage and better autumn color. A tall, woody ground cover.

COMPANION PLANTS – Fragrant sumac combines well with many other plants including sweet fern, horizontal juniper, other sumacs, Virginia sweetspire, and perennials including asters.

Rhus copallina

Shining Sumac, Flaming Sumac, Winged Sumac

ATTRIBUTES/USE IN LANDSCAPE – Shining sumac is a colony-forming shrub or small tree. It is notable for its glossy, dark green foliage that becomes an exceptional, brilliant red in autumn. The female plants have attractive red berry clusters, and it is able to thrive in hot, dry situations. Use in shrub borders, on steep slopes, at the woodland edge, for buffer strips around parking areas, and for massing and naturalizing. Shining sumac is an excellent plant for wildlife.

USDA Zones: 4–9		
SUN	**MOISTURE**	**pH**
Full sun to part shade	Dry to moist	5–7

be trained to a single trunk which can be 6–8" in diameter, in cultivation. It is relatively short-lived, to about 40–60 years. The growth rate is usually moderate.

SEASONS OF INTEREST

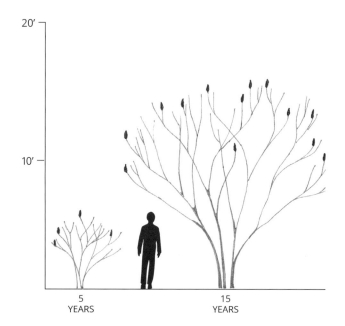

WINTER   SPRING   SUMMER   AUTUMN

FORM – Shining sumac is a tall, open, upright, irregular shrub or small tree to typically about 15'–20' (35') tall with equal spread. Shining sumac can

COLOR – The namesake foliage is a glossy dark green above. The leaves are compound, 8"–12" long with 7 to 21 leaflets arranged on a "winged" stem. The conspicuous, light yellow flower panicles, 4"–8" by half as wide, are held upright and bloom in mid-summer. The attractive, upright, showy, hairy, red berry clusters, 4"–6", ripen on female plants in early autumn and persist throughout the winter. They are particularly interesting and attractive when covered with snow. The autumn foliage color is a bright orange to vivid red. In fact, it is one of the most

20'

10'

5
YEARS

15
YEARS

Foliage and flowers in summer.

Shining sumac as a roadside border.

attractive plants for autumn foliage color. The bark is thin and reddish brown with horizontal lenticels.

TEXTURE – Coarse while dormant, medium in leaf.

CULTURE – Shining sumac is native to nearly the entire eastern United States, from southern Maine through Florida and west into Missouri and Texas.

Shining sumac is most vigorous in moist, well-drained, rich soil, and slow in drier soils. It grows well in both acid and moderately alkaline soils and in moderately dry to moist soils. Shining sumac will tolerate extreme drought. In cultivation it is tolerant of difficult sandy and gravelly soils and clay soils as long as drainage is adequate. It grows well in compacted soils and is very salt tolerant.

Shining sumac is intolerant of dense overhead shade. Full sunlight for at least eight hours per day during the growing season will produce the best results. Fruit production and autumn foliage coloration are best when planted in full sun.

Prune to remove suckers as required and to remove dead twigs and stems. Shining sumac can be trained as an upright single-trunked small tree—by pruning out stems as they appear—or allowed to become a tall, multi-stemmed colony.

Shining sumac is free from serious pests. Insects and diseases are rarely a problem unless grown in heavy shade and/or poorly drained soils. Shining sumac is rarely browsed by deer.

COMPANION PLANTS – Shining sumac combines

The brilliant autumn foliage and attractive berries of shining sumac.

well with longneedle pine, vernal witch hazel, other *Rhus* species, and sun-loving herbaceous perennials such as *Aster* spp., *Solidago* spp., *Asclepias* spp., and so on. Especially attractive when planted with those species that flower in the autumn at the time when its fall foliage is brightly colored.

WILDLIFE – The flowers of shining sumac support pollinators, while the round, fleshy fruits on the female plants are relished by many species of birds and small mammals. Shining sumac supports dozens of species of butterfly larvae.

CULTIVATED VARIETIES

'Creel's Quintet' – A compact, slower-growing form, 8'–10', a particularly attractive spreading female clone. Creamy yellow flower spikes in summer with purple-red autumn foliage. Leaves have five leaflets.

Rhus copallina var. *latifolia* 'Prairie Flame' – A usually smaller, compact form, 4"–8", a spreading male clone. Chartreuse flowers in late spring to early summer. A Morton Arboretum, Illinois, introduction.

Rhus typhina

Staghorn Sumac

ATTRIBUTES/USE IN LANDSCAPE – The staghorn sumac is a colony-forming large shrub or small tree, noted for its large, compound, dark green summer foliage and brilliant red autumn colors; stout, hairy stems; attractive red berry clusters on female plants; and ability to thrive in hot, dry situations. Use in shrub borders, the woodland edge, for stabilizing steep slopes, for buffer strips around parking areas, and for massing and naturalizing. Staghorn sumac is an excellent plant for wildlife.

SEASONS OF INTEREST

| WINTER | SPRING | SUMMER | AUTUMN |

FORM – Staghorn sumac is a tall, open, upright shrub or small tree with picturesque sparse branching. The foliage is only produced on new branch segments. The shrub form can spread to create open colonies, typically to 15'–20' (35') with equal spread.

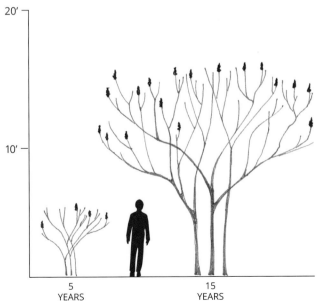

USDA Zones: 4–9		
SUN	**MOISTURE**	**pH**
Full sun to part shade	Dry to moist	5–7

Staghorn sumac is relatively short-lived, about 40–60 years. The growth rate is generally fast. The stem diameter can be 6"–8".

COLOR – The compound leaves, 16"–24" long with 11 to 31 leaflets, are a bright medium green. The conspicuous, terminal, yellow flower panicles, to 8" by half as wide, are held upright and bloom in midsummer. The attractive, dense clusters of fuzzy, dark red, round drupes ripen on female plants in late summer and persist throughout the winter. They are particularly interesting and attractive when covered with snow. The autumn foliage color is a vivid orange. In fact, it is one of the most attractive plants for autumn foliage color. The bark is thin and grayish brown, smooth with numerous lenticels; there are dense light brown hairs on the new growth.

TEXTURE – Coarse.

Staghorn sumac summer foliage and flowers.

'Bailtiger'.

CULTURE – Staghorn sumac is found in the eastern United States from Maine south through West Virginia and the Appalachians into North Carolina, and in Ohio and west through northern Indiana and north through Michigan and Minnesota.

It grows well in both acid and moderately alkaline soils and in moderately dry to moist soils. It is intolerant of poorly drained soils. Staghorn sumac will tolerate extreme drought. In cultivation, it is tolerant of difficult sandy and gravelly soils and clay soils as long as drainage is adequate. It grows well in compacted soils and is very salt tolerant.

Staghorn sumac is intolerant of dense overhead shade. Full sunlight for at least eight hours per day during the growing season will produce the best results. Fruit production and autumn foliage coloration is best when planted in full sun.

This sumac spreads rapidly out of bounds by

Early-autumn foliage.

COMPANION PLANTS – Staghorn sumac combines well with vernal witch hazel, other sumac species, and sun-loving herbaceous perennials such as asters, goldenrods, and milkweeds. It is especially attractive when planted with those species that flower in the autumn at the time when its fall foliage is brightly colored.

WILDLIFE – The flowers support butterflies and other pollinators, especially honeybees and wild bees. The round, fleshy fruit on the female plants is relished by many species of birds and small mammals. Staghorn sumac supports dozens of species of butterfly larvae.

CULTIVATED VARIETIES – Choose for fruiting (sex), autumn coloring, and attractive texture.

'Laciniata' or cutleaf staghorn sumac – The leaflets are deeply incised, giving a fine-textured appearance. It produces a beautiful orange-red to scarlet fall color. Height is to about 15'. Suckers profusely. A female clone.

'Bailtiger' (Tiger Eyes™) – A dwarf, golden-leaved, cut-leaf form. Leaves emerge chartreuse and quickly change to bright yellow. Fall color is orange-red to scarlet. The height is up to 6', and this variety does not sucker as much as 'Laciniata' of the species. A female clone.

suckering in confined areas and therefore may be invasive. Prune to remove suckers as required and to remove dead twigs and stems.

Staghorn sumac is free from serious pests. Insects and diseases are rarely a problem unless grown in heavy shade and/or poorly drained soils. It is rarely browsed by deer.

Sabal minor
Dwarf Palmetto

ATTRIBUTES/USE IN LANDSCAPE – Dwarf palmetto is a very cold-hardy palm. Some forms are as cold-hardy or perhaps more cold-hardy than needle palm. Dwarf palmetto can be used as a striking specimen or accent in an informal grouping, in borders, containers, and rain or rooftop gardens. It is good as an understory plant for use in shade or full sun, in both wet and dry soils, in sand or in heavy clays. Dwarf palmetto is a very effective plant for winter foliage interest, especially in dense shade and in regions where palms do not usually thrive due to cold temperatures. It is highly tolerant of aerial and soil salt.

SEASONS OF INTEREST

WINTER	SPRING	SUMMER	AUTUMN

FORM – Dwarf palmetto is a slow-growing fan palm, with leaves (fronds) reaching 5'–6' tall with a 10'–12' spread in some locations. The leaves can be 3' across with petioles up to 5'. It is usually "trunkless," with the leaves forming a tight mound. In most cases

USDA Zones: 6b–9		
SUN	**MOISTURE**	**pH**
Summer: part shade to shade Winter: part shade	Dry to wet	3.5–6.5

A dwarf palmetto in a Maryland garden.

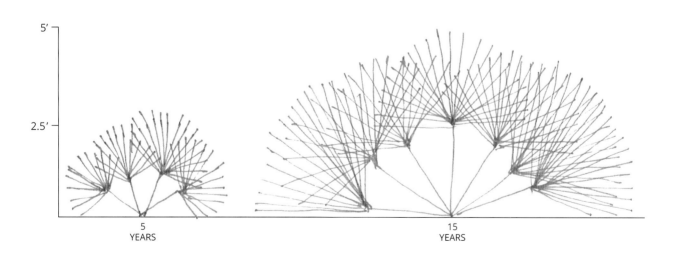

The McCurtain County strain in snow at 5°F.

the trunk actually forms below the soil. In marshy locations the trunk can extend down into the muck several feet, making old specimens of dwarf palmetto very difficult to transplant. There are some varieties of dwarf palmetto that form aboveground trunks. The trunked individuals are usually very slow growing, and wild specimens with 6' trunks may be over a century old.

TEXTURE – Coarse.

COLOR – The leaves are glossy, blue-green to green above and a dull gray-green beneath. In summer, 5'–6' flowering spikes are produced from the crown. The small, white, fragrant flowers are not particularly attractive. They are followed by ¼" black berries that are consumed by birds.

CULTURE – Dwarf palmetto is native along coastal areas of the southeastern United States from North Carolina to Florida, and westward to Texas and Oklahoma, where it is found along streams, in swamps, and along drainage ditches.

Dwarf palmetto is commonly credited with being the second most cold-hardy palm in the world, creating a tropical feel in landscapes where it may be covered in snow many times during the winter. Dwarf palmetto has been successfully grown in parts of coastal Connecticut and Rhode Island. Dwarf palmetto is both drought tolerant and tolerant of

The McCurtain County strain.

extensive flooding. Even though it is native to such a mild climate area, the plant is documented as surviving –10°F, with some literature stating that it will survive –15°F. It should be successful in USDA zones (6b) 7–11, and possibly in warmer areas of zone 6a. A word of caution in assuming these cold-hardiness ratings: High summer temperatures are required to gain this degree of winter cold tolerance. Winter shade and protection from harsh winter winds is also preferable, at least for the first several years in the colder areas. Plants growing under pines that are pruned clear of branches for the first 15' are rarely damaged at all in winters that remain above –5°F. Several dozen specimens planted at the Smithsonian's Air and Space Museum in Washington, DC, survive harsh winter winds and sun, along with the salt spray from treating snow on Independence Avenue. It is very salt tolerant.

In zones 6 and 7, it is advisable to plant container grown, in the spring, in order to give the plant an entire summer growing season to become established before the onset of winter. Volunteer seedlings are usually produced in high numbers.

The species is usually free from insect and disease pests. Deer are almost never a problem with dwarf palmetto.

COMPANION PLANTS – Dwarf palmetto is found in nature with bald cypress, longneedle pine, live oak, sweet gum, black gum, titi, Virginia sweetspire, and summersweet. It combines well with native azaleas (*Rhododendron* spp.) and other understory evergreen and deciduous plants.

WILDLIFE – Numerous bird species eat the black berries. Never or rarely browsed by deer.

CULTIVATED VARIETIES – There are no cultivated varieties (clones). The following naturally occurring strains are sold in nurseries.

'**Bluestem Dwarf Palmetto**' – A strain from Texas that may form trunks to as much as 18' and sometimes produces basal side shoots. Not as hardy as more dwarf forms. To zone 7.
'**Emerald Island Blue Giant**' – Originating in North Carolina, is reliably hardy to at least zone 7. It produces exceptionally large foliage to 8'.
Arkansas strain – Hardy to zone 6b.
Louisiana strain – Often with short trunks and large foliage. Hardy only to zone 7b (7a with protection).
McCurtain County strain – Plants native to McCurtain County, Oklahoma; very hardy when subjected to temperatures well below 0°F in their native area.

Viburnum nudum

Smooth Witherod Viburnum, Possumhaw Viburnum

Viburnum cassinoides

Witherod Viburnum

Note to the reader: These viburnum species are very similar in the landscape and are often considered as one. They are covered together here.

ATTRIBUTES/USE IN LANDSCAPE – These viburnums are medium to large deciduous shrubs known for spring flowering, exceptionally showy fruits, and striking autumn foliage. They are useful as a specimen, in shrub or woodland borders, groupings, for naturalizing or screening, and along streams and water. The witherods are valuable for parks, residential planting, highway planting, rain gardens, and rooftops. They are excellent for wildlife.

SEASONS OF INTEREST

WINTER	SPRING	SUMMER	AUTUMN

FORM – The smooth witherod, 5'–8' (12') by same, is rounded, multi-stemmed, and upright spreading. The witherod viburnum is a bit smaller, at 5'–6' (10'),

USDA Zones: Smooth witherod: 5–9 Witherod: 3–8		
SUN	**MOISTURE**	**pH**
Full sun to part shade	Dry to wet	5.5–6.8

with equal spread. They both have a moderate to fast growth rate.

COLOR – Showy, profuse, creamy white flowers appear in late spring and are arranged in flat-topped clusters (cymes) 2"–4½" wide. The flowers are followed by stunning multicolored clusters of pink berries in late summer, which progress to blue and then a dark blue-purple as they ripen in early autumn and in some varieties persist into winter. The 1½"–4", dark green leaves are oval to lanceolate with a light green underside.

The leaves of smooth witherod are a glossier green, larger, and generally lack the serrated edge

The late-spring bloom of the witherod viburnums.

of the leaves of witherod. In autumn, the foliage for both viburnums can be an attractive orange-red to maroon to dark red-purple. Choose a cultivated variety known for superior coloring when selecting for that trait.

TEXTURE – Medium in all seasons.

CULTURE – Smooth witherod is native to eastern and southeastern swamps, bogs, and low woodlands from coastal Connecticut expanding into the Piedmont as it grows south to Florida and Louisiana. Witherod viburnum is a more northern native and grows throughout the Northeast and Pennsylvania, southward through the Appalachians, then into Georgia and the Gulf States.

The witherods are easily grown in moist to wet, well-drained soil, but these sturdy plants tolerate dry soils as well. They also tolerate sand and clay soils. The witherods flower and fruit best in full sun.

Rarely seriously bothered by insect pests or disease, the witherods are generally not preferred by deer, but may be browsed in some locations.

COMPANION PLANTS – The witherod viburnums are versatile and are found with many other species including oaks, magnolias, flowering dogwood, eastern redbud, clethra, fothergilla, and Virginia sweetspire.

Witherod viburnum in spring.

WILDLIFE – The witherods are excellent plants for wildlife. They provide food for caterpillars as well as food and nesting for birds and cover for wildlife. They also produce pollen and nectar.

CULTIVATED VARIETIES – Varieties offer choices in form as well as color of berries and autumn foliage.

'Bulk' (Brandywine™) – 5'–6' (12'). More compact. Very showy berries. Glossy dark green leaves turn a maroon to dark red in autumn. Fragrance "musky."

'Winterthur' – A compact, dense variety, 6' tall by similar width. Has 4" yellow-white flower clusters, with fruit progressing from pale green to pink-red to deep blue with colors appearing simultaneously for a few weeks. The glossy green leaves turn maroon to dark red-purple in autumn.

Viburnum prunifolium

Blackhaw Viburnum

ATTRIBUTES/USE IN LANDSCAPE – The black-haw viburnum is a deciduous medium to large shrub to small tree known for spring flowering, exceptionally showy fruits, and striking autumn foliage. Use as a specimen, in shrub or woodland borders, groupings, for naturalizing and screening, and along streams and water. It is valuable for parks, residential planting, highway planting, and rain gardens. The blackhaw viburnum is excellent for wildlife.

SEASONS OF INTEREST

WINTER	SPRING	SUMMER	AUTUMN

FORM – As a shrub, blackhaw grows to 12'–15' tall × 8'–12' wide, with stiff, horizontal branching to vase-shaped habit. It may be trained as a single-trunked, rounded-crown small tree and can reach a height of

USDA Zones: 3–8		
SUN	**MOISTURE**	**pH**
Full sun to part shade	Dry to wet	5.5–6.8

30'. This form is more common in its southern range. It has a slow to moderate growth rate.

COLOR – Showy, profuse, creamy white flowers in late spring are arranged in flat-topped clusters 2"–4½" wide. This viburnum is not pleasantly fragrant. The flowers are followed by stunning multicolored pendant clusters of yellow-green to pink berries in late summer, which progress to blue and then a dark

Blackhaw viburnum spring flowering.

20'

10'

5
YEARS

15
YEARS

Blackhaw, in spring, at the woodland edge.

blue-purple as they ripen in early autumn, and in some varieties they persist into winter. The 1½"–4½" dull to shiny green leaves are oval to lanceolate with a pale green underside. In autumn, they can be an attractive bright red or maroon.

TEXTURE – Medium in leaf, coarse in winter.

CULTURE – Blackhaw is native to eastern and southeastern swamps, bogs, and low woodlands from Connecticut south to Florida and Louisiana.

It is easily grown in a moist to wet, well-drained soil, but it is a sturdy plant that tolerates dry soils. Blackhaw grows in acidic sandy to clay soils as well. It is moderately salt tolerant and resistant to drought.

Fruit and foliage in early autumn.

Blackhaw viburnum in the wild, as the leaves unfurl, in early spring.

The blackhaw is rarely seriously bothered by insect pests or disease. They are rarely browsed by deer.

COMPANION PLANTS – Companions for the versatile blackhaw, in nature and cultivation, are numerous and include oaks, magnolias, flowering dogwood, eastern redbud, clethra, fothergilla, and Virginia sweetspire.

WILDLIFE – The blackhaw viburnum is an excellent plant for wildlife. It provides food for many caterpillars and produces pollen and nectar. Blackhaw supports native bees. The berries feed birds, and the plant provides nesting and cover.

CULTIVATED VARIETIES – Varieties are listed, but at this time they are not commonly available.

Yucca spp.

Adam's Needle Yucca, Mound-Lily Yucca, Spanish Bayonet Yucca

ATTRIBUTES/USE IN LANDSCAPE – Yucca is a genus of more than 40 species of perennial shrubs and trees. They are known for their evergreen, tough, swordlike leaves and large, showy panicles of white or whitish flowers. Yuccas are very resilient plants, surviving extreme drought, wind, salt, and alkaline soils. They are very effective as specimens, dramatic accent plants, and container plants in xeriscapes, rooftops, raised parking planters, extreme urban locations, along highways, and in seashore plantings—even extending out onto dunes.

SEASONS OF INTEREST

Evergreen foliage

Flower in bloom

USDA Zones: 5–9		
SUN	**MOISTURE**	**pH**
Full sun to part shade	Dry, well drained	6.5–8

FORM AND COLOR – The yuccas are structured as rosettes of swordlike, stiff or flexible evergreen leaves. They may be trunkless, short trunked and single stemmed, or branched, depending on the species. Yuccas grow slowly and over time spread to form small colonies.

Yucca filamentosa, Adam's needle, is a low evergreen shrub, trunkless or very occasionally short-trunked species. One of the most cold-hardy of the yuccas, Adam's needle is used extensively in regions where the less cold-hardy, southern, trunked species will not flourish. The 2' long and 2½" wide evergreen leaves are

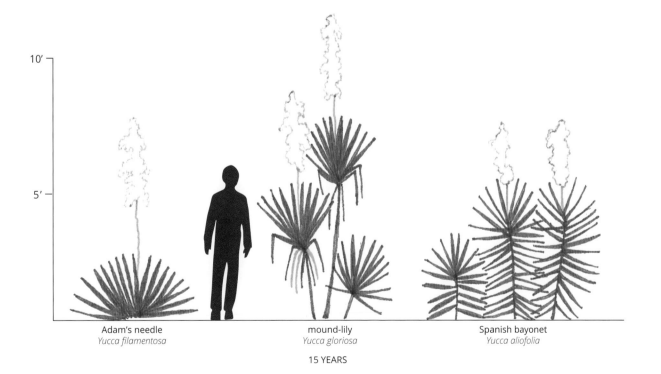

Adam's needle	mound-lily	Spanish bayonet
Yucca filamentosa	*Yucca gloriosa*	*Yucca aliofolia*

15 YEARS

Spanish bayonet and Adam's needle in the landscape.

medium green and radiate from a ground-level fibrous stem. The leaves tend to droop as they age. The margins of the leaves have white threads or "filaments." The flowers are white and produced on 3'–8' panicles, in late spring to midsummer, depending on the region as well as the individual plant and growing season. The fragrant flowers are followed by very attractive green fruit capsules. These are best pruned away to enhance the color and size of the foliage. Adam's needle will sprout from the roots to form clumps.

Yucca gloriosa, mound-lily yucca, is native from North Carolina southward. It is an erect evergreen shrub eventually forming a trunk, or multiple trunks, up to 6'–8' tall. Older plants will develop branches along the trunk. The bluish or grayish green swordlike leaves are about 2" wide and 2'–3' long. They tend to bend near the middle and point downward. In late summer to early autumn, 6'–8' panicles of fragrant white, purple-tinged flowers are produced. The flowers are followed by greenish fruit

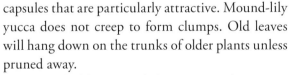

The mound-lily yucca in bloom in late summer.

Adam's needle yucca in the wild, in April.

capsules that are particularly attractive. Mound-lily yucca does not creep to form clumps. Old leaves will hang down on the trunks of older plants unless pruned away.

Yucca aloifolia, Spanish bayonet, or aloe yucca, is a short-trunked species with tight whorls of 1'–1½' long, very stiff and sharp-pointed leaves, which may pose a danger. Spanish bayonet has a distinctive unbranched trunk that will range from 5' to as

much as 20' tall. Trunks can fall over when reaching heights over 10'. They continue to grow and produce new shoots, eventually leading to a large colony of plants. Older leaves, as they die, will droop along the trunk and remain for years unless removed. The white, purple-tinged flowers are produced on 2' panicles in late summer or early to mid-autumn.

TEXTURE – Medium.

CULTURE – Yucca species occur naturally along the coastal plain of the East Coast from coastal Maine (*Y. filamentosa*, Adam's needle, USDA zones 5–10) to Mississippi excluding some of the Florida peninsula. The *Y. gloriosa*, mound-lily, and *Y. aloifolia*, Spanish bayonet, are best in USDA zone 7 and further south. (There are species that are native to the Midwestern and western states that will survive in certain microclimates, or even regional areas of the East, but generally are difficult compared to the species native to the regions within the scope of this book.)

Yuccas are usually found in dry, sandy or clay loam soils in full sun. They do not withstand saturated soils, especially in winter. Good drainage always suits them best, although they tolerate compacted soil as long as it is dry. Although they will survive in light shade, they flower best and maintain the best health in full sun. All species tolerate slightly acid to moderately alkaline soils. They are very tolerant of salt.

The yuccas are rarely bothered by insect pests or disease. Deer rarely browse on yucca.

COMPANION PLANTS – Live oak, yaupon holly, succulents, cactus, and other xeric plants.

WILDLIFE – The flowers attract butterflies and other pollinators, particularly the yucca moth. Yucca is also a larval host. Hummingbirds are attracted to the nectar.

CULTIVATED VARIETIES – Choose for foliage color.

Yucca filamentosa:
'**Bright Edge**' – Green foliage with a distinct thin yellow margin.
'**Golden Sword**' – Green foliage with an irregular yellow central streak.
'**Color Guard**' – Similar to 'Golden Sword' but with a more clearly defined central yellow streak.
'**Hofer Blue**' – Blue-green or silvery in spring fading to greenish blue in winter.

Yucca gloriosa:
'**Mobilis**' – Darker green leaves than the normal species.
'**Variegata**' – Yellow-margined leaves.

Yucca aloifolia:
'**Marginata**' – Leaves are yellow margined.

PART III

SECONDARY PLANTS

The secondary list includes those native plants that have features that are desirable in the landscape but may have problems that outweigh those desirable traits. The following traits and issues should be considered before choosing the trees and shrubs in our secondary list.

1. The plant is susceptible to serious native or exotic diseases or insects or is threatened by serious diseases or insects.
2. The plant has cultural requirements that may be difficult or costly to replicate.
3. The plant lacks cold hardiness for general use in colder locations or is susceptible to wind damage in exposed cold climates.
4. The plant lacks general heat tolerance and is difficult in hot urban areas.
5. The plant is not tolerant of prolonged drought.
6. The plant is not tolerant of air pollution.
7. The plant has a shallow root system that is too competitive for companion plants or poses a threat to roads, walkways, and/or foundations.
8. The plant is short-lived in cultivation, generally less than 50 years.
9. The plant has brittle wood that is susceptible to wind and/or ice and snow damage.
10. The plant is not as ornamental as those plants recommended in the primary lists.
11. The plant drops an unacceptable amount of fruit, twigs, or other debris.
12. The plant possesses an objectionable trait.

OPPOSITE, TOP: *Stewartia malacodendron, silky camellia*
OPPOSITE, BOTTOM: *Rhododendron canescens, mountain azalea*

Trees 50'–80'+

***Fagus grandifolia,* American beech** – 1. Magnificent tree but threatened by beech bark disease.

***Juglans nigra,* black walnut** – 1, 12. Susceptible to a new disease, thousand cankers disease, that threatens its existence.

***Liriodendron tulipifera,* tulip poplar** – 9, 12. Too tall for most landscapes; seems to be especially prone to lightning strikes. The root system is fleshy and easily damaged.

***Magnolia acuminata,* cucumber tree** – 10. The variety *subcordata* is superior in flower and size. The species is usually too large for many landscapes, with flowers usually borne too high to be appreciated.

***Picea glauca,* white spruce** – 1, 4. Susceptible to Cytospora canker, a very serious fungus disease in many areas covered by this book. White spruce is most successful in colder areas away from the coast, where humidity is lower.

***Picea pungens,* blue spruce** – 1. Similar to white spruce, it is susceptible to Cytospora canker, a very serious fungus disease in many areas covered by this book. It is more tolerant of heat than white spruce, but it dislikes heat combined with humidity in coastal zones 7b–8.

***Picea rubens,* red spruce** – 4, 6. A stately coniferous evergreen, only successful in colder parts of zone 5 and further north.

***Quercus nigra,* water oak** – 3, 7, 8, 9. Weak wooded for an oak; holds leaves late into the autumn; semievergreen.

Quercus palustris, **pin oak** – 1. Frequently used in landscapes; seems to be especially prone to bacterial leaf scorch, which ultimately leads to severe dieback or death of the tree. It is short-lived for an oak.

Quercus rubra, **northern red oak** – 1. Same issues as *Q. palustris.*

Tsuga canadensis, **Canadian hemlock** – 1, 6. Very susceptible to severe damage from hemlock woolly adelgid; not very happy in urban locations.

Ulmus americana, **American elm** – 1. Historically, this species was one of the most used and loved landscape trees. Dutch elm disease (DED) almost eliminated its use. Several resistant varieties have been introduced and are extensively used. Unfortunately, a number of new pathogens are threatening even the DED-resistant cultivars (bacterial leaf scorch; elm yellows). It is only mentioned here because some large metropolitan area public commissions and councils still demand its use.

Trees 35'–50'

Catalpa **spp., catalpa** – 1, 9, 11, 12. May be defoliated by the catalpa worm.

Diospyros virginiana, **persimmon** – 8, 10, 11, 12. Attractive bark and foliage. Fruit of female trees is messy.

Gleditsia triacanthos, **honey locust** – 1, 11. A popular landscape plant, especially its thornless cultivars, it is nonetheless very susceptible to mimosa webworm, which will greatly diminish its landscape appeal.

Halesia **spp., silver bell** – 2, 4, 5, 6, 8. As a group they are magnificent, but difficult in urban situations.

Maclura pomifera, **Osage orange** – 11, 12. Long-lived

and tolerant of many conditions. Interesting orange bark. Large, interesting fruit is messy. Deer love it.

Magnolia fraseri, **Fraser magnolia** – 2, 5, 6, 8. A very attractive, native magnolia with exceptionally fragrant flowers, especially in the variety *pyramidata.* It is not as easy to grow as other recommended magnolia species.

Magnolia tripetala, **umbrella tree** – 12. Large, attractive leaves and flowers, but flowers smell terrible.

Robinia pseudoacacia, **black locust** – 1, 7, 11. Exceptionally beautiful displays of pendulous racemes of white, very fragrant flowers in spring cannot make up for the unattractive appearance and disease and insect problems that follow. A very hardy species for use in landfill restoration and other similar projects.

Sassafras albidum, **sassafras** – 1, 8. One of the best native trees for autumn foliage color, it is very successful in some locations, but in others it dies unexpectedly. Susceptible to a new introduced species of ambrosia beetle that attacks members of the laurel family.

Tilia americana, **American linden or basswood** – 1, 10, 12. Nice foliage. Aphids relish.

Trees 15'–35'

Asimina triloba, **pawpaw** – 6, 8, 10. A good understory tree. Edible fruit. Can be invasive.

Crataegus **spp., hawthorns** – 1, 10, 12. Susceptible to lace bugs. Thorns.

Franklinia alatamaha, **Franklin tree** – 2, 3, 4, 5, 6, 7, 8, 9. One of the most beautiful native small trees for flowers and fall foliage, but very difficult in most areas other than the mid-Atlantic coastal plain and Long Island.

***Magnolia fraseri* var. *pyramidata*, pyramid magnolia** – 2, 5, 6, 8. A beautiful, large-leaved magnolia tree, uncommon in cultivation and requiring extra effort.

***Osmanthus americanus*, devilwood** – 3, 8, 10. Lovely evergreen in the South. Cultural requirements may limit its general use.

***Stewartia malacodendron*, silky camellia** – 2, 3, 5, 8. Extremely ornamental, worth the extra effort in certain landscapes, but very difficult for general use.

***Styrax americanus*, American snowbell** – 1, 5, 6, 8. A very attractive small flowering tree. It seems to be susceptible to the recently introduced granulate ambrosia beetle.

Shrubs

***Amorpha fruticosa*, false indigobush** – 10, 12. This plant has fairly attractive small spikes of flowers. It is very easy to grow in many locations, but it can be invasive. It generally does not have any qualities superior to those of other deciduous shrubs mentioned in the primary list.

***Andromeda glaucophylla*, bog rosemary** – 2, 4, 5, 6, 7, 8. For sale every spring in garden centers, this very attractive dwarf evergreen is very difficult to grow, especially in warm, humid climates.

***Arctostaphylos uva-ursi*, bearberry** – 2. Requires sandy soil and is not very tolerant of urban locations. This is a very nice shrub for seashore plantings, even on sand dunes.

***Ceanothus americanus*, New Jersey tea** – 10, 12. Attractive but more difficult to grow in cultivation than one would expect.

***Chamaedaphne calyculata*, leatherleaf** – 2, 4, 5, 6, 7, 8. Requires peaty soil and high water table.

***Cliftonia monophylla*, buckwheat tree** – 2, 3, 5. A beautiful and interesting native shrub or small tree for the South.

***Cornus amomum*, silky dogwood** – 10. Not nearly as ornamental as *Cornus sericea*.

***Corylus americana*, hazelnut** – 1, 6. Becoming more rare in the wild due to disease.

***Dirca palustris*, leatherwood** – 2, 4, 10. An attractive small shrub for late winter and small, early-spring flowers, and early-to-emerge foliage; valuable for its deer resistance.

***Euonymus americanus*, strawberry bush** – 10, 12. Euonymus scale. Deer candy.

***Gaylussacia brachycera*, box huckleberry** – 2, 4, 6, 8. This is an extremely attractive creeping evergreen shrub that can make a very nice ground cover in sandy soils or a wonderful addition to a rock garden. It is not easy to establish and usually does not last long in landscapes, especially in hot, humid areas in zones 7b and 8.

***Kalmia angustifolia*, lambkill** – 2, 6, 8, 10. An interesting but not particularly beautiful relative of mountain laurel. It is useful in rock gardens; for naturalizing, especially under pines; or as a low foundation planting in acid soils. There are several geographic races that survive in northern or southern regions, so choose the race appropriate for the region's climate.

Kalmia latifolia, **mountain laurel** – 2, 6. One of the most beautiful native evergreen flowering shrubs, or sometimes even a small tree, this species is difficult to establish in gardens. Most nursery-grown plants are produced in soil-free potting material, and they dry quickly when installed in the garden unless careful soil preparation and time-consuming watering is applied until the plant is established. I feel it is well worth the effort in some residential landscapes; however, it does not fall into the category of easy-to-grow native plants.

Leucothoe axillaris, **swamp dog laurel** – 1, 2, 4, 6, 12. Powdery mildew is a severe problem in many locations. Flowers are ill scented.

Leucothoe fontanesiana, **dog hobble** – 1, 2, 4, 6, 12. Same reasons as for *L. axillaris.*

Leucothoe racemosa, **sweetbells** – 10. Desirable for its sweetly scented racemes of bell-shaped flowers, nice autumn foliage, and rain garden use. However, it is rarely available in the trade and not superior to other recommended species.

Lyonia lucida, **fetterbush** – 2, 3, 6, 8. Beautiful evergreen for the South, where exacting requirements are met.

Paxistima canbyi, **candytuft** – 4, 6, 8. Very useful as a small evergreen ground cover, it never seems to grow with vigor in areas outside of its native mountainous regions, especially further to the south.

Physocarpus opulifolius, **ninebark** – 10. Attractive, ornamental bark. A very versatile shrub that may have a use in tough situations with full sun, drought, and flood.

Pieris floribunda, **mountain andromeda** – 2, 4. Approaching attractiveness of its exotic relative, *Pieris japonica,* it unfortunately is not as easy to grow

and not as heat tolerant. It is well worth the extra effort in cooler climates than zones 7b and 8.

Potentilla fruticosa, **shrubby cinquefoil** – 10. Tolerant of many conditions. Attractive in flower.

Rhododendron austrinum and *R. canescens,* **Florida flame azalea and mountain azalea** – 3. Both will lose flower buds in very cold winters even in zone 7.

Rhododendron canadense, **rhodora** – 1, 4, 6. A very attractive azalea, only successful in colder climates and specially prepared soils.

Rhododendron carolinianum, **Carolina rhododendron** – 2, 4, 5, 6, 8. Very beautiful in flower; the leaves are generally smaller and not as attractive as the rhododendrons recommended in the primary list. It may be worth the effort in cooler climates than zones 7–8 and away from the coastal humidity.

Rhododendron maximum, **rosebay rhododendron** – 4. A nice broad-leaved evergreen for cold climates, good only in colder zones, 5 and 6. Thrives in cooler, high-elevation locations. Usually not as successful in humid coastal locations.

Rhododendron minus, **Piedmont rhododendron** – 1, 2, 4, 5, 6, 8. Generally the same as *R. carolinianum* except it is more susceptible to leaf spot fungi.

Rhododendron prinophyllum, **roseshell azalea** – 4, 6. Grown for its wonderfully fragrant and attractive flowers, this species thrives better in cooler climates than many of the other recommended native azaleas.

Rhododendron vaseyi, **pinkshell azalea** – 4, 5, 6. A very beautiful native azalea, it is not as easy to grow in urban areas or hot, humid areas of zones 7b and 8. Worth trying in suburban gardens in regions with cooler summer temperatures.

***Ribes* spp., currants or gooseberries** – 1. Grown for fruit as well as ornamental flowers, currants and gooseberries are an alternate host for a fungus disease, white-pine blister rust. Because of this, they are illegal to grow in some states covered by this book.

***Sambucus canadensis*, elderberry** – 5, 9, 10. An interesting, weak-stemmed shrub grown primarily for its clusters of blue fruits, which follow terminal cymes of white flowers. It is useful in rain gardens but generally is not as attractive as some other recommended plants.

***Viburnum acerifolium*, mapleleaf viburnum** – 12. I grew this plant for years in shade and sun with very little extra care. Even though viburnums are listed as deer tolerant, every plant I grew, or even knew of, has been killed by deer. Being susceptible to deer is its undesirable trait.

***Viburnum dentatum*, arrowwood viburnum** – 12. Same deer issues as *V. acerifolium*. Also, after the leaves drop in the autumn they give off a very unpleasant odor.

***Viburnum lentago*, nannyberry** – 12. Mildew. Deer issues.

***Viburnum trilobum*, American cranberry bush** – 4, 6, 12. Same deer issues as well as lack of heat tolerance in the South. Much better in cooler climates.

About the Authors

TONY DOVE is a highly regarded horticulturist with over 40 years of professional experience managing public and private gardens from New York to South Carolina, as well as consulting nationally and internationally. Mr. Dove is currently with the Smithsonian Environmental Research Center in Edgewater, MD. In his 20-year tenure at the Smithsonian Institution, he has also served as chief of grounds management and acting director, Horticultural Services Division in Washington, DC. Previously, Mr. Dove served as director, Clark Botanic Garden in Albertson, NY; and horticultural director at Tryon Palace Historic Sites and Garden, New Bern, NC, and at Historic London Town and Gardens, Edgewater, MD. Mr. Dove received his education from the University of Maryland, where he graduated at the top of his class in horticulture.

Mr. Dove has consulted with important gardens and institutions. He served on the Board of Trustees of the Bayard Cutting Arboretum in Great River, NY, for over 20 years. Mr. Dove has held offices in many plant societies, including national president of the Azalea Society of America. He has enjoyed membership in organizations including the Hortus Club of New York.

Mr. Dove is a frequent speaker and has written articles for many professional journals, including those of the American Horticultural Society and the Azalea, Holly, and Rhododendron Societies of America.

GINGER WOOLRIDGE has a BS in landscape architecture from Pennsylvania State University and an MBA from the Wharton School at the University of Pennsylvania. Her professional experience has included garden design, design instruction at the USDA, commercial real estate acquisitions, commercial and residential development and construction, homeschooling her children, and presiding over a political action committee. Ms. Woolridge serves on the Board of Trustees of 1000 Friends of Maryland. She is a supporter of the Tibetan Tuberculosis Project in Dharamsala, India. She recently served as a consultant for the National Geographic Kids *Ultimate Explorer Field Guide: Trees*.

Glossary

alien: A non-native, exotic.

alluvial: Soils deposited by a river or a stream.

anthers: The pollen-containing part of the male flower.

anthracnose: A fungal disease of plants.

bioretention: A landscaped, shallow basin created to slow storm water runoff and trap sediment.

bipinnate: Twice pinnately divided, usually referring to leaves.

bisexual: Having both sexes, as in a flower having both fertile anthers and a fertile ovary.

bract: A leaflike structure, usually not resembling foliage leaves, associated with an inflorescence or flower.

buttressed trunk: A flared trunk.

capsule: A dry fruit, dehiscing at maturity to release seeds.

catkins: Dense, cylindrical flower spikes, often drooping.

chlorosis: A reduction of normal green coloration related to iron deficiency, disease, or lack of light.

circumneutral soils: Having a pH between 6.5 and 7.5.

compound leaf: A leaf with leaflets arranged on a common stalk, or petiole.

cone: A woody or leathery fruit with overlapping scales, each of which bears seed or pollen.

corymbs: A flat or nearly flat-topped floral inflorescence where the outermost flowers are the first to open.

cultivar: A plant variety, a clone, produced from a natural species and maintained by humans through cultivation. The name of the cultivar is generally set off by single quotations or different type.

cyme: A flat or nearly flat-topped floral inflorescence where the outermost flowers are the last to open.

dehiscent: Breaking open at maturity to release content.

dentate: A leaf edge with teeth standing out from the margin.

dioecious: Plants that are either male or female.

drupe: A fleshy fruit with a single seed enclosed in a stone, like a peach or cherry.

ecotype, or ecospecies: A population of a particular species, whether native or not, that has adapted to a particular set of environmental conditions through a process of natural selection; a distinct geographic variety.

endemic: A plant that is restricted to a certain area or condition.

elliptical: An elongated oval leaf shape.

ericaceous: Plants belonging to the acid-soil-requiring heath family.

espalier: To grow a plant flat against a wall.

ethnobotany: The scientific study of the relationships that exist between people and plants.

exotic: A plant not native to the continent on which it is now found.

fitness: A measure of a plant's or a plant population's sustainability. Fitness takes into account survival, seed production, and the occurrence of new seedlings or plants. It also includes a plant's susceptibility to vectors.

form: The shape of a plant.

form (f): A form usually designates a group of plants within a species with a noticeable morphological deviation; for example, a narrow-leaf form.

fruit: A seed-bearing structure formed from the ripening ovary following flowering.

hardpan: A compacted layer of soil that can be both impenetrable to roots and impervious.

hummock: A wooded, elevated area of land, raised above a marsh or swamp.

hybrid: A plant with parents of different species or even different genera.

indigenous: Plants naturally occurring in a particular environment or region.

indumentum: A general term meaning a covering of fine hairs. An example is on the underside of a magnolia leaf.

inflorescence: The arrangement of flowers along an axis and in relation to one another.

introduced: See non-native.

invasive: A non-native plant or other organism whose introduction causes or is likely to cause damage to the environment, human health, and/or human economy.

involucre: A group of one or more whorls of bracts beneath a flower or flower cluster.

lanceolate: A leaf shape where the length is much longer than the width, with the widest point being below the middle.

mesic: A type of habitat with a moderate or well-balanced supply of moisture.

monoecious: Having both female and male unisexual flowers on the same individual plant.

native: A plant that is a part of the balance of nature that has developed over hundreds or thousands of years in a particular region or ecosystem. Our definition, for this book and per the US Department of Agriculture, includes only plants found in this country before European settlement.

nipple gall: In hackberries, an abnormal growth on leaves, caused by a small psyllid wasp. In number nipple galls may cause unsightly leaves.

non-native: A plant introduced with human help. It is important to note that not all non-natives are invasive. Non-natives are often less supportive of wildlife.

oblanceolate: Leaves with a rounded apex and a tapering base.

obligate species: A species that only reproduces under certain prescribed conditions.

oblong: A simple leaf that is longer than it is broad, rounded at each end, with nearly parallel sides.

obovate: A leaf shape resembling a section through the long axis of an egg, with attachment at the narrow end.

ovate: A leaf shape resembling a section through the long axis of an egg, with attachment at the broad end.

organic soil: Soils with plant and animal residues at various stages of decomposition, cells and tissues of soil organisms, and substances synthesized by soil organisms.

palmately compound leaf: A leaf where the leaflets radiate outward from a single point on the petiole.

panicle: The compound branched racemes of a flower.

pedicel: The stalk of an individual flower.

pedicellate: Flowers that are borne on a pedicel.

peduncle: The stalk of an inflorescence.

petiole: The stalk of a leaf.

pinnate: With the same arrangement as a feather, usually referring to leaves.

plant establishment period: The period of time it takes a plant to return to normal growth on its own after planting or transplanting. In most cases, this is at least the first growing season after initial planting.

procumbent: having a stem that grows along the ground without rooting.

pubescent: Covered with short, soft hairs.

raceme: An indeterminate inflorescence with a simple, elongated axis and pedicellate flowers.

rhizome: A creeping stem, usually belowground, with nodes and internodes with adventitious roots.

rich soil: A soil high in plant nutrients.

scalelike leaves: Very small leaves that are pressed to the leaf stem.

serrated: A leaf with a margin that is "toothed" or notched like a saw.

sessile: A plant part attached by its base, without a stock.

shrub: A woody plant, usually less than 18' tall and many branched without a distinct main stem except at ground level.

specimen: An impressive plant grown as a focal point of interest.

spike: An unbranched inflorescence of sessile flowers or spikelets.

spp.: Multiple species.

stolon: A creeping stem giving rise to another plant at its tip.

stoloniferous: A plant using stolons for horizontal growth.

strain: The descendants produced from a common ancestor that share a uniform physiological or morphological characteristic.

subsp.: Subspecies.

suckering: Sprouts from a plant's lateral roots.

variety (var.): A plant that arose in nature from seed that differs in some way (e.g., flower color) from the normal population.

well-drained soil: Soil that allows water to move freely through the root zone.

winter burn: Primarily a problem of evergreens that occurs in conditions of low soil moisture, freezing temperatures, and blowing wind; results in desiccation.

xeric: A dry environment.

Acknowledgments

The godmother of *Essential Native Trees and Shrubs,* from its inception, is Della Dove. Her many skills, from photography to editing, are only surpassed by her enthusiasm. She is Tony's bright-spirited partner in life and horticulture.

Peter Biché has been a perennial supporter of our efforts and a steadfast adversary of English ivy.

We are both grateful for the love and support of our families and friends.

Kevin Mulroy of Potomac Global Media is our brilliant agent. His belief in *Essential Native Trees and Shrubs* is unwavering. Kevin is a champion communicator and problem solver. He is an invaluable member of our team.

Dan Dove, landscape architect, asked for a book of select native plants for today's landscapes, igniting the spark for our project. Kevin Conrad, curator, Woody Landscape Plant Germplasm Repository, US National Arboretum, provided ready expertise, introductions, and unfailing optimism. Raya Koren, graphic designer, laid out our first prototype and Sonia Feldman generously shared her professional design review. Editorial advice was provided by Stacie M. Cain. Drs. Babbie and Bill Adams, good friends and avid gardeners, introduced Ginger and Tony many years ago.

Ib Bellew at Bunker Hill Studio Books, and Charlesbridge Publishing recognized the commercial potential of our work.

Thank you, Joe Lops, book designer, for your talent, patience, and thoughtful attention to detail.

We hope *Essential Native Trees and Shrubs* makes a valuable contribution toward a more sustainable environment.

Tony Dove
Ginger Woolridge

Society grows great when old men plant trees whose shade they know they shall never sit in.

—Greek Proverb

Sources

Burrell, C. Colston. *Native Alternatives to Invasive Plants*. Brooklyn, NY: Brooklyn Botanic Garden, 2011.

Darke, Rick, and Doug Tallamy. *The Living Landscape*. Portland, OR: Timber Press, 2014.

Dirr, Michael A. *Manual of Woody Landscape Plants*. 2nd ed. Champaign, IL: Stipes Publishing, 2009.

Flint, Harrison L. *Landscape Plants for Eastern North America*. 2nd ed. NY: John Wiley & Sons, 1997.

Hightshoe, Gary L. *Native Trees, Shrubs, and Vines for Urban and Rural America*. NY: Van Nostrand Reinhold, 1988.

Leopold, Donald J. *Native Plants of the Northeast*. 5th printing. Portland, OR: Timber Press, 2010.

Slattery, Britt E., Kathryn Reshetiloff, and Susan M. Zwicker. *Native Plants for Wildlife Habitat and Conservation Landscaping, Chesapeake Bay Watershed*. Annapolis, MD: US Fish and Wildlife Service, 2005.

Smith, Alice Upham. *Trees in a Winter Landscape*. NY: Holt, Rhinehart and Winston, 1969.

Sternberg, Guy, with Jim Wilson. *Native Trees for North American Landscapes*. Portland, OR: Timber Press, 2004.

Tallamy, Doug. *Bringing Nature Home*. 6th printing. Portland, OR: Timber Press, 2012.

Wasowski, Sally, with Andy Wasowski. *Gardening with Native Plants of the South*. Dallas, TX: Taylor Publishing Company, 1994.

Wyman, Donald J. *Trees for American Gardens*. 3rd ed. NY: Macmillan, 1990.

Websites

There are many helpful websites addressing aspects of native plants and their relationship to our environment. Look for state- and federal-government-supported sites, land grant university sites, and major public botanical gardens, among others. We list a few good ones, but there are many more:

americanforests.org/our-programs/bigtree
nwf.org/native plant finder
missouribotanicalgarden.org
nps.gov
planthardiness.ars.usda.gov
plants.usda.gov
wildflower.org

Native Plant Societies

These groups are an excellent source of local plant information, including purchasing options. Most have websites.

Public Gardens

We have many public gardens with excellent native plant collections and education programs. The American Public Garden Association provides a list of gardens near you at **publicgardens.org**. We have been fortunate to receive technical information and other support from nearby gardens: Mt. Cuba Center in Delaware, JC Raulston Arboretum in North Carolina, Scott and Tyler Arboretums in Pennsylvania, and the US Arboretum in Washington, DC. Wherever you reside, it is likely that there is a public garden that can provide what you require.

Photography and Illustration Credits

Photography by the authors and Della Dove, with the following exceptions:

Dr. Bill Adams, p. 167 (left); Brighter Blooms Nursery, p. 215; Andrew Bunting, pp. 109, 110; Centenary College of Louisiana Arboretum, Dr. Scott Chirhart and Dr. Edwin Leuck, p.169; Young Choe, p. 197 (upper right); Kevin Conrad, pp. 57, 114; Alison Dame, p. 174; Dan Dove, p. 246; Jamie Dove Fletcher, p. 137; Don Hyatt, pp. 254, 258, 259, 261; Mt. Cuba Center, pp. iv, 45, 92 (left), 149, 187, 188, 198–199, 202, 203, 213–215, 235, 236, 280; Joyce Olin, p. 127 (right); Scott Arboretum, p. 92 (right); Frederica Struse, p. 304; Tyler Arboretum, p. 195.

Illustrations by Ginger Woolridge.

Index

Acer barbatum, southern sugar maple, Florida maple, 51

Acer pensylvanicum, striped maple, moosewood, 44–45

Acer rubrum, red maple, 46–48

Acer saccharum, sugar maple, 49–51

Aesculus parviflora, bottlebrush buckeye, 165–167

Aesculus pavia, red buckeye, 52–53

Aesculus pavia **var.** *flavescens*, yellow-flowering red buckeye, 53

Aesculus sylvatica, painted buckeye, 53

Agarista populifolia, Florida leucothoe, pipestem, tall fetterbush, 168–169

allspice, Carolina, *Calycanthus floridus*, 181–183

Amelanchier arborea **var.** *arborea*, downy serviceberry, 54–56

Amelanchier canadensis, shadblow or shadbush serviceberry, 54–56

Amelanchier × *grandiflora*, apple serviceberry, 54–56

Amelanchier laevis, Allegheny serviceberry, 54–56

Amorpha fruticosa, false indigo, 291

Andromeda glaucophylla, bog rosemary, 291

andromeda, mountain, *Pieris floribunda*, 292

anise tree, Florida, *Illicium floridanum*, 234–236

Aralia spinosa, devil's walking stick, 170–172

arborvitae, *Thuja occidentalis*, 162–164

Arctostaphylos uva-ursi, bearberry, 291

Aronia arbutifolia, red chokeberry, 173–175

Aronia melanocarpa, black chokeberry, 175

Asimina triloba, pawpaw, 290

azalea, coast, *Rhododendron atlanticum*, 264

azalea, Cumberland, *Rhododendron bakeri*, 253

azalea, flame, *Rhododendron calendulaceum*, 253–254

azalea, Florida flame, *Rhododendron austrinum*, 292

azalea, mountain, *Rhododendron canescens*, 292

azalea, pinkshell, *Rhododendron vaseyi*, 292

azalea, pinxterbloom, *Rhododendron periclymenoides*, 258–259

azalea, plumleaf, *Rhododendron prunifolium*, 260–261

azalea, roseshell, *Rhododendron prinophyllum*, 292

azalea, swamp, *Rhododendron viscosum*, 262–264

azalea, sweet, *Rhododendron viscosum* **var.** *serrulatum*, 260, 264

Baccharis halimifolia, groundsel bush, saltbush, high-tide bush, sea myrtle, 176–178

basswood, *Tilia americana*, 290

bayberry, northern, *Morella pensylvanica*, 246

bayberry, southern, *Morella cerifera*, 245–247

bearberry, *Arctostaphylos uva-ursi*, 291

beautyberry, American, *Callicarpa americana*, 179–180

beech, American, *Fagus grandifolia*, 289

beech, blue, *Carpinus caroliniana*, 62–64

Betula alleghaniensis, yellow birch, 58

Betula lenta, sweet birch, black birch, cherry birch, 57–58

Betula nigra, river birch, 59–61

birch, black, *Betula lenta*, 57–58

birch, cherry, *Betula lenta*, 57–58

birch, river, *Betula nigra*, 59–61

birch, sweet, *Betula lenta*, 57–58

birch, yellow, *Betula alleghaniensis*, 58

bog rosemary, *Andromeda glaucophylla*, 291

buckeye, bottlebrush, *Aesculus parviflora*, 165–167

buckeye, painted, *Aesculus sylvatica*, 53

buckeye, red, *Aesculus pavia*, 52–53

buckeye, yellow-flowering red, *Aesculus pavia* **var.** *flavescens*, 53

buckwheat tree, *Cliftonia monophylla*, 291

buttonbush, *Cephalanthus occidentalis*, 184–186

Callicarpa americana, American beautyberry, 179–180

Calycanthus floridus, common sweetshrub, Carolina allspice, strawberry bush, 181–183

camellia, silky, *Stewartia malacodendron*, 291

candytuft, *Paxistima canbyi*, 292

Carpinus caroliniana, American hornbeam, ironwood, musclewood, blue beech, 62–64

Carya cordiformis, bitternut, swamp hickory, 67

Carya glabra, pignut hickory, 67

Carya illinoinensis, pecan, 67

Carya laciniosa, shellbark hickory, 67

Carya ovata, shagbark hickory, 65–67

catalpa, *Catalpa* **spp.**, 290

Catalpa **spp.**, catalpa, 290

Ceanothus americanus, New Jersey tea, 291

cedar, Atlantic white, *Chamaecyparis thyoides*, 77–79

cedar, eastern red, *Juniperus virginiana*, 102–104

cedar, northern white, *Thuja occidentalis*, 162–164

cedar, southern red, *Juniperus silicicola*, 102

cedar, southern white, *Chamaecyparis thyoides*, 77–79

Celtis laevigata, sugarberry, 68–70

Celtis occidentalis, common hackberry, northern hackberry, 71–73

Cephalanthus occidentalis, buttonbush, 184–186

Cercis canadensis, eastern redbud, 74–76

Chamaecyparis thyoides, Atlantic white cedar, southern white cedar, false cypress, 77–79

Chamaedaphne calyculata, leatherleaf, 291

Chionanthus virginicus, white fringe tree, 80–82

chokeberry, black, *Aronia melanocarpa*, 175

chokeberry, red, *Aronia arbutifolia*, 173–175

cinquefoil, shrubby, *Potentilla fruticosa*, 292

Cladrastis kentukea (*lutea*), American yellowwood, 83–85

Clethra acuminata, cinnamon clethra, mountain pepperbush, 187–188

Clethra alnifolia, summersweet, sweet pepperbush, 189–192

clethra, cinnamon, *Clethra acuminata*, 187–188

Cliftonia monophylla, buckwheat tree, 291

coffee tree, Kentucky, *Gymnocladus dioicus*, 93–95

Comptonia peregrina, sweet fern, 193–194

Cornus amomum, silky dogwood, 196, 291

Cornus florida '**Appalachian Spring**', flowering dogwood 'Appalachian Spring', 86–89

Cornus racemosa, gray dogwood, 196–197

Cornus sericea, red twig dogwood, red osier dogwood, 195–197

Corylus americana, hazelnut, 291

Cotinus obovatus, American smoke tree, 90–92

cranberry bush, *Viburnum trilobum*, 293

Crataegus **spp.**, hawthorns, 290

croton, Alabama, *Croton alabamensis*, 198–200

Croton alabamensis, Alabama croton, 198–200

cucumber tree, *Magnolia acuminata*, 289

cucumber tree, yellow, *Magnolia acuminata* **var. subcordata**, 108–110

cypress, bald, *Taxodium distichum*, 159–161

cypress, false, *Chamaecyparis thyoides*, 77–79

cypress, pond, *Taxodium ascendens*, 160–161

Cyrilla racemiflora, titi, swamp cyrilla, leatherwood, 201–203

cyrilla, swamp, *Cyrilla racemiflora*, 201–203

devil's walking stick, *Aralia spinosa*, 170–172

devilwood, *Osmanthus americanus*, 291

Diospyros virginiana, persimmon, 290

Dirca palustris, leatherwood, 291

dog hobble, *Leucothoe fontanesiana*, 292

dogwood, flowering, 'Appalachian Spring', *Cornus florida*, 86–89

dogwood, gray, *Cornus racemosa*, 196–197

dogwood, red osier, *Cornus sericea*, 195–197

dogwood, red twig, *Cornus sericea*, 195–197

dogwood, silky, *Cornus amomum*, 196, 291

elderberry, *Sambucus canadensis*, 293

elm, American, *Ulmus americana*, 290

Euonymus americanus, strawberry bush, 291

Fagus grandifolia, American beech, 289

fetterbush, *Lyonia lucida*, 292

fetterbush, tall, *Agarista populifolia*, 168–169

fothergilla, coastal, *Fothergilla gardenii*, 204–207

fothergilla, dwarf, *Fothergilla gardenii*, 204–207

Fothergilla gardenii, dwarf fothergilla, coastal fothergilla, 204–207

fothergilla, large, *Fothergilla major*, 204–207

Fothergilla major, large fothergilla, mountain fothergilla, 204–207

fothergilla, mountain, *Fothergilla major*, 204–207

Franklin tree, *Franklinia alatamaha*, 290–291

Franklinia alatamaha, Franklin tree, 290–291

fringe tree, white, *Chionanthus virginicus*, 80–82

gallberry, *Ilex glabra*, 223–225

Gaylussacia brachycera, box huckleberry, 291

Gleditsia triacanthos, honey locust, 290

gooseberries, *Ribes* **spp.**, 293

groundsel bush, *Baccharis halimifolia*, 176–178

gum, black, *Nyssa sylvatica*, 120–122

gum, sour, *Nyssa sylvatica*, 120–122

gum, sweet, American, *Liquidambar styraciflua* '**Rotundiloba**', 105–107

Gymnocladus dioicus, Kentucky coffee tree, 93–95

hackberry, common, *Celtis occidentalis*, 71–73

hackberry, northern, *Celtis occidentalis*, 71–73

hackberry, southern, *Celtis laevigata*, 68–70

Halesia **spp.**, silver bell, 290

Hamamelis vernalis, vernal witch hazel, Ozark witch hazel, 208–210

Hamamelis virginiana, common witch hazel, 211–212

hawthorns, *Crataegus* **spp.**, 290

hazelnut, *Corylus americana*, 291

hemlock, Canadian, *Tsuga canadensis*, 290

hickory, bitternut, *Carya cordiformis*, 67

hickory, pignut, *Carya glabra*, 67

hickory, shagbark, *Carya ovata*, 65–67

hickory, shellbark, *Carya laciniosa*, 67

hickory, swamp, *Carya cordiformis*, 67

high-tide bush, *Baccharis halimifolia*, 176–178

holly, American, *Ilex opaca*, 98–101

holly, yaupon, *Ilex vomitoria*, 230–233

hophornbeam, American, *Ostrya virginiana*, 123–125

hornbeam, American, *Carpinus caroliniana*, 62–64

huckleberry, box, *Gaylussacia brachycera*, 291

Hydrangea arborescens, smooth hydrangea, wild hydrangea, sevenbark, 213–215

hydrangea, oakleaf, *Hydrangea quercifolia*, 216–219

Hydrangea quercifolia, oakleaf hydrangea, 216–219

hydrangea, smooth, *Hydrangea arborescens*, 213–215

hydrangea, wild, *Hydrangea arborescens*, 213–215

Hypericum densiflorum, dense St. John's wort, 222

Hypericum frondosum, golden St. John's wort, 220–222

Hypericum kalmianum, Kalm's St. John's wort, 222

Hypericum prolificum, shrubby St. John's wort, 222

Ilex decidua, possum haw, 96–97

Ilex glabra, inkberry, gallberry, 223–225

Ilex opaca, American holly, 98–101

Ilex verticillata, winterberry, 226–229

Ilex vomitoria, yaupon holly, 230–233

Illicium floridanum, Florida anise tree, 234–236

indigobush, false, *Amorpha fruticosa*, 291

inkberry, *Ilex glabra*, 223–225

ironwood, *Carpinus caroliniana*, 62–64

ironwood, *Ostrya virginiana*, 123–125

Itea virginica, Virginia sweetspire, 237–239

Juglans nigra, black walnut, 289

juniper, creeping, *Juniperus horizontalis*, 240–241

Juniperus horizontalis, creeping juniper, 240–241

Juniperus virginiana, eastern red cedar, 102–104

Kalmia angustifolia, lambkill, 291

Kalmia latifolia, mountain laurel, 292

lambkill, *Kalmia angustifolia*, 291

laurel, mountain, *Kalmia latifolia*, 292

laurel, swamp dog, *Leucothoe axillaris*, 292

leatherleaf, *Chamaedaphne calyculata*, 291

leatherwood, *Cyrilla racemiflora*, 201–203

leatherwood, *Dirca palustris*, 291

Leucothoe axillaris, swamp dog laurel, 292

leucothoe, Florida, *Agarista populifolia*, 168–170

Leucothoe fontanesiana, dog hobble, 292

Leucothoe racemosa, sweetbells, 292

linden, American, *Tilia americana*, 290

Lindera benzoin, spicebush, 242–244

Liquidambar styraciflua, American sweet gum, 105–107

Liriodendron tulipifera, tulip poplar, 289

locust, black, *Robinia pseudoacacia*, 290

locust, honey, *Gleditsia triacanthos*, 290

Lyonia lucida, fetterbush, 292

Maclura pomifera, Osage orange, 290

Magnolia acuminata, cucumber tree, 289

Magnolia acuminata var. *subcordata*, yellow cucumber tree, 108–110

magnolia, bigleaf, *Magnolia macrophylla*, 114–116

magnolia, Fraser, *Magnolia fraseri*, 290

Magnolia fraseri, Fraser magnolia, 290

Magnolia fraseri var. *pyramidata*, pyramid magnolia, 290

Magnolia grandiflora, southern magnolia, 111–113

Magnolia macrophylla, bigleaf magnolia, 114–116

magnolia, northern sweetbay, *Magnolia virginiana* var. *virginiana*, 117–119

magnolia, pyramid, *Magnolia fraseri* var. *pyramidata*, 290

magnolia, southern, *Magnolia grandiflora*, 111–113

magnolia, southern sweetbay, *Magnolia virginiana* var. *australis*, 117–119

Magnolia tripetala, umbrella tree, 290

Magnolia virginiana var. *australis*, southern sweetbay, 117–119

Magnolia virginiana var. *virginiana*, northern sweetbay, 117–119

maple, Florida, *Acer barbatum*, 51

maple, hard, *Acer saccharum*, 49–51

maple, red, *Acer rubrum*, 46–48

maple, rock, *Acer saccharum*, 49–51

maple, snakebark, *Acer pensylvanicum*, 44–45

maple, southern sugar, *Acer barbatum*, 51

maple, striped, *Acer pensylvanicum*, 44–45

maple, sugar, *Acer saccharum*, 49–51

mock orange, scentless, *Philadelphus inodorus*, 248–249

moosewood, *Acer pensylvanicum*, 44–45

Morella cerifera, southern wax myrtle, southern bayberry, 245–247

Morella pensylvanica, northern bayberry, 246

musclewood, *Carpinus caroliniana*, 62–64

nannyberry, *Viburnum lentago*, 293

New Jersey tea, *Ceanothus americanus*, 291

Ninebark, *Physocarpus opulifolius*, 292

Nyssa sylvatica, black gum, tupelo, sour gum, 120–122

oak, Darlington, *Quercus hemisphaerica*, 150–152

oak, laurel, *Quercus laurifolia*, 152

oak, live, *Quercus virginiana*, 156–158

oak, northern red, *Quercus rubra*, 149, 290

oak, pin, *Quercus palustris*, 290

oak, scarlet, *Quercus coccinea*, 147–149

oak, Shumard red, *Quercus shumardii*, 149

oak, southern red, *Quercus falcata*, 149

oak, swamp white, *Quercus bicolor*, 146

oak, water, *Quercus nigra*, 289

oak, white, *Quercus alba*, 144–146

oak, willow, *Quercus phellos*, 153–155

Osage orange, *Maclura pomifera*, 290

Osmanthus americanus, devilwood, 291

Ostrya virginiana, American hophornbeam, ironwood, 123–125

Oxydendrum arboreum, sourwood, sorrel tree, 126–128

palm, needle, *Rhapidophyllum hystrix*, 250–252

palmetto, dwarf, *Sabal minor*, 274–276

pawpaw, *Asimina triloba*, 290

Paxistima canbyi, candytuft, 292

pecan, *Carya illinoinensis*, 67

pepperbush, mountain, *Clethra acuminata*, 187–188

pepperbush, sweet, *Clethra alnifolia*, 189–192

persimmon, *Diospyros virginiana*, 290

Philadelphus inodorus, scentless mock orange, 248–249

Physocarpus opulifolius, ninebark, 292

Picea glauca, white spruce, 289

Picea pungens, blue spruce, 289

Picea rubens, red spruce, 289

Pieris floribunda, mountain andromeda, 292

pine, eastern white, *Pinus strobus*, 132–134

pine, loblolly, *Pinus taeda*, 135–137

pine, longleaf, ***Pinus palustris***, 129–131

pine, longneedle, ***Pinus palustris***, 129–131

pine, red, ***Pinus resinosa***, 136

pine, scrub, ***Pinus virginiana***, 138–140

pine, Virginia, ***Pinus virginiana***, 138–140

Pinus palustris, longneedle pine, longleaf pine, 129–131

Pinus resinosa, red pine, 136

Pinus strobus, eastern white pine, 132–134

Pinus taeda, loblolly pine, 135–137

Pinus virginiana, Virginia pine or scrub pine, 138–140

pipestem, ***Agarista populifolia***, 168–169

planetree, American, ***Platanus occidentalis***, 141–143

Platanus occidentalis, sycamore, American planetree, 141–143

poplar, tulip, ***Liriodendron tulipifera***, 289

Potentilla fruticosa, shrubby cinquefoil, 292

possum haw, ***Ilex decidua***, 96–97

Quercus alba, white oak, 144–146

Quercus bicolor, swamp white oak, 146

Quercus coccinea, scarlet oak, 147–149

Quercus falcata, southern red oak, 149

Quercus hemisphaerica, Darlington oak, 150–152

Quercus laurifolia, laurel oak, 152

Quercus nigra, water oak, 289

Quercus palustris, pin oak, 290

Quercus phellos, willow oak, 153–155

Quercus rubra, northern red oak, 149, 290

Quercus shumardii, Shumard red oak, 149

Quercus virginiana, live oak, 156–158

redbud, eastern, ***Cercis canadensis***, 74–76

Rhapidophyllum hystrix, needle palm, 250–252

Rhododendron atlanticum, coast azalea, 264

Rhododendron austrinum, Florida flame azalea, 292

Rhododendron bakeri, Cumberland azalea, 253

Rhododendron calendulaceum, flame azalea, 253–254

Rhododendron canadense, rhodora, 292

Rhododendron canescens, mountain azalea, 292

rhododendron, Carolina, ***Rhododendron carolinianum***, 292

Rhododendron carolinianum, Carolina rhododendron, 292

rhododendron, Catawba, ***Rhododendron catawbiense***, 255–257

Rhododendron catawbiense, Catawba rhododendron, 255–257

Rhododendron maximum, rosebay rhododendron, 292

Rhododendron minus, Piedmont rhododendron, 292

Rhododendron periclymenoides, pinxterbloom azalea, 258–259

rhododendron, Piedmont, ***Rhododendron minus***, 292

Rhododendron prinophyllum, roseshell azalea, 292

Rhododendron prunifolium, plumleaf azalea, 260–261

rhododendron, rosebay, ***Rhododendron maximum***, 292

Rhododendron vaseyi, pinkshell azalea, 292

Rhododendron viscosum, swamp azalea, 262–264

Rhododendron viscosum **var. *serrulatum***, sweet azalea, 260, 264

rhodora, ***Rhododendron canadense***, 292

Rhus aromatica, fragrant sumac, 265–267

Rhus copallina, shining sumac, flaming sumac, winged sumac, 268–270

Rhus typhina, staghorn sumac, 271–273

Ribes **spp.**, currants, gooseberries, 293

Robinia pseudoacacia, black locust, 290

Sabal minor, dwarf palmetto, 274–276

saltbush, ***Baccharis halimifolia***, 176–178

Sambucus canadensis, elderberry, 293

sassafras, ***Sassafras albidum***, 290

Sassafras albidum, sassafras, 290

sea myrtle, ***Baccharis halimifolia***, 176–178

serviceberry, Allegheny, ***Amelanchier laevis***, 54–56

serviceberry, apple, ***Amelanchier* × *grandiflora***, 54–56

serviceberry, downy, ***Amelanchier arborea*** **var. *arborea***, 54–56

serviceberry, shadblow, ***Amelanchier canadensis***, 54–56

serviceberry, shadbush, ***Amelanchier canadensis***, 54–56

sevenbark, ***Hydrangea arborescens***, 213–215

silver bell, ***Halesia*** **spp.**, 290

smoke tree, American, ***Cotinus obovatus***, 90–92

snowbell, American, ***Styrax americanus***, 291

sorrel tree, ***Oxydendrum arboreum***, 126–128

sourwood, ***Oxydendrum arboreum***, 126–128

spicebush, *Lindera benzoin*, 242–244
spruce, blue, *Picea pungens*, 289
spruce, red, *Picea rubens*, 289
spruce, white, *Picea glauca*, 289
St. John's wort, dense, *Hypericum densiflorum*, 222
St. John's wort, golden, *Hypericum frondosum*, 220–222
St. John's wort, Kalm's, *Hypericum kalmianum*, 222
St. John's wort, shrubby, *Hypericum prolificum*, 222
Stewartia malacodendron, silky camellia, 291
strawberry bush, *Calycanthus floridus*, 181–183
strawberry bush, *Euonymus americanus*, 291
Styrax americanus, American snowbell, 291
sugarberry, *Celtis laevigata*, 68–70
sumac, flaming, *Rhus copallina*, 268–270
sumac, fragrant, *Rhus aromatica*, 265–267
sumac, shining, *Rhus copallina*, 268–270
sumac, staghorn, *Rhus typhina*, 271–273
sumac, winged, *Rhus copallina*, 268–270
summersweet, *Clethra alnifolia*, 189–192
swamp cyrilla, *Cyrilla racemiflora*, 201–203
sweetbells, *Leucothoe racemosa*, 292
sweet fern, *Comptonia peregrina*, 193–194
sweetshrub, common, *Calycanthus floridus*, 181–183
sweetspire, Virginia, *Itea virginica*, 237–239
sycamore, *Platanus occidentalis*, 141–143

Taxodium ascendens, pond cypress, 160–161
Taxodium distichum, bald cypress, 159–161
Thuja occidentalis, arborvitae, northern white cedar, 162–164
Tilia americana, American linden, basswood, 290
titi, *Cyrilla racemiflora*, 201–203
Tsuga canadensis, Canadian hemlock, 290
tupelo, *Nyssa sylvatica*, 120–122

Ulmus americana, American elm, 290
umbrella tree, *Magnolia tripetala*, 290

Viburnum acerifolium, mapleleaf viburnum, 293
viburnum, arrowwood, *Viburnum dentatum*, 293
viburnum, blackhaw, *Viburnum prunifolium*, 280–282
Viburnum cassinoides, witherod viburnum, 277–279
Viburnum dentatum, arrowwood viburnum, 293
Viburnum lentago, nannyberry, 293
viburnum, mapleleaf, *Viburnum acerifolium*, 293
Viburnum nudum, smooth witherod viburnum, possumhaw viburnum, 277–279
viburnum, possumhaw, *Viburnum nudum*, 277–279
Viburnum prunifolium, blackhaw viburnum, 280–282
viburnum, smooth witherod, *Viburnum nudum*, 277–279
Viburnum trilobum, cranberry bush, 293
viburnum, witherod, *Viburnum cassinoides*, 277–279

walnut, black, *Juglans nigra*, 289
wax myrtle, southern, *Morella cerifera*, 245–247
winterberry, *Ilex verticillata*, 226–229
witch hazel, common, *Hamamelis virginiana*, 211–212
witch hazel, Ozark, *Hamamelis vernalis*, 208–210
witch hazel, vernal, *Hamamelis vernalis*, 208–210

yellowwood, American, *Cladrastis kentukea (lutea)*, 83–85
yucca, Adam's needle, *Yucca filamentosa*, 283–286
Yucca aloifolia, Spanish bayonet yucca, 283–286
Yucca gloriosa, mound-lily yucca, 283–286
Yucca filamentosa, Adam's needle yucca, 283–286
yucca, mound-lily, *Yucca gloriosa*, 283–286
yucca, Spanish bayonet, *Yucca aloifolia*, 283–286